THE HISTORICAL JESUS

ANCIENT EVIDENCE FOR THE LIFE OF CHRIST

THE
HISTORICAL
JESUS

ANCIENT EVIDENCE FOR
THE LIFE OF CHRIST

GARY R. HABERMAS

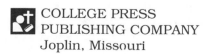
COLLEGE PRESS
PUBLISHING COMPANY
Joplin, Missouri

Unless indicated otherwise, Scripture quotations are from
THE NEW KING JAMES VERSION of the Bible.
Copyright © 1979, 1980, 1982,
Thomas Nelson, Inc., Publishers.

Cover Design by Mark A. Cole

Inernational Standard Book Number: 978-0-89900-732-8

The Library of Congress has cataloged an earlier printing as follows:

Library of Congress Cataloging-in-Publication Data

Habermas, Gary R.
    The historical Jesus: ancient evidence for the life of Christ/
Gary R. Habermas.
        p.   cm.
    Rev. ed. of: Ancient evidence for the life of Jesus.
    Includes bibliographical references and index.
    ISBN 0-89900-732-5 (pbk.)
    1. Jesus Christ—Historicity.   2. Bible. N.T. Gospels—
Evidences, authority, etc.   3. Jesus Christ—Biography—
History and criticism.   4. Bible. N.T. Gospels—Extra-
canonical parallels.   I. Habermas, Gary R. Ancient evidence
for the life of Jesus.   II. Title.
BT303.2.H29 1996
232.9'08—dc20   96-14876
                                                        CIP

With love,

to my brother Bud and Linda

and also to Sue and Al.

Acknowledgments

I am grateful for the assistance of several people who contributed to the present volume. Grant Osborne of Trinity International University and William Lane of Seattle Pacific University both read most of the manuscript and presented helpful suggestions, especially concerning the Bibliography. Edwin Yamauchi of the University of Miami of Ohio and Russell File of Liberty University also provided bibliographic assistance.

My friends at College Press, particularly John Hunter, Steve Cable, Ron Zimmerman, and Dan Rees, deserve special thanks for their careful work on the manuscript. This especially applies to their quick and efficient work in editing. The ministerial interests of these men were also gratifying.

As always, I also appreciate the tolerance of my family during my long hours of writing and editing.

Table of Contents

Introduction

The subject of the historical Jesus is of primary interest today, both in scholarly and popular circles. More attention has been given to various aspects of Jesus' life, death, and resurrection than has been the case in many years. This interest has even extended across the theological spectrum. The number of published books has been staggering, and not at all easy to review and survey.

Of all these subjects, the resurrection of Jesus is like a many-faceted diamond. Turned one way, it is the very center of the Christian Gospel. From another angle, it is the best-attested miracle-claim in Scripture (or in any other "holy book," for that matter). Turned again, it provides an evidential basis for Christian theism. Further, in the New Testament it is a bridge to almost every major doctrine in the Christian faith, as well as being related to multiple areas of Christian practice, as well.

For over twenty years, this incredible event has been the focus of my professional studies. Earlier volumes have dealt with the failure of naturalistic theories to provide an alternative account of the resurrection data, an initial work on sources for the life of the historical Jesus, an apologetic from the resurrection to Christian theism as a whole, a public debate on this subject, and two books on the enigmatic

Shroud of Turin. A forthcoming text maintains that this event is the center of both Christian theology and practice. This present volume is another puzzle piece in the overall topic, but a piece that can stand alone in producing a crucially significant element in the total case for the resurrection. During these years of study, I have never failed to be amazed at the majestic aspects of this occurrence.

This book is chiefly an effort to examine the life, death and resurrection of Jesus from a different perspective. It is largely concerned with pre- and nonbiblical evidence for these events. The main body is devoted to a study of sources that date from before, during, and just after the New Testament, including creedal traditions recorded for the first time in the pages of Scripture. These fascinating subjects seem to be too frequently left unexplored.

The volume is divided into three sections. Part One critiques a number of recent attempts, both scholarly and popular, to undermine in various ways the historicity of Jesus.

Part Two presents the central thesis: the historical evidence for Jesus' life. Here the material is usually dated from approximately AD 30–130, or within 100 years after the death of Jesus. Several sources do extend beyond this time frame. An effort has been made to include virtually all of the sources during these years, but it may not be an exhaustive treatment, depending on the date given to a few other documents.

Part Three consists of the appendixes that will hopefully provide some additionally helpful material. While the information included there is diverse, it is certainly relevant to our topic.

An Important Concern

An important question is often raised as to why we should be so concerned with pre- or even extrabiblical material when we have plenty of information about Jesus in the New Testament. There are both positive points to be raised and warnings to be given with regard to such a methodology.

Positively, there are a couple of related reasons for exploring sources for Jesus' life that are found outside of the New Testament. Initially, such an effort has much apologetic value because of the possibility that this data might corroborate our present knowledge on this subject. In other words, we may find additional evidence for the events of Jesus' life, death, and resurrection that strengthens our case derived from the Scripture. Additionally, this entire topic is one on which comparatively little published research has been done. Therefore, since at least some important evidence is to be gleaned from these sources, it ought not be largely ignored by Christian scholarship, as so often happens.

On the other hand, there are some implicit dangers that we cannot ignore. Therefore, a warning must be issued along with the plea that readers not take this concern lightly. Namely, by pursuing this line of pre- and extrabiblical evidence, we run the risk of implying that Scripture is not a sufficient source of knowledge about Jesus or that we must have additional information about his life. As a consequence, one might ignore Scripture as the primary witness to Jesus or doctrine might be questioned unless extrabiblical evidence could be adduced.[1] By such explicit or implicit beliefs, much of New Testament theology would be ignored or compromised.

This writer does not wish to be a part of such efforts that teach or even imply that Scripture is not a sufficient basis for Christian belief. This book is devoted to developing a new area of apologetics and not to questioning the basis of Scripture. In fact, this writer believes that the best approach to apologetics (in general) is one that begins with the evidence for the trustworthiness of Scripture and then proceeds on this basis.[2]

---

[1]We will deal with a similar outlook in Chapter 3.

[2]Other writings that defend the trustworthiness and inspiration of Scripture, both by the author and by other writers, will be listed in the footnotes throughout the volume.

Part One
Contemporary Challenges to the Historicity of Jesus

1 The Modern Quest for the Historical Jesus

Throughout church history, there has always been an interest in expressing the story of Jesus in terms of a historical survey of his life, frequently in a more-or-less chronological manner. Many differing stances have motivated such enterprises. For example, a desire to combine the four Gospel accounts into a single narrative has always been popular. Other writers have concentrated on limited aspects of his life, such as his birth, preaching, death, or resurrection. Many such attempts have sought to be faithful to the New Testament record, believing it to be fully accurate in all it recorded.

Other approaches to the life of Jesus have not shared the conviction that the Gospels were totally accurate. Some scholars think that the Gospels are poor records, dominated not by historical concerns, but written as religious propaganda for the purpose of communicating a particular message. Many such critical surveys have sought to reinterpret the story of Jesus in manners that emphasize non-traditional roles, viewing him as a political revolutionary, or as a Jewish prophet, or even as a magician.

But of course there are far more than just two general approaches that view the Gospels either as historical or as less than reliable. There is a myriad of possible "resting places" along the conservative-liberal spectrum. There are also attempts to address the life of Jesus in other than strictly historical terms, preferring fictional settings that often imagine Jesus' life during the years over which the Gospels say almost nothing — from his birth to the beginning of his public ministry.

In brief, there has been no shortage of different approaches to what is often called the most influential life ever lived. A brief overview of some of the more dominant trends during the last two centuries may be a helpful backdrop for the remainder of this volume.

The Fictitious Lives of Jesus

From the late eighteenth through the nineteenth centuries, both before and during the heyday of Protestant Liberalism, there were numerous attempts to formulate what Albert Schweitzer called the "fictitious lives of Jesus." In his view, these volumes were chiefly characterized as the words of "a few imperfectly equipped free-lances." Yet, in spite of the preponderance of fictional elements, Schweitzer considers them the first of the modern lives of Jesus.[1]

Such works often attempted to invent Jesus' internal motivations and speculate on other aspects of his life, even in areas where the Gospels are silent. The typical approach was to postulate the existence of a secret organization or association. Often this was the Essenes, who were portrayed as being leading, but secret, members of society, and hence were able to manipulate events and circumstances in Jesus' life. But Schweitzer refers to these plot theses as "rather a sorry makeshift."[2]

---

[1]See Schweitzer's classic treatment, *The Quest of the Historical Jesus: A Critical Study of its Progress from Reimarus to Wrede*, transl. by J.W. Montgomery from the first German edition of 1906 (New York: Macmillan, 1968), pp. 38-39.

[2]Ibid., p. 38.

Karl Bahrdt wrote one of the earliest attempts, a multi-volumed effort, from 1784–1792. For Bahrdt, Nicodemus and Joseph of Arimathea were Essenes who sought to keep secret their identity. At an early age, Jesus got involved with this clandestine order and later was viewed as a valued member. Through the efforts of this secret group, Jesus staged his "miracles." Luke was particularly responsible for the healings. The Essenes also plotted Jesus' death, and Luke administered drugs, causing Jesus to survive crucifixion. Afterwards, Jesus was nursed back to health, which allowed him to make several visits to his followers.[3]

Perhaps the best known and most imitated of the fictitious lives of Jesus was written by Karl Venturini from 1800–1802. From his youth, Jesus was protected and trained by the Essenes. The "miracles" he performed during his public ministry were not really supernatural. His healings, for example, were effected by medicines. Venturini did not invent a plot surrounding Jesus' death, and Jesus actually expected to die. But Joseph of Arimathea and Nicodemus noticed signs that Jesus might still be alive while they were preparing his body for burial. They signaled the Essenes, who later removed his body. After having recovered somewhat, Jesus was periodically seen by his disciples.[4]

Later, fictitious lives by writers such as Gfrörer (written between 1831 and 1838), Hennell (1838) and Salvator (1838) all postulated that the Essenes were involved in many aspects of Jesus' ministry. All three authors likewise asserted that Jesus was nursed back to health by the Essenes after his crucifixion so that he could visit his followers.[5]

Each of these writers conjectured that Jesus did not die by crucifixion, but was nursed back to health by the members of a secret group, and recovered sufficiently enough to visit with his disciples.[6] Such attempts to construct a speculative

---

[3]Ibid., pp. 39-44.

[4]Ibid., pp. 44-47.

[5]Ibid., pp. 161-166.

[6]For a detailed analysis and critique of several versions of the swoon theory, see Chapter 4.

life of Jesus attracted very little scholarly attention. They were plainly based on supposition and thus could add little to more serious historical studies, as noted by Schweitzer.

The Classical Period

The nineteenth century was the classical period of Protestant Liberalism. Often dated from the publication of Schleiermacher's *On Religion*[7] in 1799 until World War I, these decades probably produced the largest number of "lives of Jesus." In fact, this period of thought is sometimes characterized by these volumes.

However, Jesus was not depicted as he was portrayed in the Gospels. The emphasis in the majority of these studies was on Jesus as a great example for living, with the implication that we should pattern our lives after his. But at least two key elements in the Gospels were usually either denied or ignored. Supernatural aspects such as Jesus' miracles were treated as nonhistorical. Further, dogmatic theology was eschewed, especially the doctrine of Jesus' deity. It was assumed that, while Jesus was an outstanding moral pattern, he was only a man.

An example may serve to illustrate the liberal methodology. In the early phase of the movement, the predominant approach to Jesus' miracles was to rationalize them, most often by explaining how something that the Gospel writers considered to be supernatural could really be understood better as the normal operation of nature. This was a carry-over from the deistic thinking of the previous century.[8] In his life of Jesus, published in 1828, Heinrich Paulus treated a fair amount of the New Testament text as historical, but he supplied naturalistic explanations of the miraculous elements.

---

[7] Friedrich Schleiermacher, *On Religion: Speeches to its Cultured Despisers*, transl. by John Oman (New York: Harper and Brothers, 1958).

[8] An example of deistic diatribe against Jesus' miracles is Thomas Woolston's "A Defence of the Discourses on Miracles" (1729), included in Peter Gay, ed., *Deism: An Anthology* (Princeton: Van Nostrand, 1968).

He thought that understanding the secondary causes behind the purported miracles would serve to explain what "really" happened.[9]

David Strauss' *Life of Jesus*, published just a few years later in 1835, presented a serious and influential challenge to Paulus' classic approach. Strauss supplanted the rationalistic replacement method with a mythical strategy that questioned many reports about the historical Jesus. He held that the Gospels were chiefly mythological documents that utilized normal description in order to depict transcendental ideas in seemingly historical garb. The overall purpose of the New Testament language was to express essentially inexpressible truths in a manner that allowed them to be more readily applied to life.[10]

Most obviously, the mythical approach popularized by Strauss and others denied the basic historicity of the Gospels, thereby challenging the orthodox position. Not as evident, however, is how this method even undermined the earlier rationalistic strategies of those such as Paulus, inasmuch as they, too, relied on a certain amount of factual reliability in the Gospel accounts of Jesus.

These two methodologies serve not only to typify the major Liberal treatments of miracles, but provide models for the entire subject of the life of Jesus. As such, they present two distinct methods of approaching the Gospel data.

Still, Classical Liberalism as a whole fell on hard times earlier this century. It espoused an overly optimistic outlook, holding an evolutionary anthropology that involved humans reaching higher levels of consciousness. But such a view was overwhelmed by the realities of World War I and the recognition of intrinsic weaknesses within human nature. Those scholars who could not abandon their idealistic beliefs in the goodness of man, who still clung tenaciously to their convictions, struggled past the greatest slaughter of human lives in

---

[9]Schweitzer, *Quest*, chapter V.

[10]David Strauss, *A New Life of Jesus*, 2 vol. (Edinburgh: Williams and Norgate, 1879).

history, only to be confronted by the carnage of World War II. Liberalism was unable to maintain its leadership in the theological realm.

Liberalism suffered setbacks for other reasons, as well. For our purposes, the major issue is not only whether there is warrant for the belief that Jesus lived and acted in history. On this subject, there was little dispute. But we are also interested if there is any *basis* for supernatural events in his life. This remains to be seen.

De-emphasizing the Historical Jesus

The publication of Barth's *Epistle to the Romans*[11] in 1918 seemed to entail a message that was not only more fitted to the troublesome political climate, but matched an emerging theological conviction, as well. Barth insisted on a revitalized belief in God's sovereignty, along with the reality of sin. The book hit the kind of nerve accomplished by very few volumes, serving as a monumental call away from a groundless trust in the goodness of human abilities, along with a restored focus on God.

Barth's Neo-orthodoxy replaced Liberalism in the forefront of contemporary theological dialogue. However, while opposing a variety of the Liberal theological emphases, Barth and his followers were rather uninterested in the historical Jesus, preferring to divorce evidential concerns from the exercise of faith.[12] Even late in his career, Barth continued to express his lack of support for those who sought to study the historical Jesus.[13]

The work of Rudolf Bultmann was another major influence against the pursuit of the historical Jesus. His 1941 essay

---

[11] Karl Barth, *Epistle to the Romans*, transl. by Edwyn C. Hoskyns (London: Oxford University Press, 1933).

[12] For one early discussion of such matters, see Karl Barth, *The Resurrection of the Dead* (New York: Revell, 1933), pp. 130-145.

[13] Karl Barth, *How I Changed My Mind* (Richmond: John Knox, 1966), p. 69.

"New Testament and Mythology" popularized the theological methodology of demythologization, including a de-emphasis on utilizing any evidential foundations for faith.[14] Biblical descriptions of the supernatural were thought to be crucial indicators of early Christian belief, but simply could not be understood today in any literal sense. Yet, transcendent language was significant in itself. Rather than discard it, such should be reinterpreted in terms of its existential significance for present living and decision-making.[15]

While Barth and Bultmann were quite different in their theological agendas, to be sure, and often radically opposed to one another,[16] they agreed that the historical Jesus was an illegitimate quest. Many of their followers agreed, but not everyone followed them in their conclusions.

The New Quest for the Historical Jesus

For years many theologians remained under the influence of Bultmann's existential approach. But there were also signs of some dissatisfaction. In a landmark 1953 lecture, Ernst Käsemann argued that early Christian commitment to a

---

[14]Rudolf Bultmann, "New Testament and Mythology," in *Kerygma and Myth: A Theological Debate*, ed. by Hans Werner Bartsch (New York: Harper and Row, 1961), pp. 3-8 for example.

[15]Ibid., pp. 9-16; Rudolf Bultmann, *Jesus Christ and Mythology* (New York: Scribner's, 1958), pp. 16-18.

[16]Barth and Bultmann had a famous disagreement over the reason for Paul's citation of the resurrection appearances in 1 Cor. 15:3ff. Bultmann's conclusion that Paul's chief purpose was to present proof for Jesus' resurrection (even though Bultmann thought that such was misguided) is important for our purposes. A brief synopsis of Bultmann's response is found in his *Theology of the New Testament*, transl. by Kendrick Grobel (New York: Scribners, 1951), vol. I, p. 295. Barth registered his complaints against Bultmann on several occasions. One interesting claim is that, apart from the problems that he perceived in Bultmann's program of demythologization, Barth thought that Bultmann's agenda was a return to the old Liberal emphasis (*How I Changed My Mind*, p. 68), a claim that Bultmann vehemently denied. We will return to a critique of Bultmann's views in Chapters 3-4.

particular message did not require believers to be uninterested in at least some minimum amount of historical facts in the life of Jesus. Rather, belief in Jesus actually requires the presence of some historical content.[17]

Other Bultmannian scholars soon joined Käsemann in a modest critique of skeptical approaches that attempted to eliminate any historical basis in early Christianity. At the same time, scholars like Günther Bornkamm also continued certain other Bultmannian emphases: a rejection of the Nineteenth Century quest for the historical Jesus, and the assertion that faith does not depend on historical scholarship. Nevertheless, a substantial amount could be known about the life of Jesus.[18]

Citing the influence of Käsemann, Bornkamm, and others, James Robinson rejected the old quest, while calling for a new approach to the historical Jesus. In agreement with others that faith was not dependent on historical research, he still asserted that the Christian *kerygma* (the core teachings) required an historical basis:

> This emphasis in the *kerygma* upon the historicity of Jesus is existentially indispensable, precisely because the *kerygma* . . . proclaims the meaningfulness of life 'in the flesh'.
>
> It is this concern of the *kerygma* for the historicity of Jesus which necessitates a new quest.[19]

The "New Quest" for the historical Jesus scholars, as they came to be called, popularized a test for historical authenticity in the life of Jesus. Often termed the "criterion of dissimilarity," this test dictates that we can only know that material

---

[17]Käsemann's essay is included in *Essays on New Testament Themes*, transl. by W.J. Montague (Naperville, IL: Allenson, 1964), pp. 15-47.

[18]Günther Bornkamm, *Jesus of Nazareth* transl. by Irene and Fraser McLuskey with James M. Robinson (New York: Harper and Row, 1960), chapter I.

[19]James M. Robinson, *A New Quest of the Historical Jesus*, Studies in Biblical Theology, First Series, 25 (London: SCM, 1959), pp. 85-92; cf. pp. 9-22.

in Jesus' life is authentic if it is not derived either from primitive Christian teachings or from Judaism. When Gospel material originates from neither of these sources, one can be reasonably sure that the material is historical.[20]

However, the resulting application of the criterion of dissimilarity yields significantly less material than the methodology employed by the old quest. One major criticism is that this test would allow Jesus to share neither Jewish nor Christian beliefs, which is ludicrous in that he was raised in the former milieu and is the chief inspiration for the latter. Thus this approach fails to extricate itself from the historical skepticism that it is critiquing.

Further, the question is whether additional data can be justified, and on what grounds. Other scholars went much further in their critique of those who would severely curtail the search for history in the life of Jesus, which was the dominant trend until at least the middle of this century. Sometimes conclusions seemed more sympathetic to the stance of traditional Christianity, especially in arguing for some of the supernatural elements contained in the Gospels.

Wolfhart Pannenberg headed a group of intellectuals who argued forcefully for the concept of God's revelation in time-space history.[21] The resurrection of Jesus, in particular, was singled out for defense.[22] Jürgen Moltmann championed an eschatological perspective that acknowledged the importance of God's participation in both past and present history.[23]

---

[20]Ibid., pp. 99-100.

[21]For the seminal work written by a group of theologians sometimes called the "Pannenberg circle," see Wolfhart Pannenberg, ed., *Revelation as History*, transl. by David Granskou (London: Collier-Macmillan, 1968).

[22]Ibid., chapter IV; cf. also Wolfhart Pannenberg, *Jesus – God and Man*, transl. by Lewis Wilkins and Duane Priebe (Philadelphia: Westminster, 1968), pp. 88-105.

[23]Jürgen Moltmann, *Theology of Hope: On the Ground and the Implications of a Christian Eschatology*, transl. by James W. Leitch (New York: Harper and Row, 1967).

The Third Quest for the Historical Jesus

It is probably accurate to say that, at the present, there has been a somewhat positive assessment of attempts to understand Jesus in historical terms. Interestingly enough, this attitude often crosses liberal-conservative lines. Although there is no identifiable consensus among current scholars, current trends have led to what some have called the "Third Quest" for the historical Jesus.[24]

More positive in its assessment of the historical Jesus than was the "New Quest," it is also more difficult to produce certain common earmarks of the latest installment of Jesus research, due to the inclusion of such a wide spectrum of views. Perhaps the chief characteristic is the emphasis on anchoring Jesus against the backdrop of his own time, especially with regard to the Jewish setting and context for Jesus' life and teachings. Any interpretation that does not recognize the "Jewishness" of Jesus may be judged not to fit into this category.

Accordingly, emphasis has been placed on such factors as the religious, political, economic, and social influences in the land of Palestine. Recent archaeological findings have fueled a debate concerning the amount of Hellenistic and Roman influence in the Galilee of Jesus' day.

A few brief examples will perhaps reveal some threads that tie together this loose-knit group of studies. For Geza Vermes, himself a Jew, Jesus was a popular Jewish rabbi and Galilean holy man.[25] A treatise by Ben Meyer portrays Jesus

---

[24]This designation was probably first given by Stephen Neill and Tom Wright in *The Interpretation of the New Testament: 1961–1986*, Second Edition (Oxford: Oxford Univ. Press, 1988). The best treatment and evaluation is that by Ben Witherington III, *The Jesus Quest: The Third Search for the Jew of Nazareth* (Downers Grove: InterVarsity, 1995). For a popular overview of recent works on Jesus, see Tom Wright, "The New, Unimproved Jesus," *Christianity Today*, vol. 37, no. 10, September 13, 1993, pp. 22-26.

[25]Geza Vermes, *Jesus the Jew: A Historian's Reading of the Gospels* (New York: Macmillan, 1973); cf. Geza Vermes, *The Religion of Jesus the Jew* (Minneapolis: Fortress, 1993).

as preaching to Israel, God's chosen people, with a renewed offer of community.[26] E.P. Sanders centers on Jesus' cleansing of the temple, which, seen in the context of the Judaism of Jesus' day, was an act that seriously offended his Jewish audience and eventually led to his death.[27] Richard Horsley interprets Jesus as favoring nonviolent social dissent.[28] Other important volumes add to the emphasis on Jesus and the Jewish background of his thought.[29]

A notable exception to this fairly positive trend is the position taken by the Fellows of the Jesus Seminar. While agreeing with the need to research the historical Jesus, these scholars follow more in the tradition of Strauss and Bultmann, and favor a return to a mythical approach to the Gospels.[30]

Summary and Conclusion

It would appear that, for at least the last two hundred years, there has usually been a keen interest in studying the life of Jesus. Although there have also been times (such as a few decades earlier this century) when this interest has waned among scholars, it seems to reassert itself periodically.

---

[26]Ben F. Meyer, *The Aims of Jesus* (London: SCM, 1979).

[27]E.P. Sanders, *Jesus and Judaism* (Philadelphia: Fortress, 1985).

[28]Richard Horsley, *Jesus and the Spiral of Violence: Popular Jewish Resistance in Roman Palestine* (San Francisco: Harper and Row, 1987).

[29]Examples include James H. Charlesworth, *Jesus Within Judaism* (Garden City: Doubleday, 1988); John P. Meier, *A Marginal Jew: Rethinking the Historical Jesus*, Vol. 1 (Garden City: Doubleday, 1991) and *Mentor, Message, Miracle*, Vol. 2 (Garden City: Doubleday, 1994).

[30]Some representative volumes include the following: Robert W. Funk, Roy W. Hoover, and the Jesus Seminar, *The Five Gospels: The Search for the Authentic Words of Jesus* (New York: Macmillan, 1993); John Dominic Crossan, *The Historical Jesus: The Life of a Mediterranean Jewish Peasant* (San Francisco: Harper Collins, 1991); John Dominic Crossan, *Jesus: A Revolutionary Biography* (San Francisco: HarperSanFrancisco, 1994); Marcus J. Borg, *Jesus: A New Vision: Spirit, Culture, and the Life of Discipleship* (San Francisco: Harper Collins, 1987). A volume that exhibits some similarities is Burton L. Mack, *The Lost Gospel: The Book of Q and Christian Origins* (San Francisco: HarperSanFrancisco, 1993).

It is within such a contemporary context, then, that studies in the life of Jesus proceed. And like so many other areas, there are those scholars who will defend the biblical accounts, those who will deny their authority, and those who line up somewhere in between.

But not all interpretations of Jesus' life attempt to pay strict attention to historical detail. Some, like the fictitious lives earlier in this chapter, have admittedly set out to construct rather imaginary portrayals of his time on the earth. But in spite of the fact that scholars deny the validity of such efforts, they have arguably played an influential role in the popular understanding of Christianity. In the last few decades, many popular lives of Jesus have appeared, and are quite similar in many respects to the fictitious works of about 150 years ago. We will discuss several in subsequent chapters.

Perhaps surprisingly to some, there is still a conclusion to be gained from all of this variety. As in so many other matters, the question is not how many scholars hold such-and-such a view, or what trends have dominated intellectual thought, or even how surveys tell us the majority of people think.

The real issue is what the data tell us about the Jesus of history. What sources do we have at our disposal? Is there any material from non-Christians? When did Jesus live? What did he do? What did he teach? How did he die? Is there any truth to the New Testament contention that Jesus was raised from the dead? It is our purpose to pursue the answers to many of these questions both by addressing critical challenges and by ascertaining what sources support a traditional understanding of Jesus.

2   Did Jesus Ever Live?

Very few scholars hold the view that Jesus never lived. This conclusion is generally regarded as a blatant misuse of the available historical data. Even Rudolf Bultmann, in his program of demythologizing the New Testament, said, "By no means are we at the mercy of those who doubt or deny that Jesus ever lived."[1]

However, this idea is a persistent one and does appear from time to time. This especially seems to be the case with more popular treatments of the life of Jesus. What would such an argument look like? Here we will examine the views of two scholars who hold such a position.

G.A. Wells

In several recent writings,[2] G.A. Wells has explained his

---

[1]Rudolf Bultmann, "The Study of the Synoptic Gospels," in *Form Criticism*, transl. by Frederick C. Grant (New York: Harper and Brothers, 1962), p. 60.

[2]Wells' thesis is set forth in several writings, such as: *Did Jesus Exist?* (Buffalo: Prometheus, 1975); *The Historical Evidence for Jesus* (Buffalo: Prometheus, 1982); "Was Jesus Crucified Under Pontius Pilate? Did He Even Live at All?" *The Humanist*, vol. XXXVIII, no. 1, January-February, 1978, pp. 22-27.

position that Jesus may be a historical personage, although an obscure one. He even asserts the possibility that Jesus never existed at all, but that New Testament authors patterned his story after the ancient mystery religions.

A central theme in Wells' writings is the chronological order of the New Testament books, an arrangement that supposedly reveals much Christological development. Wells delineates four stages, the earliest being Paul's epistles, all of which were written before AD 60. These are followed by the non-Pauline canonical epistles, then the pastoral epistles and non-canonical writings of Ignatius, with the fourth stage being the Gospels. With the exception of Paul's epistles, Wells believes that the rest of these books are rather late. He dates the last three stages between AD 70 and 120.

Wells believes that the comparative lack of historical details about Jesus in Paul's writings meant that he knew virtually nothing about Jesus' life, including neither the time of his birth, death, nor when the reported resurrection appearances occurred. Paul is said to have conceived of Jesus as "a supernatural being who spent a brief and obscure period on earth in human form and was crucified," perhaps even centuries before Paul's own time.[3]

The second stage of New Testament writings, the non-Pauline epistles, denotes a slight shift in thinking. They assert that Jesus lived on earth *recently*, an element that Wells believes is absent from Paul altogether. The pastoral epistles and Ignatius' non-canonical writings indicate a later stage in the early second century when Jesus was linked with the governorship of Pilate, meeting his death at Roman hands. The Gospels, which are more-or-less fabricated, represent the fourth stage in which there is an interest in a full history of Jesus. According to Wells, the early church simply accepted any reconstruction of Jesus' life as long as there was no conflict with other well-established beliefs. Mark was the earliest Gospel (AD 90), followed by Matthew and Luke, with

---

[3]Wells, "Was Jesus Crucified Under Pilate?" pp. 22, 25. Details are included in *Did Jesus Exist?*, chapter 5.

John being the last one written (early second century).[4]

Armed with his own reconstruction, Wells concludes that the historical facts of Jesus' life were mostly a later addition to the New Testament, since Paul, the author of the earliest books, did not know and was not too interested in such details. Neither did the earliest Christians emphasize the historical Jesus, but only the divine Christ who was little different from the mystery gods of other ancient peoples. Besides the mystery religions, Jewish wisdom concepts helped to inspire the early picture of Jesus.

It is thus possible that Jesus never existed at all or, if he did, that he attracted very little attention. At any rate, Christianity got its start, according to Wells, without any contact with a historical Jesus who supposedly died about 30 AD, because "only in later documents is his sojourn on earth assigned to a specific time and place." Nothing precise was known about him, since no firsthand information is presented in the New Testament.[5]

1. Early interest in historical Jesus

Of the numerous problems with Wells' thesis, we will mention five major points here. First and perhaps most important, the earliest books of the New Testament exhibit sufficient interest in the life of the historical Jesus, especially in his death and resurrection. This includes the preservation of eyewitness testimony to these facts.

It is no coincidence that Paul is the author who includes one of the most important indications of this interest in 1 Corinthians 15:3ff.,[6] where he incorporates a very early

---

[4]Besides his discussion in *Did Jesus Exist?*, cf. "Was Jesus Crucified Under Pilate?" pp. 24, 26.

[5]Wells, "Was Jesus Crucified Under Pilate?" pp. 22, 24-26.

[6]This text is so important and figures so prominently in contemporary critical discussions, that we will devote a lengthy portion of chapter 7 to the subject. Here we will only be able to hint at some of the relevant details. The reader interested in some of the more scholarly particulars should consult the later chapter.

Christian creed that is much older than the book in which it appears. Such early traditions appear frequently in the New Testament and consist of oral teachings and proclamations that were repeated until recorded in the book itself. These creeds, then, actually predate the New Testament writings in which they occur. This particular tradition reports the death, burial, resurrection, and appearances of Jesus, reciting that he rose the third day after his death. A list of persons to whom he appeared then follows.

This confession links the historical life of Jesus, and the central Christian message of the gospel, in particular (vv. 3-4), with those eyewitnesses who testified to his resurrection appearances, beginning on the third day after his death (vv. 5-7). In addition, Paul had not only met some of these witnesses personally (Gal. 1:18-19; 2:9), but he explains that his message concerning these facts is identical with their eyewitness testimony (1 Cor. 15:11; cf. 15:14, 15). So the eyewitnesses of Jesus, and especially of his resurrection, were relating the same findings as Paul. It is crucially important that this information is very close to the actual events, and therefore cannot be dismissed as late material or as hearsay evidence. Critics not only admit this data, but were the first ones to recognize the early date.[7]

Paul shows just how much he values the historical facts concerning Jesus' resurrection appearances when he points out that, if they are not true, then there are absolutely no grounds for any distinctly Christian faith (1 Cor. 15:12-19, 32). This early creed and the subsequent testimony disprove Wells' thesis concerning the lack of early interest in the facts of Jesus' life, for they demonstrate clearly that Paul is even willing to base the Christian faith on the truthfulness of Jesus' death and resurrection.

---

[7]For example, after providing arguments for the trustworthiness of this information, Jewish New Testament scholar Pinchas Lapide declares that this formula "may be considered as a statement of eyewitnesses." See his volume, *The Resurrection of Jesus: A Jewish Perspective* (Minneapolis: Augsburg, 1982), pp. 97-99.

2. Jesus lived in the first century

A second problem proceeds from this discussion. Wells admits that his position depends on the assertion that Christianity could have started without a historical Jesus who had lived recently. He suggests that, for Paul, Jesus may have lived long before "and attracted no followers until he began, in Paul's own day, to make resurrection appearances."[8] But this is one place where Wells' thesis is the weakest. We have said that Paul bases his entire message on the *facticity* of this gospel data, presenting the reports of eyewitnesses to Jesus' appearances, persons that he knew personally, in order to further corroborate these recent events. That this creed is also very early and close to the actual events further assists in substantiating the testimony. Other portions of Paul's writings confirm this conclusion, in opposition to Wells.

Paul is also aware of the fact that Jesus lived *recently*. Paul refers to Jesus' contemporaries: Cephas and the twelve (1 Cor. 15:5); the apostles, brothers of Christ, and Cephas (1 Cor. 9:5); James, the brother of the Lord, and the apostle Peter (Gal. 1:18-19); the apostles Peter, James, and John (Gal. 2:8-9); Peter alone (Gal. 2:11). The best explanation for the phrase "the third day" (1 Cor. 15:3-4) is that Paul had temporal interests in mind, and that these witnesses began to see Jesus three days after he was raised from the dead.[9] Further, Paul points out that most of the 500 people who saw the resurrected Jesus at one time were still alive when he wrote

---

[8]Wells, "Was Jesus Crucified Under Pilate?" pp. 24-25.

[9]Some scholars favor interpreting "on the third day" in 1 Cor. 15:4 in other than literal terms. For an in-depth explanation and critique of such an option, see William Lane Craig, *Assessing the New Testament Evidence for the Historicity of the Resurrection of Jesus* (Lewiston: Mellen, 1989), pp. 94-115. However, it should be noted carefully here that, in spite of the serious problems with such interpretations, and *regardless of the view one takes*, Wells would still have other major problems. As we have seen, Paul personally spoke to Peter and other apostles, and most of the 500 witnesses were still alive when Paul wrote. Additionally, Paul also knew James, the brother of Jesus. It is not surprising that it is clear to the vast majority of interpreters that Paul thought of Jesus' appearances as having occurred very soon after his death and certainly contemporaneously with his own life.

the book of 1 Corinthians, about AD 55–57. In the evaluation in our next section, we will list other problems of this nature.

Wells' explanation of these texts is insufficient, as well as being faulty.[10] For instance, he actually suggests, in describing James as the Lord's brother, that Paul is referring not to an actual brother (in the sense of a blood relation) but to a group of individuals in the early church called the brethren of the Lord!

Perhaps almost needless to say, several decisive problems plague this supposition. This is far from the most normal way of understanding Paul, either in Galatians 1:19 or 1 Corinthians 9:5. Further, all four Gospel writers did not hesitate to speak of Jesus' brothers in the clear context of his physical family.[11] Whether these four volumes were written later or not, they all agree against Wells' position. Additionally, the ancient historian Josephus calls James "the brother of Jesus, who was called Christ."[12] This is certainly not a reference to any Jerusalem faction of believers (see discussion below)! Lastly, there is no ancient evidence at all that supports Wells' position, not to mention the sense one gets of special pleading.

Wells' explanation is a good example of the informal logical fallacy known as "pettifogging," where one raises a smoke screen instead of dealing directly with the material. But this is not the same as explaining these historical references to the earthly ministry of Jesus. We may not like what the texts state, but we cannot thereby cause Jesus and his contemporaries to disappear from recent history simply by this type of *reductio ad absurdum*.

For reasons such as these, New Testament scholars, with virtually no exceptions, recognize the clear meaning of the texts that indicate that Jesus was a contemporary of Paul and the other apostles, having lived recently. While Paul's epistles

---

[10]Wells, "Was Jesus Crucified Under Pilate?" pp. 24-25; also *Did Jesus Exist?*, chapter 5.

[11]Matt. 12:46-47; Mark 3:31-32; Luke 8:19-20; John 7:5.

[12]Josephus, *Antiquities* 20:9.1.

do not contain myriads of details about the life of Jesus, there is no reason to claim that he was largely uninterested, either. An impressive compilation of facts concerning Jesus and his ministry, learned from persons who knew him best, can be built from the epistles of Paul alone.[13] Since Wells recognizes Paul's major epistles as the earliest and most crucial material here, this information militates against his skeptical position.

3. Ancient mystery religions

The third major problem with Wells' approach concerns his usage of the ancient mystery religions to explain the early Christian worship of Jesus. Such a reliance on the development of legends was a popular thesis late last century, but has been dismissed today by the majority of researchers, and for good reasons.

The basis for two serious problems with the legend theory has already been mentioned above. Paul's use of the creed in 1 Corinthians 15:3ff. reveals that the proclamation of Jesus' death and resurrection was both early and dependent on the reports of *eyewitness* testimony. Thus an adequate account must be made of the report of reliable witnesses that they actually saw Jesus alive after his death. Pannenberg concludes:

> Under such circumstances it is an idle venture to make parallels in the history of religions responsible for the *emergence* of the primitive Christian message about Jesus' resurrection.[14]

In other words, that it was Paul and the other apostles who had these actual experiences rules out legend as the cause for the resurrection, since the original teaching concerning Jesus' appearances is based on real eyewitness experiences of

---

[13]For one list, see Amedee Brunot, "The Gospel Before the Gospels," *The Sources for the Life of Christ*, ed. by Henri Daniel-Rops, transl. by P.J. Hepburne-Scott (New York: Hawthorn, 1962), pp. 110-114; cf. pp. 114f.

[14]Pannenberg, *Jesus – God and Man*, p. 91.

something that was seen and not on later legends. These experiences require an adequate explanation.

Even Otto Pfleiderer, an advocate of the mythical thesis almost one hundred years ago, agrees here. He points out that myths cannot provide the direct cause for the resurrection appearances to the disciples, for these occurrences were real experiences linked to historical facts and not legendary parallels.[15]

Other problems also abound with this legendary thesis, examples of which can only be briefly mentioned here. It is common for the similarities with the mystery religions to be reported without also noting the great differences between them and the origins of Christianity. Again, Pfleiderer acknowledges the validity of this concern.[16] For example, Wells notes the pagan mythical deities who were said to have returned to life on the *third* day, without mentioning those believed to have regained life on the first, second, or fourth days.[17]

Even more persuasively, there is no known case of a mythical deity in the mystery religions where we have both clear and early evidence that a resurrection was taught prior to the late second century AD, obviously much later than the Christian message. Whether or not the mystery religions borrowed this aspect from Christianity is not the issue. Rather, it would appear fruitless to charge that the earliest believers were inspired by such later teachings.[18]

Further, the mystery gods were not even historical

---

[15]Otto Pfleiderer, *The Early Christian Conception of Christ: Its Significance and Value in the History of Religion* (London: Williams and Norgate, 1905), pp. 157-158; cf. pp. 77-78, 102.

[16]Ibid., pp. 153-154, 159.

[17]Compare Wells, "Was Jesus Crucified Under Pilate" p. 24 with Bruce M. Metzger, *Historical and Literary Studies: Pagan, Jewish and Christian* (Grand Rapids: Eerdmans, 1968), especially pp. 18-19.

[18]Metzger, *Historical and Literary*, pp. 11, 20-22; cf. Edwin Yamauchi, "Easter — Myth, Hallucination, or History?" *Christianity Today*, vol. XVIII, no. 12, March 15, 1974, pp. 4-7 and vol. XVIII, no. 13, March 29, 1974, pp. 12-16.

persons. This is certainly in contrast to the early Christian insistence that its beliefs have solid, factual underpinnings.

Lastly, scholars now realize that there was very little influence from the mystery religions in first century Palestine. Michael Grant notes that this is a major problem with Wells' thesis: "Judaism was a milieu to which doctrines of the deaths and rebirths of mythical gods seems so entirely foreign that the emergence of such a fabrication from its midst is very hard to credit."[19] Other scholars agree with this assessment.[20]

4. Late-dating of the Gospels

A fourth major problem in Wells' thesis is his late-dating of the Gospels, in conjunction with his belief that no New Testament source prior to AD 90 links the death of Jesus with Pilate. Such dates for the Gospels may have been popular in the nineteenth century, but are abandoned today by the vast majority of critical scholars, and for good reason. Although it is not in the scope of this book to take an in-depth look at the dates of the Gospels, most critical scholars date Mark about AD 65–70, and Matthew and Luke about AD 80–90, which is about twenty to twenty-five years earlier than Wells' dates. John is usually dated at the end of the first century (AD 90-100) rather than in the second century. Some even accept dates earlier than these, but the vast majority of critical scholars differ with Wells' conclusions.[21] Even historians such as Michael Grant accept the earlier dates, again contrary to Wells' view.[22]

Of course, the issue here is not a battle of how many scholars hold these positions, but the reasons behind their

---

[19]Michael Grant, *Jesus: An Historian's Review of the Gospels* (New York: Scribner's, 1977), p. 199.

[20]Examples include Metzger, *Historical and Literary* (p. 7) and Pannenberg, *Jesus – God and Man* (p. 91).

[21]Donald Guthrie surveys the recent state of Gospel studies on this issue, in his *New Testament Introduction* (Downers Grove: InterVarsity, 1990), pp. 53-56, 84-89, 125-131, 297-303.

[22]Grant, *Jesus: an Historian's Review*, pp. 183-189.

views. Still, if the majority of contemporary scholars is correct over against Wells' position on the dating of the Gospels, then Wells' assertion that the New Testament does not link Jesus to Pilate prior to AD 90 is also in error.

Even apart from the issue of dating, Wells employs another highly questionable line of reasoning to explain how the early church unanimously chose Pilate's name — because "Pilate would naturally come to mind . . . . for he was just the type of person to have murdered Jesus."[23] Here we must ask why would the Gospels all agree in this choice of names, even if Pilate did fit the description? Would Herod not be an even better choice? Wells obviously prefers his thesis because it facilitates his four-stage development of the New Testament. Yet his view is not compelling because it conflicts with the facts.

5. Historical methodology

A fifth criticism of Wells' thesis is his lack of application of normal historical methodology to the Gospel material.[24] When this is done, historically reliable material about Jesus can be gleaned. Michael Grant specifically notes that this is the major problem with Wells' thesis:

> But, above all, if we apply to the New Testament, as we should, the same sort of criteria as we should apply to other ancient writings containing historical material, we can no more reject Jesus' existence than we can reject the existence of a mass of pagan personages whose reality as historical figures is never questioned.[25]

By normal historical standards used to ascertain other events in ancient history, we can learn about Jesus as well.

Wells postulates that the lateness of the Gospels and the

---

[23]Wells, "Was Jesus Crucified Under Pilate?" p. 26.

[24]See Appendix 1 on the nature of historical methodology.

[25]Grant, *Jesus: An Historian's Review*, pp. 199-200.

lack of reliable information caused their writers to do much guessing and made them accept almost anything reported about Jesus. Yet we have just seen several ways in which Wells' lack of application of the historical method has contributed to the major problems with his thesis.

For example, if the majority of critical scholars is right in dating the Gospels earlier than Wells postulates, then these writings are much closer to the events that they record. The basis for the Gospel report of the death and resurrection of Jesus is firmly grounded in history, without being inspired by the mystery religions, again contrary to Wells' thesis. That eyewitnesses had considerable influence is a definite pointer in the direction of the reliability of the material.[26] The trustworthiness of the Gospels follows from the earlier dating of the Gospels, especially if we can show that the writers were those who were either eyewitnesses or still in a position to know the truthfulness of their report.[27] The result of our overview is that the early Christian writings are far different from those envisioned by Wells.

Michael Martin

One of the only scholars to follow G.A. Wells in his thesis about the historical Jesus is philosopher Michael Martin, who makes the claim that we are justified in questioning any but the barest data concerning the historical Jesus.[28] Martin agrees with the thesis of G.A. Wells that in the earliest layer of Christian teaching, "Jesus is not placed in a historical context and the biographical details of his life are left unspec-

---

[26]Cf. John Drane, *Introducing the New Testament* (San Francisco: Harper and Row, 1986), chapter 12; Robinson, *Can We Trust the New Testament?* (Grand Rapids: Eerdmans, 1977); Robert M. Grant, *An Historical Introduction to the New Testament* (London: Collins, 1963); Henri Daniel-Rops in Daniel-Rops, ed., *Sources*; Archibald Hunter, *Introducing the New Testament* (Philadelphia: Westminster, 1957).

[27]These subjects will be addressed further in chapter 5 below.

[28]Michael Martin, *The Case Against Christianity* (Philadelphia: Temple Univ. Press, 1991), chapter 2.

ified." Rather, most of the well-known particulars such as those in the Gospels were not proclaimed until the end of the first century or later.[29] Therefore, Martin writes, "a strong prima facie case challenging the historicity of Jesus can be constructed."[30]

In an intriguing move, however, Martin not only acknowledges the lack of scholarly support for Wells' thesis, but he even opts not to employ it in the main portion of his book, since it "is controversial and not widely accepted."[31] While such a maneuver can be made for other reasons, Martin's decision does raise an interesting question: is there a possibility that he is perhaps less convinced of Wells' thesis than he is willing to acknowledge? Perhaps he, too, is aware of some of the serious problems with the entire proposal.

Following Wells, Martin postulates "four layers of Christian thinking," the earliest of which "consists of Paul's teaching of 'Christ crucified' in which Jesus is not placed in a historical context and the biographical details of his life are left unspecified."[32] Wells and Martin do not deny that there are *some* details about Jesus in these early sources. But the issue concerns whether the New Testament writers knew more than a minimal amount of data about Jesus and whether they even knew that he lived during the time traditionally assigned to him. Martin states: "there is no good evidence that they believed that these events occurred at the beginning of the first century."[33] Rather, these details emerged "only at the end of the first century."[34]

In order to further evaluate this scenario, we will look at the three chief avenues pursued by Martin himself: Paul's admittedly early information about Jesus, the dating of the

---

[29]Ibid., pp. 59, 65, 85, 90-91, 95-96.

[30]Ibid., p. 37. Martin concludes: "Wells's argument against the historicity of Jesus is sound . . . ." (p. 67).

[31]Ibid., p. 67.

[32]Ibid., p. 59.

[33]Ibid., p. 85; cf. pp. 65, 67.

[34]Ibid., pp. 95-96.

Gospels, and extrabiblical sources. It is my contention that Martin errs in an extraordinary number of his central claims, and in each of these areas.

1. The earliest epistles of Paul

Martin admits that from the genuine Pauline letters we do learn some claimed information about Jesus, especially concerning his death and resurrection. In spite of this, Paul does not seem to know many details about Jesus; we cannot even conclude that he knew that Jesus was a first century figure.[35]

Here we are not interested in whether or not Paul was right, but what Paul thought about the chronology of Jesus. However, using only the Pauline epistles that Martin accepts, there is no shortage of data showing that Paul knew Jesus was an earlier contemporary. We have already seen that Jesus died and was raised, appearing to his followers just three days later (1 Cor. 15:3ff.). Those eyewitnesses who saw him afterwards included Peter, Jesus' disciples, 500 believers, most of whom were still alive, James, and the apostles. Then Paul informs us that he was contemporary with these apostolic witnesses (15:9-11, 14-15).

If there is any doubt on the last point, Paul states that, right after his conversion, at least some of the apostles could still be found in Jerusalem (Gal. 1:17). Three years later Paul visited there, and specifically tells us that he spent 15 days with the apostle Peter and also saw "James, the Lord's brother" (1:18-19). Then, 14 years later, Paul went to Jerusalem again and met with Peter and James, as well as seeing John, the "pillars" of the church (2:1-10). Later, he met with Peter in Antioch (2:11-14).

Plainly, Paul considered himself a contemporary of the other apostles[36] as well "the Lord's brothers" (1 Cor. 9:5).

---

[35]Ibid., pp. 53, 85.

[36]See Rom. 16:7; 1 Cor. 1:12; 3:22; 9:5; 2 Cor. 11:4-5; 12:11; 1 Thess. 2:4-7.

Having seen the Lord was a prerequisite for the position of apostle (1 Cor. 9:1; cf. Acts 1:21-22).

Taking these declarations fairly and in a straightforward manner, there are several indications that Paul unquestionably thought of a direct chain from Jesus to the present. Jesus had died recently, as indicated by his resurrection appearances that began three days afterwards to hundreds of persons who were still alive in Paul's day. Further, not only were Peter and James specifically included in Paul's list of eyewitnesses, but along with John, they were singled out as apostolic leaders in the early church. James and others are even called the brothers of Jesus.

It is exceptionally difficult to see how anyone could know all this and still agree with Martin: "To be sure, Paul and other earlier epistle writers thought Jesus was crucified and was resurrected. But there is no good evidence that they believed that these events occurred at the beginning of the first century."[37]

Initially, it does no good (and Martin does not suggest it) to assert that Paul *believed* items like the resurrection appearances and their proximity to the life of Jesus but that he was mistaken. Although we can argue forcefully against the latter point, it is not the issue here. As Martin says in the words just quoted, the question is precisely whether Paul believed the proximity of these events. So how does Martin answer this material?

He does not really explain the connection between Paul and contemporary apostle-eyewitnesses like Peter and John, or the other apostles. But he does challenge the claim that the James that Paul knew was really the brother of Jesus. Repeating what he terms the "plausible" suggestion of Wells, Martin postulates that, since there were factions in the early church who favored Paul, Apollos, or Peter, "there may well have been one at Jerusalem called the brethren of the Lord, who would have had no more personal experience of Jesus than Paul himself."[38] Later, Martin confidently asserts that "it

---

[37]Ibid., p. 85.

[38]Wells as cited by Martin, *Case Against Christianity*, p. 55.

is dubious that 'James the Lord's brother' means 'James, Jesus' brother.'"[39] Thus, James would have been the member of a Christian faction called "the brethren of the Lord" that had no physical, familial relation to Jesus!

Having already discussed this suggestion by Wells, we will only summarize our response here. Several decisive problems that plague this interpretation include the most natural way of understanding Paul in Galatians 1:19 and 1 Corinthians 9:5, the testimony of all four Gospel writers, Josephus (who calls James "the brother of Jesus, who was called Christ"[40]), as well as the lack of any ancient evidence to support Wells' position.

One gets the distinct impression in reading the dubious interpretations of Wells and Martin that the point is not to fairly explain Paul's meaning, but to say anything in order to avoid the clear meaning of the texts. The reason in this instance is plain. If James is the actual brother of Jesus, then this defeats the supposition that Jesus could have lived much earlier and still be believed by early Christians to have appeared in the first century. But the sense of special pleading here is strong. Martin himself appears to recognize the weakness of Wells' position when he adds: "Wells's interpretation may seem ad hoc and arbitrary."[41] I think most scholars would agree, and for reasons such as these.[42]

---

[39]Ibid., p. 92.

[40]Josephus, *Antiquities* 20:9.1

[41]Martin, *Case Against Christianity*, p. 55.

[42]In a discussion about what can be known of Jesus' life, even Helmut Koester lists James as one of Jesus' brothers (p. 73). Concerning Peter, he asserts "*it cannot be doubted* that Peter was a personal disciple of Jesus . . . ." (p. 164). Of further interest, Koester remarks about a first century dating for Jesus: "*It is certain*, however, that Jesus was arrested while in Jerusalem for the Passover, probably in the year 30, and that he was executed" (p. 76). (The italics in both quotations above have been added.) Helmut Koester, *Introduction to the New Testament*, vol. 2 (Philadelphia: Fortress, 1982).

2. The dating of the Gospels

Martin devotes just one page to a discussion that is crucial to his thesis — the dating of the four Gospels. Even here he does not present Wells' arguments, but simply relates what he thinks is the state of current scholarship. His typical approach is to report that the majority of scholars favor a date that is significantly later than most, in fact, actually hold.

A case in point concerns what is usually considered to be the earliest gospel. Martin confidently asserts that Mark is dated from 70–135, and adds that "most biblical scholars date Mark around AD 80." He provides no grounds other than a citation of a single page in Wells.[43]

However, the dates Martin provides by no means represent the current attitude of "most biblical scholars." John Drane, quoted approvingly by Martin in the same chapter, lists the most common date for Mark as 60–70,[44] which is up to 65 years earlier! Guthrie agrees, noting "the confidence of the majority of scholars that Mark must be dated AD 65–70."[45] It is certainly true that the views of current scholars do not determine the issue. However, Martin not only likes to cite and summarize scholarly opinion, but his case is hurt by his misunderstandings of the current state of New Testament scholarship.

Unfortunately for Martin, his inaccuracies concerning the Gospels do not end with his late and incorrect datings. He compounds the issue by making other claims that are, at best, misleading. He declares that "Mark was not mentioned by other authors until the middle of the second century."[46] Yet he does not discuss the important mention by Papias, usually placed about 25 years earlier, linking this gospel to the apostle Peter.[47]

---

[43]Martin, *Case Against Christianity*, p. 43. In the name of fairness, we must agree with Martin that a detailed discussion would be far too complex to present as a chapter sub-section of any book.

[44]Drane, *Introducing New Testament*, p. 184.

[45]Guthrie, *New Testament Introduction*, p. 88.

[46]Martin, *Case Against Christianity*, p. 43.

[47]See Eusebius, *Ecclesiastical History*, III:XXXIX.

Further, Martin asserts that Luke (and probably Matthew) was unknown to either Clement of Rome or Ignatius, being known first by Polycarp, whom he dates from 120–135.[48] However, citations of the sayings of Jesus found in all three synoptic Gospels are found in Clement, while Ignatius cites a text on a resurrection appearance of Jesus found in Luke.[49] Additionally, while Martin admits that Polycarp knows Matthew and Luke, he dates this ancient writer much later than most others would place him.

On a related matter, Martin charges that Clement "is not clear" about whether the disciples received their instructions from Jesus "during his life on earth," citing *Corinthians* 24. But chapter 42 seems quite clear, with a fair reading most likely referring to Jesus' sojourn on earth: "The apostles received the Gospel for us from the Lord Jesus Christ; Jesus Christ was sent forth from God . . . ."[50] Jesus and his apostles were contemporaries.

Martin's radical conclusions are unfounded, but he nonetheless bases still other claims upon them. Contending the possibility that the earliest Gospel was not written "until the beginning of the second century," he concludes that these books were "not written by eyewitnesses."[51] Yet he fails to establish any of these claims.

3. Extrabiblical sources

A last area that Martin investigates is whether sources outside the New Testament provide viable data concerning the historicity of Jesus. But here, once again, Martin's research exhibits several flaws.

---

[48] Martin, *Case Against Christianity*, p. 43.

[49] See Clement, *Corinthians* 13, 46; Ignatius, *Smynaeans* 3. Whatever view one takes on the sources of these quotes, the minimal point here is that Martin seems unaware of the errors in his statements or the critical case that could easily be mounted against him.

[50] See J.B. Lightfoot, transl. and ed., *The Apostolic Fathers* (Grand Rapids: Baker, 1971), p. 31.

[51] Martin, *Case Against Christianity*, pp. 44-45.

Concerning Josephus' major reference to Jesus,[52] Martin thinks there is "almost uniform agreement that this passage is spurious."[53] While he is, of course, entitled to his opinion about the current state of scholarship, the endnote is curious. Martin lists five scholars who apparently support his view, while accusing Habermas of holding a dissenting position without being aware of those who oppose him.

Yet, upon closer inspection, at least two of the remaining five scholars cited by Martin actually *oppose* Martin's position! While F.F. Bruce explains in the page cited by Martin that words were added to Josephus' text, the reader who continues will discover that Bruce favors the view that this is an authentic reference to Jesus that records several key facts, including Jesus' crucifixion at the hands of Pontius Pilate.[54] Further, Martin seems to miss the fact that John Drane not only disagrees with his thesis, but Drane adds that "most scholars have no doubts about the authenticity" of the majority of the passage.[55] Thus, with three of six scholars listed by Martin himself disagreeing with him, and Drane saying that *most* others also object, it is difficult to understand how Martin's note corroborates his additional conclusion that "this passage is almost universally acknowledged by scholars to be a later Christian interpolation."[56]

Citing what some call the "Negative Evidence Principle," Martin seeks to discount the testimony of several extrabiblical sources for Jesus. But one of the conditions for this principle is that "all the available evidence used to support the view that p is true is shown to be inadequate."[57] Yet, Martin

---

[52]Josephus, *Antiquities* 18:3.

[53]Martin, *Case Against Christianity*, p. 48.

[54]F.F. Bruce, *Jesus and Christian Origins Outside the New Testament* (Grand Rapids: Eerdmans, 1974), pp. 37-41.

[55]Drane, *Introducing New Testament*, p. 138. Incidently, after a detailed look at the issue in question, Charlesworth concludes that we can now be sure that Josephus **did** write about Jesus in the major reference in his *Antiquities* (*Jesus Within Judaism*, p. 96).

[56]Martin, *Case Against Christianity*, p. 85. Later, he calls Josephus' text a "clearly forged passage" (p. 91).

[57]Ibid., p. 46.

has not shown this to be the case, especially with Josephus. Questions arise with regard to his treatment of several other non-New Testament sources, as well.[58]

Therefore, Martin is far from proving his declaration that pagan writers present "no reliable evidence that supports the historicity of Jesus." It simply does not follow that "we are justified in disbelieving that Jesus existed."[59]

In conclusion, there is a substantial body of data that argues for a historical Jesus who lived early in the first century. We have mentioned a few of the key strands (and we will investigate many others in Chapter 7). Paul knew of Jesus' disciples and visited with Peter and John. Another acquaintance, James, was the brother of Jesus. Hundreds who had witnessed the risen Jesus were still alive in Paul's day. Further, the Gospels are written within a time frame that at least raises the possibility of recording much reliable historical information about Jesus. Certain extrabiblical texts record other data about Jesus, as well. Martin's charges at each of these points involve arguments that strain the limits of reason and even border on credulity.

While we will turn below to a positive case for the historicity of Jesus, we have argued here that the central tenets of Martin's theses fail to account for the available data at a very basic level. Many of his problems stem from what might be considered, at best, a failure to assess carefully the available evidence on this topic. Along with Wells, one distinctly gets

---

[58]For examples, **why** should we question Josephus' second reference to Jesus as the brother of James (Martin, p. 49)? Do many but the most radical scholars doubt it? How do we know for sure that Tacitus couldn't have obtained data about Jesus from Roman or other sources (p. 51), especially when he records data not found in the New Testament? Should we reject all secondary citations in ancient accounts like Martin questions Africanus' citing of Thallus (p. 51)? While some scholars may question whether Suetonius' mention of "Chrestos" is a reference to Jesus (pp. 51-52), what about those who think that it **is** Jesus (such as Bruce, p. 21)? Although Martin questions why I don't mention some of the texts from the Talmud (p. 70, note 44), I plainly say that these passages are dated much later. (See Gary R. Habermas, *Ancient Evidence for the Life of Jesus*, [Nashville: Nelson, 1984, 1988], p. 99.)

[59]Both quotations are from Martin, *Case Against Christianity*, p. 52.

the sense that this thesis is held in the face of myriads of data to the contrary. That the view lacks scholarly appeal (as readily admitted by Martin himself) is not because some scholars are unwilling to embrace such a radical thesis, but that the conclusions are simply unwarranted.

Summary and Conclusion

Surprisingly few scholars have asserted that Jesus never existed or have attempted to cast almost total doubt on his life and ministry. When such efforts have occurred, they have been met by rare outcries from the scholarly community.[60] We have seen that these attempts are refuted at almost every turn by the early and eyewitness testimony presented by Paul and others, as well as by the early date of the Gospels. Such evidence caused Charlesworth to conclude specifically concerning Wells' position: "Many solid arguments can be presented against such distortions and polemics."[61]

---

[60]For instance, when John M. Allegro wrote a rather bizarre work (*The Sacred Mushroom and the Cross* [London: Hodder and Stoughton, 1973]) to argue that Jesus probably never lived, he was greeted by intense criticism from his peers, even though he admitted that his views were only speculation on his part. Norman Anderson reports that, in England, Allegro's thesis was dismissed by fifteen experts in Semitic languages and related fields who lodged their protest in a letter that was published in the May 26, 1970 issue of *The Times* (apparently referring to the American edition). They judged that Allegro's views were "not based on any philological or other evidence that they can regard as scholarly." The book was also "met with scathing criticism in review after review." See Anderson's *Jesus Christ: The Witness of History* (Leicester: InterVarsity, 1985), p. 15, fn. 2. John A.T. Robinson concurs, mentioning Allegro's volume in a section of his book entitled "The Cynicism of the Foolish." Robinson asserts that if such reasoning was found in other disciplines, it "would be laughed out of court." See Robinson's *Can We Trust the New Testament?* p. 15.

[61]Charlesworth, *Jesus Within Judaism*, p. 98.

3 Limitations on the Historical Jesus

While few scholars doubt that Jesus ever lived, several approaches have been popular over the years that propose to limit what we can know about the historical Jesus. We will investigate a number of common misconceptions that would restrict research on our topic. Each challenge will be presented, followed by an initial critique. Many of the criticisms in this chapter will anticipate the research that will be presented subsequently.

A Demythologized Jesus

From about 1930–1960, a popular view was that the Gospels do not present a historical record of Jesus, but a witness to early Christian belief. Since the writers were more concerned about faith and the application of the Christian message to daily concerns than about actual events in the life of Jesus, we know much less about the historical Jesus than the Gospels actually record.

The most influential version of such a view was popularized by Rudolf Bultmann, who held that the Gospels were essentially a later interpretation of Jesus' person and teachings, largely in mythical terms. The early post-Easter faith allowed a free modification of the historical Jesus into a partially mythical figure. According to this theory, the Gospel writers used imagery to express spiritual concepts in mundane terms.

For instance, God's transcendence might be described as immense spatial distance. Or God's use of a miracle to control nature would really reveal his omnipotence. However, these mythical expressions were said to be literally meaningless today. The chief job for theologians, according to Bultmann, was to demythologize the Gospels by ascertaining what the writers were really trying to communicate and by reinterpreting it into a message that was existentially valid for twentieth century humanity.[1]

A major example was Bultmann's treatment of the resurrection of Jesus, which was accomplished without a historical investigation of any sort. He concludes at the very outset, "Is it not a mythical event pure and simple? Obviously it is not an event of past history."[2]

While the earliest disciples' faith in the resurrection was a historical fact, it is not even important to know the cause of this belief.[3] Thus, the historicity of the resurrection was rejected *a priori* as a myth, without any attempt to investigate the facts. Even the importance of such historical research was rejected. Because the early church was said not to have been interested in recording history, legend was mixed into the Gospel accounts. The result was that Bultmann thought there was much uncertainty concerning historical aspects of Jesus' life and teachings.[4]

In his earlier writings, Bultmann expressed this conclusion quite strongly, such as his belief that "we can know almost nothing concerning the life and personalty of Jesus."[5] Still,

---

[1]Bultmann, *Jesus Christ and Mythology*, pp. 16-21, 35-38.

[2]Bultmann, "New Testament and Mythology," p. 38.

[3]Ibid., p. 42. Bultmann expresses the same view in his *Theology*, vol. I, p. 45.

[4]Bultmann, "The Study of the Synoptic Gospels," pp. 60-61, 64, 72.

[5]Rudolf Bultmann, *Jesus and the Word*, transl. by Louise Pettibone Smith and Erminie Huntress (New York: Scribner's, 1934), p. 8.

there is no doubt that Bultmann accepted a number of historical facts concerning the life and message of Jesus, especially in his later writings.[6] Bultmann's view will be presented in Chapter 7, where we will list a number of historical facts that are even accepted by historical skeptics.

While the works of Rudolf Bultmann are probably the best known source for the position that little can be known about the historical Jesus, other critics have also held this view as well, including a number of his disciples. But as we said in Chapter 1, several reasons have accounted for the decline in the influence of this postion over the last thirty years. We will emphasize four important problems.

1. Historical grounding needed

As already mentioned, Bultmann's own disciples noted the initial problem with their mentor's approach. By deemphasizing the historical basis for the life of Jesus, Bultmann failed to provide both early and modern Christians with the grounding that is indispensable for the founding and present existence of the Christian faith. If no such factual support exists, then this critique is not entirely effective. But if Bultmann's position was due more to a philosophical bias, which many thought was the case, and if there is a historical foundation, then he was mistaken to proclaim otherwise.

The New Testament often claims to be based on historically accurate accounts.[7] Paul reminds us that, apart from a historical Gospel, there is no basis for faith whatsoever, since it would be vain and groundless (1 Cor. 15:1-20). The point here is that, without a historical core of knowledge concerning Jesus, Christianity would have little initial impetus to encourage faith in an otherwise unknown person.

This criticism was probably the single most influential

---

[6]Bultmann, *Theology*, vol. I, chapter I in particular.

[7]For some instances, see Luke 1:1-4; John 1:14; 20:30-31; Acts 2:22-38; 17:30-31; Heb. 2:3-4; 2 Pet. 1:16-18; 1 John 1:1-3.

contribution to the dissatisfaction with Bultmann's thought. John Macquarrie, while supporting Bultmann in a number of areas, takes issue with him here:

> It is very doubtful whether the Christian faith could have been built upon the foundation of a historic Jesus who, as Bultmann presents him, was little more than a teacher of a practical philosophy with certain resemblances to existentialism, and who is stripped of the numinous characteristics which the Gospels attribute to him.[8]

Many of Bultmann's disciples agreed with this critique that there had to be some adequate historical knowledge of Jesus. We saw in Chapter 1 that the major thrust came from the "new quest for the historical Jesus" scholars like Ernst Käsemann, Gunther Bornkamm, and James Robinson.[9] While they did not emphasize historical facts as the basis for faith, they did agree that, without such data, violence is done both to the apostolic *kerygma* (the kernel of their message) and to the present understanding of Jesus.[10]

Although Bultmann never endorsed the search for a historical Jesus, he was perhaps affected by some of these critiques, and in his later years he admitted more historical knowledge about Jesus.[11] Christianity proclaimed a historical basis for its message. If an investigation reveals that such a basis exists, then these facts must have a more important function than Bultmann allowed.

2. Assumption of myth

Second, the major problem for Bultmann in terms of this study is that he dismissed the historicity of Jesus' resurrection

---

[8]John Macquarrie, *An Existentialist Theology: A Comparison of Heidegger and Bultmann* (New York: Harper and Row, 1965), p. 23.

[9]For details, see "The New Quest for the Historical Jesus" in Chapter 1.

[10]For an excellent treatment of this issue, see Carl F.H. Henry, *Frontiers in Modern Theology* (Chicago: Moody, 1965), pp. 15-24.

[11]See Ibid., pp. 21-22 for an interview with Bultmann, where he lists some of these historical facts.

without any investigation at all. Rather than consider the evidence, he simply rejected it *a priori*. Again it is Macquarrie, himself an eminent commentator on Bultmann's thought, who sharply criticizes him on this point:

> And here we must take Bultmann to task for what appears to be an entirely arbitrary dismissal of the possibility of understanding the resurrection as an objective-historical event . . . . The fallacy of such reasoning is obvious. The one valid way in which we can ascertain whether a certain event took place or not is not by bringing in some sweeping assumption to show that it could not have taken place, but to consider the historical evidence available, and decide on that.[12]

The problem is that Bultmann made his decision against the historicity of the resurrection apart from factual observation. Again it is Macquarrie who comments:

> But Bultmann does not take the trouble to examine what evidence could be adduced to show that the resurrection was an objective-historical event. He assumes that it is myth.[13]

This is a crucial critique, because it just might be the case that the historical facts are enough to demonstrate the resurrection, but that Bultmann simply ignores what could provide an excellent basis for the Christian faith. Interestingly enough, we will argue below that the methodology of form criticism, which he popularized, even backfired into an argument *for* miracle-claims.

3. Faulty historiography

The third problem with Bultmann's methodology is that even contemporary historians oppose the form and redaction criticism that he popularized as the proper approach to New Testament studies. Whereas Bultmann's use of these meth-

---

[12]Macquarrie, *Existentialist Theology*, pp. 185–186.
[13]Ibid., p. 186.

ods revealed the minimal historical results noted above, ancient historians have employed their normal patterns of investigation and found an adequate basis for history in the New Testament. Oxford ancient historian A.N. Sherwin-White leveled the following indictment at form critics:

> So, it is astonishing that while Graeco-Roman historians have been growing in confidence, the twentieth-century study of the Gospel narratives, starting from no less promising material, has taken so gloomy a turn in the development of form-criticism . . . that the historical Christ is unknowable and the history of his mission cannot be written. This seems very curious.[14]

Sherwin-White asserts that the same standards that are commonly applied to ancient secular history can also be applied to the New Testament records, with the result that a factual account emerges. Michael Grant, another historian, likewise applies the techniques of normal historical methodology to the New Testament and also concludes that much can be known about the historical Jesus, in spite of the efforts of Bultmann, whose methodology Grant specifically rejects.[15]

Here an objection is often advanced. It is sometimes claimed that the New Testament authors cannot be compared to ancient secular writers, since the latter attempted to write history, while form critics hold that the biblical authors allowed their beliefs to significantly color their recording. To this challenge and to the larger issue of the form criticism advocated by Bultmann and others, Sherwin-White and Grant provide numerous responses.

(1) There are several examples of ancient historians like Herodotus, Livy, or Tacitus whose works show similarities in several respects to that in the Gospels, including a moralizing intent "which the evangelists would have applauded," yet

---

[14]A.N. Sherwin-White, *Roman Society and Roman Law in the New Testament* (London: Oxford Univ. Press, 1963), p. 187.

[15]Michael Grant, *Jesus: An Historian's Review*, especially pp. 175-184, 198-201.

they are well accepted as historical. And even though there were differences, too, this does not keep us from discovering a good amount of factual material in the Gospels.[16]

(2) Literature of the sort the form critics believe the Gospels to be is not known elsewhere in ancient history. As Sherwin-White asserts, "We are not acquainted with this type of writing in ancient historiography."[17]

(3) The Gospels are quite close to the period of time that they record, while ancient histories such as those by Plutarch and Livy often describe events that took place even centuries earlier. Yet, modern historians are able to successfully delineate data even from these early periods of time.[18]

(4) Ancient histories sometimes "disagree amongst themselves in the wildest possible fashion," such as the four ancient sources for the figure of Tiberius Caesar, yet the history they record can still be ascertained.[19] Another contemporary historian, Paul Maier, makes the same point in reference to the contradictory material in the sources for the great (first century AD) fire in Rome.[20]

(5) Form critics speak much of the experiences of the earliest disciples, but history looks for adequate causes behind these experiences.[21]

(6) Some portions of the New Testament, like the book of Acts, are confirmed by external indications of historicity.[22]

(7) The principles of form criticism do not preclude an important place for history in the Gospels. Although the primary interest of the Gospel writers was spiritual, history was also very important. There is no good reason why they

---

[16]Ibid., p. 182.

[17]Sherwin-White, *Roman Society*, p. 189.

[18]Ibid., p. 186.

[19]Ibid., pp. 187-188.

[20]Paul Maier, *First Easter: The True and Unfamiliar Story* (New York: Harper and Row, 1973), p. 94.

[21]Grant, *Jesus: An Historian's Review*, pp. 181-182.

[22]Sherwin-White, *Roman Society*, p. 189. Throughout this volume, Sherwin-White investigates various claims in the book of Acts.

would pervert the historical in order to preserve the spiritual, when both were so important and even complemented one another.[23]

Sherwin-White and Grant are examples of modern historians who have pointed out some of the many weaknesses in the form-critical method as espoused by Bultmann.[24] Both scholars conclude that if the same criteria which are applied to other ancient writings are applied to the New Testament, we can delineate a historical basis for the life and teachings of Jesus.[25]

4. Textual attestation

Our fourth critique is not really aimed specifically at Bultmann, but at any critics who would challenge the text of the New Testament, which measures exceptionally well against ancient classical works. This is especially the case in three areas: manuscript number, the time of the writing in relation to the time of the events described, and the completeness of the text. So, in addition to our previous subject concerning factual content, as noted by historians, the New Testament texts can be ascertained.

The New Testament is easily the best attested ancient writing in terms of the number of manuscripts. Ancient classical works have comparatively few manuscripts, with twenty entire or partial copies generally being an excellent number. By comparison, the New Testament has over 5000 copies. Such a wide difference would provide the New Testament with a much better means of textual criticism, which is crucially important in ascertaining the original readings.[26]

---

[23]Ibid., pp. 189-193.

[24]For more complete data concerning these points of critique, see Sherwin-White, *Roman Society*, pp. 186-193 and Grant, *Jesus: An Historian's Review*, especially p. 180-184.

[25]Sherwin-White, Ibid., pp. 186-187; Grant, Ibid., pp. 199-200.

[26]See F.F. Bruce, *The New Testament Documents: Are They Reliable?* (Grand Rapids: Eerdmans, 1967), especially p. 16; John A.T. Robinson, *Can We Trust*, especially p. 36.

Perhaps the strongest manuscript evidence concerns the date between the original and the earliest copy. For most of the ancient classical works, a gap of only 700 years would be excellent, while 1000–1400 years is not at all uncommon. By comparison, the Chester Beatty Papyri and Bodmer Papyri contain most of the New Testament and are dated about 100-150 years after its completion. An entire copy of the New Testament (Codex Sinaiticus) and a nearly complete manuscript (Codex Vaticanus) date only about 250 years after the original autographs. Such early dates for the New Testament help to insure its authenticity.[27]

Additionally, while we have the entire New Testament text, this is not the case with every ancient work. For instance, of the 142 books of Roman history written by Livy, 107 books have been lost! Only four and a half of Tacitus' original fourteen books of Roman *Histories* remain in existence and only ten full and two partial books remain from the sixteen books of Tacitus' *Annals*. In contrast, each New Testament book is complete, which is also a factor in establishing the authenticity of these writings.[28]

The fact that the New Testament is so well-attested is seldom even disputed by critics. In a two-volume work dedicated to his former teacher Rudolf Bultmann, Helmut Koester summarizes nicely the excellent state of the text:

> Classical authors are often represented by but one surviving manuscript; if there are half a dozen or more, one can speak of a rather advantageous situation for reconstructing the text. But there are nearly five thousand manuscripts of the NT in Greek, numerous translations that derive from an early stage of the textual development, and finally, beginning in II CE, an uncounted number of quotations in the writings of the church fathers. . . . the manuscript tradition of the NT begins as early as the end of II CE; it is therefore separated by only a century or so from the time at which the autographs were

---

[27]Bruce, *Documents*, pp. 16-18; John A.T. Robinson, *Can We Trust*, pp. 36-37; Daniel-Rops, *Sources*, pp. 41-42.

[28]Bruce, *Documents*, p. 16; Robinson, *Can We Trust*, pp. 37-38.

written. Thus it seems that NT textual criticism possesses a base which is far more advantageous than that for the textual criticism of classical authors.[29]

Other critiques could be raised against Bultmann's form-critical approach to the Gospels. For instance, some have noted his outdated, nineteenth century view of science that causes him to refer to anything which does not fit his system as "myth."[30] Others note that he is also dated in his heavy reliance on Hellenistic influences for much of the New Testament teaching, instead of turning to the now demonstrated Jewish milieu.[31] One serious claim is that his lack of emphasis on the historicity of Jesus qualifies his system as a type of twentieth century gnosticism.[32]

Some even believe that Bultmann's lack of emphasis on the historical Jesus leaves him in the precarious position of having to demythologize Jesus himself in order to be logical.[33] Additionally, an entire host of other historical and textual problems could be raised against these and other critical approaches to the New Testament text.[34]

Nonetheless, these four major critiques of Bultmann and others who employ more radical versions of form and redaction criticism are sufficient to show that these methods are unsuccessful in pre-empting an historical approach to Jesus.

---

[29]Koester, *Introduction*, vol. 2, pp. 16-17.

[30]Macquarrie, *Existentialist Theology*, p. 168; Gordon H. Clark, "Bultmann's Three-Storied Universe" in *Christianity Today*, ed. by Frank Gaebelein (Westwood: Revell, 1966), pp. 218-219.

[31]Carl F.H. Henry, "Cross-Currents in Contemporary Theology," in *Jesus of Nazareth: Saviour and Lord*, ed. by Carl F.H. Henry (Grand Rapids: Eerdmans, 1966), p. 15; Clark, "Bultmann's Universe," pp. 217-218.

[32]Avery Dulles, "Jesus of History and Christ of Faith" in *Commonweal*, Nov. 24, 1967, pp. 225-232.

[33]Schubert Ogden, *Christ Without Myth* (New York: Harper and Row, 1961).

[34]For an excellent treatment of the general trustworthiness of the Gospels, see Craig Blomberg, *The Historical Reliability of the Gospels* (Downers Grove: InterVarsity, 1987). Part Two specifically addresses the efforts of recent forms of criticism.

The lack of an adequate historical basis for Christian faith, the improper dismissal of supernatural claims such as Jesus' resurrection, historical problems with radical form and redaction criticism, and the reliability of the New Testament texts all argue against such approaches. Many other criticisms could be added to the list, contrary to efforts that minimize the historical facts in the life of Jesus.

An Historical Jesus Without Theology or Miracles

A less radical but very popular model for pursuing history in the life of Jesus involves accepting the Gospels as fairly reliable historical records. While the historicity of many aspects of Jesus' life may be affirmed in this way, it is at the expense of the miraculous and the theological portions of the material, which are usually either ignored or rejected.

Such an approach is appealing to Michael Grant, who judges that, while much history can be gained by such a method, the miraculous elements in the life of Jesus are not within the purview of the historian, but belong in the realm of faith.[35] Nevertheless, Grant does find a considerable amount of history in the life of Jesus.

In addition to historians, this approach of ascertaining historical facts from the Gospels was made famous by the theological movement known as nineteenth century Liberalism, as we discussed in Chapter 1. Often termed "Old" or "German Liberalism" to distinguish it from other modern alternatives, the chief methodology was to reconstruct Jesus' life chiefly by using the synoptic Gospels. These sources were generally viewed as quite adequate materials for this endeavor, with the general exceptions of doctrinal portions and miracles. In other words, the Liberals usually accepted the facts presented in the synoptic Gospels, but endeavored to get to the man behind the early theological creeds and to provide naturalistic explanations for the miracles.[36]

---

[35]Grant, *Jesus: An Historian's Review*, p. 13.

[36]James M. Robinson, *A New Quest*, chapter II.

On the one hand, the doctrinal affirmation of Jesus being both divine and human was viewed by the Liberals as being untenable, so their desire was to "unmask" the historical Jesus from the Christ of faith and doctrine. They attempted to strip the Christ of dogma from the human Jesus.[37]

On the other hand, the historicity of miracles was also rejected. The most common way[38] to deal with the subject was to accept as factual the biblical accounts containing them, minus the supernatural portion. This element was explained by normal, naturalistic phenomena. For example, in the early nineteenth century, Heinrich Paulus accepted most of the Gospel reports pertaining to the death and resurrection of Jesus with one major exception: Jesus was said to have been removed from the cross while he was still alive. The resulting view attempted to remove the supernatural element from the resurrection.[39]

This approach presents some seemingly compelling ideas, such as viewing the Gospels as generally historical sources, an attitude that takes the supporting evidence and historical data seriously. However, there are several reasons why it falls short, and this led to the rejection of Old Liberalism. We will present four major critiques of this view.

1. A priori *rejection of miracles*

First, why should miracles be rejected as actual events, unless we have prior knowledge that they can *never* be factual? Neither history, science, nor any other discipline can rule out miracles without an investigation. The claim that miracles are contrary to the laws of nature and therefore invalid is itself based on faulty reasoning and thus cannot rule out miracles *a priori*.[40]

---

[37]Schweitzer, *Quest*, pp. 3-4.

[38]It should be noted that the other major approach to miracles that we outlined in Chapter 1, the mythical strategy of David Strauss, is very similar at this point to Bultmann's position that we just covered above.

[39]Schweitzer, *Quest*, pp. 49-55.

[40]See Gary R. Habermas, "Skepticism: Hume" in *Biblical Errancy: An*

Current science is no longer able to postulate absolutes that can rule out possibilities in an *a priori* manner, as was often believed in the past. We can only speak in terms of probabilities for any given occurrence. Even more important, the technique of examining all of the evidence before conclusions are drawn is required by the proper use of inductive research methodology. Accordingly, such an approach is utilized not only in physics, but in such varied disciplines as law, medical science, criminal justice, and journalism. Historians also investigate the known facts to find whether an event actually happened or not.[41]

As former Oxford lecturer William Wand remarks, there is no scholarly reason for rejecting possibilities before an investigation. An *a priori* dismissal cannot be allowed, even if we do not like the conclusion that is indicated by the facts. One must decide on the basis of the known evidence.[42]

Then if miracles cannot be rejected without an investigation, on what grounds can we accept part of the Gospel record and reject part of it? Such picking and choosing seems arbitrary unless there is some objective criterion for determining such a practice.

For reasons such as these, conclusions that are drawn before and against the facts are both non-historical and non-scientific. To rule out the possibility of miracles *a priori* is not a valid procedure. We must investigate the evidence and then draw our conclusions.

Analysis of its Philosophical Roots, ed. by Norman L. Geisler (Grand Rapids: Zondervan, 1981), pp. 23-49 for an examination and critique of Hume's argument against belief in miracles and their relation to the laws of nature, as well as an evaluation of a number of other scholars who are inspired by Hume's account. See also Richard Swinburne, *The Concept of Miracle* (London: Macmillan, 1970).

[41]For details on historical methodology and inductive research, see Appendix 1.

[42]William Wand, *Christianity: A Historical Religion?* (Valley Forge: Judson Press, 1972), pp. 29-30, 70-71.

2. Miracle-claims and historical investigation

The second major problem with this approach is the common assumption that miracle-claims cannot be investigated by historical methodology at all. Often the charge is made that miracles belong in the realm of religious faith and, as such, are out of the reach of the tools of historical or any other investigation.[43]

It should be repeated that it is not the purpose of this book to determine if a miracle, as an act of God, has actually occurred. Our intention is to investigate the life of Jesus in general, and his resurrection in particular, according to historical standards. We are asking about the historical basis that we have for these events, not whether God performed any certain occurrences. For such a philosophical investigation of the resurrection as an actual miracle, which is an entirely appropriate study, the interested reader is referred to Habermas', *The Resurrection of Jesus: An Apologetic*.[44]

As indicated in Appendix 1, we distinguish between a miracle-*claim* and a miracle. We can historically investigate the Christian claim that Jesus was raised from the dead without, in this present study, raising the attendant question of whether it is a miracle caused by God in a theistic universe. Nonetheless, the historical question of the resurrection is quite important even by itself, for *if* a miracle did literally occur, it did so in the time-space realm. Our approach will be to examine the historical side of the claim that Jesus was raised. Did Jesus, after dying on the cross by crucifixion, appear to his followers alive? This is our major focus.

Therefore, the charge that historical methodology cannot take us all the way to the conclusion that a miracle has actually occurred is a worthwhile concern. But this is entirely different from the assertion that historical inquiry *cannot* do any part of the important research. We need to distinguish between the historical and the philosophical dimensions of

---

[43]This charge is also investigated in depth in Appendix 1.

[44]Gary R. Habermas, *The Resurrection of Jesus: An Apologetic* (Grand Rapids: Baker, 1980; Lanham: University Press of America, 1984).

the issue. While knowledge is united, the research paths to it are multiple and each discipline has its strengths.

The original charge that miracles cannot be investigated at all would only be correct if we knew in advance that miracles do not literally occur in history. If they happen only in some non-objective realm or if they do not occur at all, then they cannot be investigated by historical methodology and this would be a correct assessment. However, since the claim that miracles literally occur in normal history is an open question, then it would at least be possible to investigate the historical portion of these claims as to their accuracy.

While some will object to even a partial investigation of a miracle-*claim*, this assertion is often simply a form of *a priori* objection just answered in the first critique above. In other words, since we cannot rule out the possibility of miracles without an inquiry, and since it is claimed that miracles have happened in space-time history, they can be investigated as such.

For those who object to investigations of any sort with regard to miracle-claims, holding that they are only tenets of faith, it must be remembered that the New Testament teaches that Jesus' resurrection is an actual event (1 Cor. 15:1-20, for instance). Further, salvation consists of trust in the facts of the gospel, including the resurrection (vv. 1-4). Paul asserts that faith is built on these firm facts.

But if faith is not placed in a trustworthy source, how can we know that it is legitimate? Again, we do not need sight as a basis for our belief, but historical facts provide a stronger foundation than does a hopeful "leap." If strong evidence for the resurrection is found, this would be the final indication that this event can be investigated historically, for it would bear up well under examination.

Some historians have called for just such an investigation. They hold that any data for the resurrection must be examined. Then we can judge whether it is an actual event of history.[45]

----

[45]Some examples are Yamauchi, "Easter," March 15, 1974, pp. 4-7 and March 29, 1974, pp. 12-16; Maier, *First Easter*, pp. 105-122; Wand,

3. The failure of naturalistic theories

A third problem with this approach to history in the life of Jesus, especially with Old Liberalism, is that the naturalistic theories that were proposed to account for the resurrection are disproven by the known historical facts. Interestingly enough, it was the liberals themselves who attacked their own theories, in spite of their theological dispositions.

These naturalistic views were very popular in the nineteenth century. There was no consensus of opinion on which theory was the best alternative explanation for the literal resurrection. In fact, many of those who popularized these theories did so only after attacking and revealing the weaknesses in the other theories of fellow liberals. For instance, Paulus' swoon theory mentioned above was disarmed by David Strauss, who, according to Schweitzer, dealt it its "death-blow."[46] We will examine the swoon theory in detail in Chapter 4.

It is not the purpose of this book to take an in-depth look at these alternative theories proposed to explain away the facticity of Jesus' resurrection. Suffice it to remark here that, as with Paulus' theory, each of the naturalistic theories was disproven by the liberals themselves. By this process, and by the critiques of others outside their camp, the weaknesses of these attempts were revealed. In other words, each of the alternative theories was disproven by the known historical facts.[47]

It is also instructive to note that twentieth century critics usually rejected these theories wholesale. Rather than deal with each proposal separately, the naturalistic attempts to disprove the resurrection were generally dismissed in their

---

Christianity, pp. 29-31, 51-52, 93-94; A.J. Hoover, *The Case for Christian Theism: An Introduction to Apologetics* (Grand Rapids: Baker, 1976), chapter 16.

[46]Schweitzer, *Quest*, p. 56.

[47]See the excellent 1908 work by James Orr, *The Resurrection of Jesus* (Grand Rapids: Zondervan, 1965). Cf. Gary R. Habermas, *The Resurrection of Jesus: A Rational Inquiry* (Ann Arbor: University Microfilms, 1976), especially pp. 114-171.

entirety by recent critical scholars. For example, Karl Barth, probably the most influential critical theologian of this century, listed the major naturalistic theories and concluded that "Today we rightly turn our nose up at this," a conclusion derived at least partially from "the many inconsistencies in detail." He also notes that these explanations "have now gone out of currency."[48]

Similarly, Raymond Brown also provides a list of these theories and then concludes: "the criticism of today does not follow the paths taken by criticism in the past. No longer respectable are the crude theories . . . popular in the last century."[49] These are just examples of the many contemporary critical theologians who, in spite of their diverse theological persuasions, have agreed in rejecting the alternative theories against the resurrection.[50]

Therefore, not only were the naturalistic theories disproven by the historical facts, but nineteenth century Liberals critiqued these views individually, while twentieth century critics have generally dismissed them as a whole. These hypotheses have not stood the test, even from a critical perspective. These are important indications of the failure of the alternative approach to Jesus' resurrection.

---

[48]Karl Barth, *The Doctrine of Reconciliation*, in *Church Dogmatics*, 14 vols., transl. by G.W. Bromiley and T.F. Torrance (Edinburgh: T. & T. Clark, 1956), vol. IV, p. 340.

[49]Raymond E. Brown, "The Resurrection and Biblical Criticism," in *Commonweal*, November 24, 1967, p. 233.

[50]See Paul Tillich, *Systematic Theology*, 2 vols. (Chicago: Univ. of Chicago Press, 1971), vol. II, especially p. 156; Bornkamm, *Jesus of Nazareth*, pp. 181-185; Joachim Jeremias, "Easter: The Earliest Tradition and the Earliest Interpretation," *New Testament Theology: The Proclamation of Jesus*, transl. by John Bowden (New York: Scribner's, 1971), p. 302; Robinson, *Can We Trust the New Testament?*, pp. 123-125; Pannenberg, *Jesus – God and Man*, pp. 88-97; Ulrich Wilckens, *Resurrection*, transl. by A.M. Stewart (Edinburgh: Saint Andrew, 1977), pp. 117-119; Lapide, *The Resurrection of Jesus*, pp. 120-126; cf. A.M. Hunter, *Bible and Gospel* (Philadelphia: Westminster, 1969), p. 111.

4. The possibility of theology

The fourth critique of this historical approach will only be mentioned briefly since it cannot be dealt with in this book. But the attempt of both contemporary historians and nineteenth century liberals to ignore the theological teachings in the life of Jesus might also be subject to revision if it is found that Jesus did, in fact, rise from the dead.[51] If the resurrection were shown to be an historical event, it would have much possible relevance for Jesus' theological teachings, which could not then be ruled out as irrelevant.

For reasons such as these, we must therefore rule out this erroneous attempt to pursue historical facts in the life of Jesus. It fails because it usually rejects the possibility of miracles in an *a priori* manner, and also because it frequently rejects any investigation of miracle-claims at all. Additionally, its naturalistic approach to Jesus' resurrection has failed, as even critics admit, and it also ignores the possibility that, if Jesus literally arose from the dead, then there is certainly a possible relevance for the theology that he taught.

No Extra-New Testament Sources for Jesus

The last view that we will examine in this chapter is the often-mentioned opinion that everything we know about Jesus is recorded in the New Testament, and in the Gospels in particular. These are sometimes said to be our *only* sources for the life of Jesus, meaning that ancient secular history knows nothing of him.

Actually, this position is compatible with any number of possible positions regarding the historicity of Jesus, including the two other views set forth in this chapter. On the other hand, it need not be a critical theory at all, in that believers could hold the view that the uniqueness of Jesus is increased because only Christian records know of his teaching and life.

---

[51]The lengthy chain of argument can be found in Habermas, *The Resurrection of Jesus: An Apologetic*, especially Part One.

But sometimes this position is held as a challenge to Christians. It may be asked that if Jesus made such an impact on the people of his time, then why do we know nothing of him from ancient (and especially secular) history?

Whatever the motivation or belief of the one holding this opinion, it certainly is held by a seemingly wide spectrum of persons. As one history text proclaims:

> Historical information about the beginnings of Christianity is unfortunately very limited. No external source, Jewish or classical, records the career of Jesus, and our entire knowledge comes from the subsequent writings of his followers gathered together in the *Gospels*. Modern scholarship no longer doubts the authenticity of these writings . . . (emphasis added by the authors).[52]

The authors certainly do not sound overly critical and perhaps they are speaking of a fully developed life of Jesus in ancient history. Nevertheless, this view is echoed by many persons. Consider a statement in a modern novel, spoken by a fictitious archaeologist who is very skeptical of Christianity:

> The church bases its claims mostly on the teachings of an obscure young Jew with messianic pretensions who, let's face it, didn't make much of an impression in his lifetime. There isn't a single word about him in secular history. Not a word. No mention of him by the Romans. Not so much as a reference by Josephus.[53]

Although the character who uttered this pronouncement is fictitious, the charge is a frequent one and, as in this case, sometimes used in an attempt to discredit Christianity. We will simply make two responses to this view here, especially since it is not necessarily a critical attempt to reject the pursuit of the historical Jesus.

---

[52]Shepard Clough, Nina Garsoian and David L. Hicks, *Ancient and Medieval*, in *A History of the Western World*, 3 vols. (Boston: D.C. Heath and Co., 1964), vol. I, p. 127.

[53]Charles Templeton, *Act of God* (New York: Bantam, 1979), p. 152.

1. A false notion

First, it is simply false to hold that there are no ancient sources outside of the New Testament that speak of Jesus. It is true that none of these extrabiblical sources give a *detailed* account concerning Jesus, but there are nevertheless well over a dozen non-Christian sources from ancient history that mention him. There are also a number of early Christian sources that provide more information concerning him. We will have to wait until Part Two to specifically substantiate this claim, but it is enough to note here that it is incorrect to assert that the ancient non-Christian world knew nothing of Jesus. It may even be the case that he is one of the most-mentioned figures of the ancient world!

2. Communications in the ancient world

Second, Daniel-Rops notes a few considerations that help explain why even more was not written about Jesus in ancient times. For instance, the first century was certainly not characterized by advanced communications, at least by any modern standards. Any number of events, persons, or situations could be newsworthy in a regional setting and get hardly any attention on the international scene. Furthermore, there were very few ancient writers, comparatively speaking. Consequently, they would have plenty to write about and often confined themselves to situations that were "official" or of international interest.

At the beginning, we cannot be sure that Jesus or the earliest Christians made any such international commotion. Lastly, Jesus' background as a peasant from a humble family would mitigate against him receiving any great amount of attention. Even the Christian teaching of his messiahship might look to an outsider to be a Jewish sectarian dogma, making Jesus just another "pretender" to be the king of the Jews.[54]

---

[54]Daniel-Rops, "The Silence of Jesus' Contemporaries," *Sources*, pp. 13-14, 17-18.

Again, we must not be misled by these considerations into the mistaken conclusion that extra-New Testament sources ignore Jesus. There are a surprising number of non-Christian sources that do tell us a number of things about him. There are also several reasons why even more is not reported.

Summary and Conclusion

In this chapter we have investigated some misconceptions concerning the historicity of Jesus, reaching the conclusion that none of them presents compelling reasons to disregard all or part of our source material about him.

A popular view in the mid-twentieth century taught that Jesus did exist but that very little can be known about him. This approach was disproven by the data, and has lost most of its appeal. The disregard for details concerning the historical Jesus and their relation to faith, an *a priori* dismissal of the possibility of miraculous events such as Jesus' resurrection, historical objections to radical form and redaction criticism, and the demonstrated reliability of the New Testament text are some of the reasons we rejected this option. Other problems are also apparent.

Many prefer a more historical view that constructs a life of Jesus from the available records, apart from either doctrine or miracles. However, this view, while seemingly more compelling, suffers both from ruling out miracles *a priori*, and by its frequent denial of a historical investigation of miracle-claims. Further, this approach failed in its attempt to offer naturalistic alternative theories concerning the resurrection, as even critics admit, and by ignoring the possibility that Jesus' theological teachings would very possibly be relevant if it could be shown that he was literally raised from the dead in time-space history.

Lastly, some charge Christianity with having no extrabiblical references for Jesus' life whatsoever. Not only is such a claim false, as we will show in Part Two, but there are good reasons why there are not even more secular sources for the life of Jesus than the surprising number of ancient non-Christian sources that *are* available.

These alternative approaches to the historical Jesus therefore present no roadblock to our investigation of his life. Applying normal historical methodology to early Christian creeds, archaeological evidence, ancient non-Christian, and Christian (non-New Testament) sources, we will examine what history tells us about the life of Jesus. But first we will study some more or less popularized presentations of Jesus that portray atypical views of his life, as well as examine two recent movements that seek to explain the life of Jesus in non-orthodox terms.

4 Reinterpretations of the Historical Jesus

In addition to the major historical approaches presented in the last chapter, many have attempted to write more-or-less popular lives of Jesus. These authors often advocate unorthodox interpretations: Jesus never died on the cross; he was connected with the Qumran community; someone else changed his message to fit their own desires; he traveled to various parts of the world during the so-called "silent years" or even after the crucifixion.

While such works are given virtually no attention by careful scholars, these attempts are sometimes very popular with those who are unfamiliar with the data behind such questions. Many are bothered by nonfactual or illogical presentations, but are not quite able to locate the problems involved. This is the major reason that these approaches are included in this book. We will investigate several of the most popular recent attempts to present unorthodox pictures of Jesus' life.

The Rise of the Swoon Theory

Each of the fictitious lives of Jesus surveyed in Chapter 1 taught that Jesus survived death on the cross and was later revived. His "appearances" to his disciples were not miraculous, of course, for he had never died in the first place. The swoon theory, espoused by Heinrich Paulus and others during the heyday of the liberal naturalistic theories, was quite popular in the first half of the nineteenth century. It was disproven by the facts and indicted by liberals like David Strauss. Before examining this view, it will be helpful to present an overview of two contemporary attempts to write similar lives of Jesus.

Hugh Schonfield's *The Passover Plot* created quite a sensation when it appeared.[1] However, very few readers were aware of the similarity between this book and earlier fictitious lives of Jesus. For Schonfield, Jesus had carefully planned his career of public ministry in accordance with his belief that he was Israel's Messiah.[2] Accordingly, he plotted events such as his triumphal entry into Jerusalem, on which occasion Lazarus helped him make the appropriate arrangements.[3] Jesus made especially intricate plans concerning his upcoming crucifixion, which required especially accurate timing. On this occasion his chief confidant was Joseph of Arimathea.[4]

While Jesus was on the cross, Joseph made arrangements for an unidentified man to give Jesus a drink that had been drugged. As a result, Jesus slipped quickly into a state of unconsciousness, which made him appear dead. Nonetheless, Jesus was in a very serious condition when he was removed from the cross, especially complicated by John's report of the spear wound in his chest.[5] On Saturday, Jesus' body was removed from the tomb, after which he regained consciousness briefly, but died shortly thereafter and was reburied.[6]

At this point, Schonfield turns to his proposed reconstruction of events that account for the disciples' belief in Jesus' resurrection. The unidentified man at the cross who adminis-

---

[1]Hugh Schonfield, *The Passover Plot* (New York: Bantam Books, 1965).

[2]Ibid., pp. 37-38.

[3]Ibid., pp. 112-115.

[4]Ibid., pp. 153-161.

[5]Ibid., pp. 160-161.

[6]Ibid., p. 165.

tered the drug is the key figure in this reconstruction. He helped carry Jesus to the tomb, then returned on Saturday to rescue him. During Jesus' brief period of consciousness, Jesus asked this man to convey to his disciples that he had risen from the dead. However, Jesus died shortly after and this person helped bury him. It is also this anonymous person who was present in the tomb when the women came early on Sunday morning and was the one mistaken by Mary Magdalene as the gardener. Later this same man visited the disciples on the road to Emmaus, at the seashore and in Galilee. The disciples mistook this stranger for Jesus and proclaimed his resurrection from the dead.[7]

It should be obvious to the reasonably impartial reader that this incredible sequence of events, where an unidentified man simply "appears" very conveniently whenever there is a need to explain anything away, is extremely questionable, to say the least. The entire plot closely parallels the fictitious lives of Jesus which are now so outdated and ignored by serious scholars. Indeed, even Schonfield admits that much of his account "is an imaginative reconstruction."[8] Later he explains that "We are nowhere claiming for our reconstruction that it represents what actually happened."[9] According to John A.T. Robinson, *The Passover Plot* is an example of a popularistic book which is factually groundless enough that, if the public were not so interested in virtually anyone who writes on Christianity, it "would be laughed out of court."[10] Therefore, we assert that there is a very high improbability against Schonfield's reconstruction of Jesus' life.

One other example of the swoon theory in popular literature is Donovan Joyce's *The Jesus Scroll*.[11] The thesis of this book, which contains an even more incredible string of improbabilities than Schonfield's, will be left for a later

---

[7]Ibid., pp. 166-172.

[8]Ibid., p. 6.

[9]Ibid., p. 165; cf. pp. 171-173.

[10]J.A.T. Robinson, *Can We Trust the New Testament?*, p. 15.

[11]Donovan Joyce, *The Jesus Scroll* (New York: New American Library, 1972).

section of this chapter. However, Joyce's account of the
swoon theory is discussed here.

For Joyce, Jesus was also planning his escape from death
on the cross. Accordingly, he was drugged and the Roman
soldiers did not examine Jesus too closely, perhaps because
they had been bribed. Neither did they stab him in the side
with a spear in order to ensure his death. As a result, Jesus
did not die on the cross. Rather, he was resuscitated in the
tomb, apparently by a doctor who had been concealed inside
ahead of time.[12]

This account of Jesus' swoon likewise smacks of fictitious
aspects, similar to both Schonfield and the eighteenth and
nineteenth century attempts.

The Fall of the Swoon Theory

The swoon theory was perhaps the most popular naturalistic theory against the historicity of Jesus' resurrection in the
early nineteenth century. But David Strauss, himself a liberal
theologian, disproved this theory to the satisfaction of his
fellow scholars.

1. Strauss' critique

Strauss raised a very important issue. Even if it was imag-
ined that Jesus was able to survive Roman crucifixion, what
could he do about the heavy stone in the entrance to the
tomb? In his extremely weakened physical condition, could
he move an object which even a healthy man would have a
great problem with (according to tradition)? This would be
even more difficult when it is remembered that the stone
would have to be rolled uphill out of its gully. Additionally,
the inside of the stone would provide no edge against which
Jesus might at least use his weight to push. Then, even if he
could have escaped from the tomb, could he walk the
distance to the disciples' hiding place after having his weight

---

[12]Ibid., pp. 106-110, 118.

suspended on a Roman crucifixion spike just a short time previously?

Yet, Strauss' most convincing point concerned Jesus' condition upon reaching his disciples. Very few would doubt that he would be in sad physical shape, limping badly, bleeding, pale and clutching his side. He would obviously be in need of physical assistance and, at any rate, would not appear to be the resurrected and glorified Lord of Life! As Strauss pointed out, the disciples would have gone for a doctor's help rather than proclaim Jesus the risen Son of God! Strauss asserted that even if the swoon theory was conceivable, it still could not account for the disciples' belief in the risen Jesus. Since they did proclaim him to be the resurrected and glorified Lord, the swoon theory is not able to account for the facts.[13]

Shortly after the turn of the century, Schweitzer referred to Strauss' critique as the "death-blow" to such rationalistic approaches.[14] After Strauss' views were circulated, the liberal "lives of Jesus" usually shunned the swoon theory.[15] By the early twentieth century, other critical scholars proclaimed this theory to be nothing more than a historical curiosity of the past. Even critics no longer considered it to be a viable hypothesis.[16]

2. Death by asphyxiation

Modern medical research has leveled at least two additional critiques against the swoon theory. First, crucifixion is essentially death by asphyxiation, as the intercostal and pectoral muscles around the lungs halt normal breathing while the body hangs in the "down" position. Therefore, faking death on the cross still would not permit one to breathe; one cannot fake the inability to breathe for any

---

[13]David Strauss, *A New Life of Jesus*, vol. 1, pp. 408-412.

[14]Schweitzer, *Quest*, pp. 56-67.

[15]Ibid., cf. pp. 161-166 with 166-179, for example.

[16]Eduard Riggenbach, *The Resurrection of Jesus* (New York: Eaton and Mains, 1907), pp. 48-49; James Orr, *The Resurrection of Jesus*, p. 92.

length of time. Breaking the victim's ankles insured death even quicker, since the person could not push up in order to free the lungs for breathing. The Romans were knowledgeable in these matters, as indicated by the broken leg bones of a first century crucifixion victim whose skeleton was recently discovered (see Chapter 8 for details). Since Jesus' ankles were not broken, we have the Roman's assurance that he was previously dead. Otherwise, this method would have killed him. Either way, the end result of Jesus' death is very probable.

3. Heart wound

Further, an even stronger refutation of the swoon theory is gained from the medical conclusion that the Roman lance entered Jesus' heart, the final assurance of death by crucifixion as recorded by Roman author Quintilian (*Declarationes maiores* 6.9). The gospel writer probably never understood the medical significance of what he recorded, for which eyewitness testimony is claimed (John 19:34-35). Medical doctors who have studied this issue usually agree that this is a very accurate medical description. The water probably proceeded from the pericardium, the sac that surrounds the heart, while the blood came from the right side of the heart. Even if Jesus was alive before he was stabbed, the lance would almost certainly have killed him.[17] Therefore, this chest wound also disproves the swoon theory.

We have noted three major problems that are sufficient to refute the swoon hypothesis. The physical condition of Jesus

---

[17]For examples of physicians who deal with this issue, see William D. Edwards, Wesley J. Gabel, and Floyd E. Hosmer, "On the Physical Death of Jesus Christ," *Journal of the American Medical Association* vol. 255, No. 11, 21 March 1986; Robert Bucklin, "The Legal and Medical Aspects of the Trial and Death of Christ," *Medicine, Science and the Law* (January, 1970); C. Truman Davis, "The Crucifixion of Jesus: The Passion of Christ from a Medical Point of View," in *Arizona Medicine*, March, 1965, pp. 183-187; Pierre Barbet, *A Doctor at Calvary* (Garden City: Doubleday, 1953); Robert Wassenar, "A Physician Looks at the Suffering of Christ" in *Moody Monthly*, 79/7, March 1979, pp. 41-42; James H. Jewell, Jr., and Patricia A. Didden, "A Surgeon Looks at the Cross," in *Voice*, 58/2, March-April, 1979, pp. 3-5.

(as advocated by Strauss), the nature of death on the cross by asphyxiation, and the study of Jesus' chest wound combine to eliminate this theory. Additionally, we witnessed the difficulties above (with Schonfield and Joyce) in the actual implementation of this view. Neither are these the only key problems. For example, this thesis cannot account for the conversions of James, the brother of Jesus, and especially Paul, from their skepticism to Christianity. Therefore, it is no surprise that this hypothesis is rejected today by critics.[18]

Qumran Connections

Another popular picture of Jesus is that he was a member of the Essene Community at Qumran, which is said to have influenced his teachings tremendously. Sometimes, but seldom, he is even connected with the Essene "Teacher of Righteousness," a priest who called the people to obey the Law and to live a holy life before the Lord and was perhaps even martyred for his teachings.

For instance, Upton Ewing's *The Essene Christ* asserts that Jesus was raised as an Essene and belonged to the sect, as did John the Baptist.[19] It is even hinted that Jesus thought of himself as the "Teacher of Righteousness."[20] Because of this background of both John and Jesus, their followers were likewise influenced by Essene teachings. Subsequently, the four Gospels are said to have borrowed much from the Qumran community.[21]

Strangely enough, Ewing sees the major theme of the Essene community, including Jesus and the early Christians, as the teaching of monistic ethics. This teaching involves a

---

[18]For examples, Barth, *Church Dogmatics*, vol. IV, p. 340; and Brown, "The Resurrection," p. 223.

[19]Upton Ewing, *The Essene Christ* (New York: Philosophical Library, 1961).

[20]Ibid., pp. 48-51, 62-63.

[21]Ibid., pp. 52, 62-64.

type of pantheistic oneness of the entire universe with God, each other and all of life. As a result, no violence should be perpetrated on any creature or person, but we should live in peace and love with all.[22]

Another writer to link Jesus and Christian origins with the Qumran community is Charles Potter. He also suggests that both John the Baptist and Jesus studied at Qumran while growing up. This would explain where Jesus was during his so-called "silent years" between the ages of twelve and thirty.[23] During these years, Potter postulates that Jesus either wrote, or at least read and was very influenced by an apocalyptic book named *The Secrets of Enoch*, which is closely connected with the ideas taught by the Essenes. While, at the very least, Jesus was inspired by these teachings, Potter is careful to point out that Jesus was not the Essene "Teacher of Righteousness," who lived long before Jesus.[24]

These works of Ewing and Potter are examples of popularistic attempts to explain the inner motivations and secret events of Jesus' life that are not recorded in the New Testament. Like the fictitious lives of Jesus described by Schweitzer, not only do we find an interest in these inner workings, we also confront the secretive organization of the Essenes once again. And like Schweitzer's examples, so are these works refuted by the facts. Four critiques of these views are now presented.

1. Faulty logic

First, there is a train of illogic employed in these works. For Ewing, the connection between Jesus and the Essenes is based on the opinion that, since he was neither a Sadducee nor a Pharisee, Jesus must have been an Essene![25] Again,

---

[22]Ibid., see pp. 62-64, 368-369, 393, 397, for examples.

[23]Charles Potter, *The Lost Years of Jesus Revealed* (Greenwich: Fawcett Publications, Inc., n.d.).

[24]Charles Potter, *Did Jesus Write This Book?* (Greenwich: Fawcett Publications, Inc., n.d.), pp. 16, 77, 133-141.

[25]Ewing, *Essene Christ*, p. 51.

since the Gospels depict Jesus as opposing both the Sadducees and the Pharisees but never opposing the Essenes, then he must have been one of the latter.[26]

Both of these statements are textbook examples of arguments from silence. Just because there is an absence of evidence in the Gospels as to what group Jesus favored, we cannot argue from that silence to the fact that he favored the Essenes. For instance, the Talmud fails to mention the Essenes, so does this make it an Essene book? These statements also commit the black-white fallacy of logic. They assume that either Jesus had to be a Sadducee or Pharisee on the one hand or an Essene on the other. But this conclusion only follows if it is known that these are the only options. Jesus could have been a member of another group or of no group at all. Indeed, the Gospels depict him as one who was "his own man" without explicit support for any sectarian politics.

Potter argues similarly. He states that he applied the logic which he learned in college to the facts concerning *The Secrets of Enoch* and decided that there was "no convincing reason against Jesus' authorship."[27] With this logic he surely should have noticed that his argument was also from silence. An absence of reasons against Jesus' authorship provides no evidence that he did, in fact, write the book. Potter additionally argues that *The Secrets of Enoch* was written by one author, from AD 1–50.[28] That is also an argument from the absence of evidence. There were surely an enormous number of intelligent people who lived between these years who would, given accurate dates, also be candidates for authorship. But this is not evidence that Jesus was the author. In concession, Potter even admits that his thesis is somewhat "imaginative."[29]

---

[26]Ibid., p. 78.

[27]Potter, *Did Jesus Write This Book?* p. 14.

[28]Ibid., pp. 134-135.

[29]Ibid., p. 136.

2. Major differences with Qumran

The second major reason for rejecting this thesis is that, while there are similarities between Jesus and Qumran,[30] there are also many differences that oppose any close connection. As asserted by Brownlee, "The Qumran literature tells us much about the background of primitive Christianity, but it can tell us nothing directly about Jesus."[31] A number of scholars have noted numerous differences between Jesus and Qumran beliefs.[32]

(1) Jesus opposed legalism, whereas the Essenes held strictly to it.

(2) Jesus also opposed ceremonial purity, while the Essenes, again, adhered meticulously to it.

(3) Jesus associated with common people and "sinners," whereas such activity was appalling to the Essenes.

(4) The sinlessness of Jesus is in contrast to the Essene teaching that even the Messiah would be purified from sin by suffering.

(5) Jesus combined several messianic aspects, while the Qumran community was looking for two (or even three) different messiahs.

(6) Jesus did not teach a strong hierarchy among his followers, while the Essenes imposed strict social rules.

(7) Jesus' group was open, but the Essene community was closed.

---

[30]For an extensive list of similarities, see especially James H. Charlesworth, "The Dead Sea Scrolls and the Historical Jesus," in *Jesus and the Dead Sea Scrolls*, ed. by James H. Charlesworth (New York: Doubleday, 1992), pp. 9-22; Jean Daniélou, "What the Dead Sea Scrolls Tell Us About Jesus," in Daniel-Rops, *Sources*, pp. 23-28; John M. Allegro, *The Dead Sea Scrolls* (Baltimore: Penguin, 1956), pp. 148-151; William Brownlee, "Jesus and Qumran," in *Jesus and the Historian*, ed. by F. Thomas Trotter (Philadelphia: Westminster, 1968), p. 75.

[31]Brownlee, "Jesus and Qumran," p. 52.

[32]Charlesworth, "Dead Sea Scrolls," pp. 22-35; Daniélou, "Dead Sea Scrolls," pp. 28-29; Allegro, *Dead Sea Scrolls*, pp. 161-162; Brownlee, "Jesus and Qumran," pp. 62-76; Charles Pfeiffer, *The Dead Sea Scrolls and the Bible* (Grand Rapids: Baker, 1969), pp. 97-99, 130-134; F.F. Bruce, *Second Thoughts on the Dead Sea Scrolls* (Grand Rapids: Eerdmans, 1956), pp. 79-84.

(8) Jesus' ministry was public, while the Essenes were very private.

(9) Jesus' teachings were oral, whereas the Essenes emphasized writing and copying.

(10) Jesus' manner of teaching was clear, not obtuse as in the Dead Sea Scrolls.

(11) Jesus had no formal training, in contrast to those from the Qumran community.

(12) Healing was a major part of Jesus' ministry, but this aspect was not emphasized at Qumran.

(13) The teaching of love was Jesus' major ethical message, but does not appear in Essene teachings.

(14) Jesus' ethics are closer to Rabbinic literature than to Qumran.

(15) Jesus had a more positive admiration for the Old Testament prophets than did the Essenes.

(16) Jesus did not emphasize angelology as much as did the Qumran community.

(17) Jesus' central teaching was the Kingdom of God, whereas the Essenes give little or no place to the concept.

(18) For Jesus, salvation was straightforward, while the Essenes had an elaborate initiation system.

(19) Jesus taught that salvation would also be extended to the Gentiles while the Essenes were more exlusivistic.

(20) Jesus was missionary-minded, while the Essenes were not.

(21) According to Josephus, the Essenes taught the immortality of the soul, in contrast to the Christian teaching of the resurrection of the body.

As a result, a close connection between Jesus and Qumran is very improbable.[33] Daniélou even states:

> Must we then conclude that he was an Essene, at least at some period of his life? Here historians are unanimous in affirming the contrary. There is nothing either in his origins or in the

---

[33]Allegro, *Dead Sea Scrolls*, p. 160.

setting in which he habitually lived, to justify such a conclusion.[34]

3. Major differences with the "Teacher of Righteousness"

Our third critique opposes the minority opinion that Jesus was the Essenes' "Teacher of Righteousness." Although very few hold this view, we will still list several problems noted by scholars.[35]

(1) The Essenes' Teacher was a priest, as opposed to Jesus' plural office.

(2) The Teacher considered himself a sinner in need of purification, while Jesus was sinless.

(3) The Teacher perceived that he was separated by an infinite gulf from God, while Christians hold that Jesus is the very Son of God.

(4) There is no evidence of any atoning value being placed on the Teacher's death, while such is the special significance of Jesus' shed blood and death.

(5) There is no claim or evidence that the Teacher was raised from the dead, while this is the central event for Christianity.

(6) Jesus is worshiped by Christians as God, while such was not the practice of the Essenes and even opposed their belief.

(7) Additionally, the Essenes' Teacher lived long before Jesus did.

4. View not necessarily critical of Christ

Our fourth critique of this position is the strongest. While the point is often missed, this view is not necessarily critical of Christ or his teachings even if it was shown that he had affinities to Essene thought or even that he was a member of the group. As Pfeiffer explains:

---

[34]Daniélou, "Dead Sea Scrolls," p. 28.

[35]Ibid., pp. 30-32; Brownlee, "Jesus and Qumran," pp. 69-70; Allegro, *Dead Sea Scrolls*, pp. 161-162; Bruce, *Second Thoughts*, p. 98.

It should be observed that there is nothing derogatory to the person of Christ in the assumption that He or His followers were of Essene background. The Scriptures make it clear that the mother of our Lord was a Jewess, and that He became incarnate in the midst of a Jewish environment. If it were proved that this environment was also Essene, Christian theology would lose nothing and the uniqueness of Jesus would be no more disproved than it is disproved by the assertion of the Jewish origin after the flesh.[36]

In other words, Jesus had to be born somewhere and he went to school somewhere. To assert that this background was influenced by the Essenes is not in itself critical of Christianity, as long as his teachings are not adjusted or his uniqueness modified. His person and teachings are still validated by a trustworthy New Testament (see Chapter 2) and, if his resurrection is verified, this could also serve to confirm his message.[37]

Yet, we must still reject this approach to the life of Jesus. The illogical argumentation, the differences between Christianity and Qumran and the differences between Jesus and the Teacher of Righteousness all invalidate it. However, even if this hypothesis was demonstrated, it would affect nothing of major importance in Christianity since Jesus did have some type of background and his message can be shown to be trustworthy and unique anyway.

Jesus' Message Is Changed by Others

The charge is often made that Jesus' message was actually quite different from the one which Christians have traditionally taught concerning him. This sometimes is said to be the case, for instance, because the Gospels represent the teachings of the early church and not those of Jesus himself (compare the discussion about Bultmann above). We saw

---

[36]Pfeiffer, *Dead Sea Scrolls*, p. 97.

[37]Although this argument cannot be pursued here, see Habermas, *The Resurrection of Jesus: An Apologetic.*

how this approach is invalidated as an attempt to ascertain Jesus' teachings.

Hugh Schonfield postulated another reason for this change in Jesus' message. He holds that Jesus was a teacher who was true to Judaism and who had no desire to start any new religion. That is why, for instance, he never proclaimed his own deity.[38] While Paul did present some different teachings,[39] he is not the real culprit. Rather, Schonfield asserts that the church at Rome perverted Paul's teachings about Jesus in order to turn him into a deity who set up a new religion.[40] The Roman church did this by consciously writing some of the New Testament books and by influencing others to rewrite the story of Jesus. Books said to be either written or influenced strongly by this effort include the synoptic Gospels, Hebrews and Peter's epistles.[41] The general movement is from Jesus' original teachings, to Paul's assessments, to the Roman redirection.[42] The result is that Christian theology as it is taught today is not the teachings of Jesus and the apostles.[43] By such progress, the teachings of Jesus and Paul have been changed by a plot to make Christianity palatable to Roman Gentiles. In spite of Schonfield's new "twists," his thesis is vulnerable to four criticisms.

1. No factual basis

First, since Schonfield rejects the testimony of the Gospels,[44] he presents no valid basis on which to assert that Jesus' original teachings were different from what traditional Christianity believes about him. The problem here is actually

---

[38]Hugh Schonfield, *Those Incredible Christians* (New York: Bantam, 1969), pp. IX, 50-51.

[39]Ibid., p. 67.

[40]Ibid., pp. 135-155.

[41]Ibid., pp. 136-149.

[42]Ibid., pp. 149, 211, 230.

[43]Ibid., pp. XVII, 170.

[44]Ibid., pp. 142-146, 259-272.

twofold. Initially, Schonfield is opposed by all of the evidence for the authenticity and trustworthiness of the Gospels (and the New Testament). Additionally, and more specifically, how can one rule out the Gospels' testimony and still have a basis on which to assert that the original teachings of Jesus were different? How can Schonfield know that Jesus did not present the message of the Gospels? What is his basis of comparison between Jesus and what the earliest sources say about him? It becomes apparent that there are no grounds of distinction between Jesus and the Gospels.

Schonfield might respond that Jesus could not have taught the message that traditional Christianity affirms, since it was contrary to what first century Jews believed. Yet Schonfield uses the Gospels to establish this response,[45] a basis which he rejects. And since it is not proper hermeneutical method to pick and choose the verses which one will accept and those which one will reject, he is again left without any valid basis for his position.

For those who contend that the Gospels are dependable sources that reveal a non-divine Jesus and that Paul (and others) perverted this message, it should be mentioned here that even the synoptic Gospels reveal that Jesus claimed deity for himself. For example, he referred to himself as "Son of God" and "Son of Man," he taught that salvation was found only in himself and claimed that only he had the power to forgive sin.[46] He certainly claimed to be in a privileged relationship with God; his usage of "Abba" (Aramaic for "Daddy") is a very unusual name for God and is an indication of his unique sonship, as many critical scholars admit.[47]

---

[45]Ibid., pp. 50-51.

[46]See Habermas, *The Resurrection of Jesus: An Apologetic*, chapter 3 for several additional indications of Jesus' claims to deity. For an argument for the deity of Christ even for those who do not accept the trustworthiness of the New Testament, see Terry L. Miethe and Gary R. Habermas, *Why Believe? God Exists!* (Joplin: College Press, 1993), chapter 27.

[47]Joachim Jeremias, *The Central Message of the New Testament* (Philadelphia: Fortress, 1965), pp. 9-30; Reginald Fuller, *The Foundations of New Testament Christology* (New York: Scribner's, 1965), p. 115, for instance.

At any rate, we cannot follow Schonfield and attempt to divorce Jesus' message from what the earliest sources indicate concerning him, for in so doing we destroy the basis that is needed to establish that division. Additionally, to assume that Jesus did not consider himself deity while ruling out the Gospels, is to do so on the grounds of the presumed first century Jewish thought, which is a circular argument that presupposes Jesus did not teach anything different. This is the very point to be demonstrated.

2. No evidence for the Roman plot

Second, there is no evidence for any such plot on the part of Christians at Rome, as presumed by Schonfield. Of course, one can argue anything without the appropriate support, but others are not obliged to accept it. Similarly, no one is constrained to accept Schonfield's thesis without the proper evidence.

Since we do not know that Jesus denied deity and especially since there are reasons to assert that he did claim such deity then why would there be a need for Roman Christians to "invent" the message? In other words, we can only begin to contemplate the alteration of Jesus' words if we know that he did not teach the message of his deity in the first place. But since the point is invalid, as just shown, one cannot leap to the next step of a conspiracy by the Christians at Rome.

3. Paul attests to Jesus' deity

Third, the Pauline epistles, which even Schonfield accepts as valid texts, attest to the orthodox view of Jesus' deity. Thus, while Schonfield holds that Paul followed Jesus' own teachings in rejecting the deity of the Messiah,[48] the writings of Paul which are accepted by Schonfield teach otherwise. This is revealed by even a brief survey. In Romans 1:3-4, Paul gives Jesus the titles "Son," "Lord" and "Christ." Although

---

[48]Schonfield, *Those Incredible Christians*, pp. 98, 257.

completely ignored by Schonfield in a treatment of this verse,[49] the usage of "Lord," in particular, indicates Paul's view of Jesus' deity. As said Oscar Cullmann in his classic Christology, this term indicates that Paul could give Jesus the title of "God," since "Lord" itself "clearly expresses Jesus' deity."[50]

Even stronger is Paul's statement in Romans 9:5, where Jesus is, in all probability, actually called "God."[51] Similarly, Paul affirms Christ's full deity in Colossians 2:9. While Schonfield clearly mistranslates this latter verse,[52] Cullmann, agreeing with virtually all scholars, renders the key phrase as "the whole fullness of deity dwelt bodily" in Jesus Christ.[53] As philologist A.T. Robertson points out, this verse indicates that all the fullness of the very essence of God dwells in Jesus in bodily form.[54] These two references, in particular, reveal Paul's view of the full deity of Jesus.

Other passages are additionally helpful. Philippians 2:6-11 asserts that Jesus has the form or very nature of God and commends worship of the exalted Jesus. In Colossians 1:15, Paul points out that Jesus is the "image of God" and in 2 Corinthians 12:8, Paul prays to Christ.[55] By these means, then, Paul does teach the deity of Jesus. This is not a doctrine added by unscrupulous Christians from Rome, but a teaching of Jesus himself and of Paul.

4. Jesus' claim to deity

Fourth, even if a divine messiah was not what first century

---

[49]Ibid., p. 155.

[50]Oscar Cullmann, *The Christology of the New Testament*, transl. by Shirley Guthrie and Charles Hall (Philadelphia: Westminster, 1963), pp. 311-312.

[51]Ibid., pp. 312-313; Raymond E. Brown, *Jesus: God and Man* (Milwaukee: Bruce, 1967), pp. 20-22.

[52]Schonfield, *Those Incredible Christians*, p. 252.

[53]Cullmann, *Christology*, p. 311.

[54]A.T. Robertson, *Word Pictures in the New Testament*, 6 vols. (Nashville: Broadman, 1931), vol. 4, p. 491.

[55]Cullmann, *Christology*, pp. 235, 311-312.

Jews were looking for, there is a good reason why Jesus may still have made this very claim, as the evidence indicates he did. If he was truly deity, then he may have been attempting to correct the first century Jewish understanding of the messiah. And if he was, in fact, raised from the dead, this at least raises the possibility that his claims were verified. Again, any verification of Jesus' teachings is beyond the scope of this book, but if the resurrection is demonstrated as history, then claims in this area can no longer be disregarded.[56] Schonfield might then have to face his thesis in reverse.

At any rate, Schonfield's thesis (as well as others who claim that Jesus' teachings were changed) is invalid. This is especially so when the Gospels have been rejected, for there is then no basis for this conclusion. It is thereby circular to assume that Jesus' views did not differ from first century Jews, for this is the very point to be demonstrated. But then the presumed plot of the Christians at Rome also fails because there is no evidence that Jesus did not teach his own deity. In fact, there is much evidence in the Gospels that he did teach this.

If one rejects the Gospels there is little basis for rejecting the traditional Christian testimony concerning Jesus, and we arrive at a circular argument. If the texts are accepted, then we are faced with Jesus' claims to be deity. Additionally, Paul's firm teaching on the deity of Jesus invalidates this thesis, as does a possible verification of Jesus' claims if his resurrection is demonstrated as historical.

Paul did not corrupt Jesus' teachings

It should be carefully noted, however, that Schonfield represents only one version of the thesis that Jesus' message was changed. This claim is a very common one. In general, the frequent charge is that Paul either originated or corrupted Christianity, usually on the subjects of the deity of Jesus and

---

[56]See Habermas, *The Resurrection of Jesus: An Apologetic*, especially chapters 1-3 for the details of such an argument.

the nature and extent of the gospel message. It is to this more general charge that we wish to offer seven brief critiques.

(1) It has been mentioned above that Jesus made various statements regarding his own deity. He claimed to be the Son of Man, the Son of God, to forgive sin and that he was the actual means of salvation. There are also additional indications of his own teachings concerning his deity, such as his use of the word "Abba." It is quite significant that Jesus' first century contemporaries were convinced of his claim to deity (Mark 2:6-7; John 5:17-18).[57] Therefore, the thesis which asserts that the deity of Jesus is a later doctrine fails largely at this point.

(2) Numerous ancient, pre-Pauline creeds also teach the full deity of Jesus. Philippians 2:6-11 not only attributes Old Testament praise of God (as the one true God) to Jesus (cf. Isa. 45:22-23), but it also calls Jesus "Christ" and "Lord." On this latter title, Cullmann asserts that it is even loftier than the passages which address Jesus as God, since Lord is the name for God. This allowed Christians to attribute what the Old Testament says about God to Jesus, as evidenced in this passage.[58] Additionally, and even stronger, Jesus is said in verse six to have the same nature or essence as God. Reginald Fuller states that here Jesus is "equal with God."[59] Cullmann speaks of Jesus' "identity of form with God," which shows that he is "equal with God" in his exaltation.[60] Other pre-Pauline creeds also teach the deity of Jesus. Romans 1:3-4 calls Jesus "Son," "Christ" and "Lord." First Corinthians 11:23ff., which Joachim Jeremias states "goes back . . . to Jesus himself,"[61] also calls Jesus "Lord." First Corinthians

---

[57]The subject of Jesus' self-designations is an intricate issue and cannot be dealt with in detail here. For some justification of these claims, see Oscar Cullmann, *Christology*. On the last point, see Reginald Fuller, *Foundations*, p. 115.

[58]Cullmann, *Christology*, pp. 235, 237, 307.

[59]Fuller, *Foundations*, pp. 208, 248.

[60]Cullmann, *Christology*, p. 321; see also p. 235.

[61]Joachim Jeremias, *The Eucharistic Words of Jesus*, transl. by Norman Perrin (London: SCM Press, Ltd., 1966), p. 101.

15:3ff., perhaps the oldest New Testament creed, calls Jesus "Christ." It is also significant that these creeds pre-date Paul and extend back to the earliest church, which completely complement Jesus' own self-claims.

(3) Paul did not teach a new religion. He taught that Christianity was a fulfillment of Judaism (Rom. 10:4, 9-11; Col. 2:16-17), which is what Jesus taught, as well (Matt. 5:18; Luke 16:16-17).

(4) Paul also agreed with Jesus as to the nature of the gospel. Both taught that men are sinners (Mark 3:38; Rom. 3:23; 6:23) and that Jesus died, with his shed blood providing atonement for that sin (Matt. 26:28; Mark 10:45; Eph. 1:7; Rom. 5:8). The death and burial of Jesus was completed by his resurrection (Luke 24:46-47; John 20:25-29; Rom. 10:9). Yet man cannot save himself, but needs God's grace and leading (Matt. 19:25-26; John 4:44; Eph. 2:8-9), which is imparted through faith and surrender to Christ (Mark 1:15; Rom. 10:9-11). The result is a changed life and commitment (Luke 14:25-35; John 15:1-11; 2 Cor. 5:17; Eph. 2:10).

(5) Paul was the apostle to the Gentiles (Rom. 11:13-14). Jesus also taught the disciples to take the gospel to the Gentiles (Matt. 28:19-20; Luke 24:47; John 10:16; Acts 1:8) and that non-Jews would be found in the Kingdom of God (Matt. 8:11-12; John 17:20). These teachings are actually the fulfillment of Old Testament promises (Gen. 12:3; Isa. 19:18-25), not a new doctrine.

(6) Paul's message of the gospel was both checked and approved by the original apostles (Gal. 2:1-10), providing official recognition that his message was not opposed to that of Jesus. It was also shown earlier that Paul's epistles were accepted as Scripture immediately after being written (2 Pet. 3:15-16; Clement of Rome; Ignatius and Polycarp).

(7) We have also introduced the significance of Jesus' resurrection with regard to the truthfulness of his teachings. Since Paul agrees with Jesus, any such confirmation would also apply to Paul's teachings.

---

[62]C.H. Dodd, *The Apostolic Preaching and its Developments* (Grand Rapids: Baker, 1980), p. 16.

Therefore we conclude that Paul was not the founder of Christianity and neither did he corrupt Jesus' teachings. They agree on the essentials of the faith. Furthermore, the early pre-Pauline creed in 1 Cor. 15:3ff. presents the same view of the deity of Jesus and the nature of the gospel. As the eminent New Testament scholar C.H. Dodd pointed out, Paul's preaching coincided with that of primitive Christianity and those who would assert otherwise bear the burden of proof.[62]

Jesus As International Traveler

In surveys of popular lives of Jesus, it is not long before one discovers a prevalent tendency to view Jesus as an international traveler. It is sometimes asserted that he took journeys to such exotic places as India, Japan, or Egypt during his eighteen so-called "silent years" (between the ages of twelve and thirty), or trips after his crucifixion; the latter usually necessitating a swoon theory. We looked briefly at one similar thesis already, with Potter's *The Lost Years of Jesus Revealed*. Although Jesus did not travel too far, it is said that he spent his "silent years" in the Qumran community. (See the discussion of this thesis above.)

Oriental legend

Another persistent legend states that Jesus traveled east to India and Japan. According to family documents which were purportedly uncovered in 1935 by Shinto priest Kiyomaro Takeuchi, Jesus reportedly sailed to Japan at the age of eighteen. He stayed in that country for about seven or eight years and studied Japanese philosophy and culture in his search for wisdom. Armed with both this knowledge and with some magic tricks which he had learned, Jesus went back to Palestine. Upon his return, Jesus preached the Kingdom of God. When it became clear that he was going to be killed, the Japanese legend relates that his brother, Isukiri, volunteered to die in Jesus' place so that Jesus could continue with his work on earth. Having convinced Jesus by such rationale, his brother Isukiri died and was buried. Afterwards, Jesus and Judas went to the tomb and reburied Isukiri's dead body.

The legend continues by teaching that Jesus then left Palestine and took four years to get to Shinjo, Japan. There he changed his name to Torai Taro Tenkujin, got married and fathered three children. After living a full life as a prophet and teacher, Jesus is said to have died at the age of 112 years. The Japanese of Shinjo commemorated his death with what they claim is Jesus' tomb located in a small valley not far from the village. However, when asked if Jesus is really buried in this tomb, Shinjo mayor Genki Kosaka replied that he could not say either way.[63]

Joyce's hypothesis

Another hypothesis involving Jesus as a traveler is related by Donovan Joyce, who asserts that in 1964 he was told of a scroll which was stolen by a professor who would not give him his true name. This professor claimed that the scroll was found at Masada, on the Dead Sea, and was written by a man identifying himself as "Jesus of Gennesareth, son of Jacob," an eighty-year-old defender of Masada who apparently died while fighting the Romans during the Jewish revolt of AD 66–73. Unfortunately Joyce never found out the professor's real name and, in the meantime, the scroll has disappeared so that no one knows the whereabouts of it or of the professor![64] Yet Joyce claims that there is a chance that this scroll was written by Jesus before his death at the age of eighty years. Therefore, there must be a history of what happened to Jesus during the almost fifty years from the time of his crucifixion until his death.

So Joyce suggests that Jesus never died on the cross, but "plotted" to remain alive in spite of crucifixion. He was drugged on the cross, but the guards, apparently bribed, did

---

[63]John Peterson, "A Legend Says Jesus Died in Japan at 112," *The Detroit News*, August 9, 1971, pp. 1A, 6A. There are other parallels of a similar nature in Ethiopia and Egypt.

[64]Joyce, *The Jesus Scroll*, pp. 7-14.

not examine Jesus' comatose body too closely. A doctor was concealed in the tomb in order to nurse Jesus back to health again, assisted by Joseph of Arimathea, Jesus' uncle. As Jesus recovered he paid one last visit to his disciples and then retired as a monk at Qumran.[65] But Jesus was not to live out the remainder of his days in the quiet Qumran setting. Joyce postulates that Jesus was a part of the Hasmonean line, and connects him with the Zealots as an open revolutionary against Rome. In accord with his background, Jesus had married Mary Magdalene even before his crucifixion, according to Hasmonean tradition, and fathered at least one son. Jesus was opposed to the Roman rule and left Qumran for Masada, where he died while fighting the Romans.[66]

Holy Blood, Holy Grail

Another recent attempt to present Jesus as a traveler is the book *Holy Blood, Holy Grail*. Acknowledging the usage of Joyce's presentation, this work also holds that Jesus was married to Mary Magdalene (who is identified as Mary of Bethany). The children from this marriage were heirs of Jesus' kingly bloodline.[67] Jesus was said to have been crucified for crimes perpetrated against Rome, not against the Jews. However, he did not die on the cross, but was drugged to make him appear dead. Pilate was bribed in order to allow Jesus to be removed from the cross alive. The Essenes then took his body, which was laid in the tomb of Joseph of Arimathea, a relative of Jesus. After nursing Jesus back to health, Joseph, Mary Magdalene and Lazarus (Jesus' brother-in-law) went to France to live. However, no one knows where Jesus went after his recuperation. The authors suggest India, Egypt, Masada or somewhere else in Israel.[68] The vast bulk of

---

[65]Ibid., pp. 100-110, 131-140, 160.

[66]Ibid., pp. 54-59, 76-99, 141-158.

[67]Michael Baigent, Richard Leigh and Henry Lincoln, *Holy Blood, Holy Grail* (New York: Delacorte, 1982), pp. 301-320, 324.

[68]Ibid., pp. 322-332, 347.

the book is devoted to the remains of Jesus' bloodline, through Mary Magdalene, as they settled and spread in France. This supposed bloodline is traced through royal families, secret organizations and age-old mysteries. But, as even the authors recognize, the major question is whether this French lineage did, in fact, come from Jesus.[69]

Problems with International Travel Theory

These attempts to have Jesus avoid death and then travel afterward are laden with more difficulties than any other approach that we have studied. This is largely due to the presence of so much conjecture combined with an absence of facts. We present four major objections to such approaches to the life of Jesus.

1. Gospels are trustworthy

First, in our earlier discussions we determined that the New Testament, and the Gospels in particular, are authentic and trustworthy documents for the life and teachings of Jesus. We will not belabor this point any further, except to note that this conclusion is based on both the early and eyewitness testimony behind the Gospels, including authors who were close to the facts, as well as the attestation of the earliest church and overwhelming manuscript evidence. Such facts reveal that the Gospels are a valid basis for the teachings of Jesus, in opposition to these theses which almost always involve vast alterations of New Testament data. On this point alone these theses fail.

2. Swoon theory disproven

Second, most of these theses involve the swoon theory concerning Jesus' resurrection, without which there would be

---

[69]Ibid., see chapters 1-11, 13 for details. See p. 286 for the author's statement concerning the need to have evidence of such a bloodline.

no basis for any post-crucifixion travels followed by a later, obscure death. But as stated above in our examination of this hypothesis, this hypothesis falls prey to numerous problems which will not be repeated here.

Some sources, such as the Japanese legend cited here, assert that someone else died on the cross in place of Jesus. Other such claims include the Gnostic writing "The Second Treatise of the Great Seth" (55:15-20)[70] and the Muslim *Koran* (Surah IV: 156-159).[71] Whereas the Japanese tale claims that the crucified person was Jesus' brother, the Gnostic source claims that Simon of Cyrene was killed while the glorified Jesus sat in the heavens and laughed at the error. A popular Muslim teaching is that it was Judas who died instead of Jesus.

Such strange "twists" to the swoon theory have been virtually ignored by scholars with good reason, for serious problems invalidate each of these theses.

(1) The sources that report these theories are exceptionally late. While the date of the Gnostic writing is difficult to obtain, it was probably written two or more centuries after Jesus and definitely manifests theological rather than historical interests, since one Gnostic belief is that Jesus could not have died physically on the cross, hence a substitute would be needed. The Japanese legend was not known until about AD 500 when it was introduced in Japan by the Chinese. The *Koran* is a seventh century AD writing. Works of the third to seventh century are rather late to have much authoritative claim, while the Gnostic and Muslim sources plainly exhibit theological interests for their assertions.

(2) Why would Jesus' disciples, friends and relatives not recognize a substitute, especially when several were present at the crucifixion and burial? This is almost beyond credulity.

(3) How could Jesus' enemies have missed the oversight?

---

[70]See James M. Robinson, *The Nag Hammadi Library in English* (San Francisco: Harper and Row, 1977), pp. 329-338.

[71]*The Meaning of the Glorious Koran*, transl. by Mohammed Marmaduke Pickthall (New York: New American Library, n.d.), p. 93.

Since they knew what his appearance was from his trips to Jerusalem and certainly had strong motives to kill him, including the desire to be present at the crucifixion to witness his death, such a mistake would be simply incredible.

(4) Such theories would not be able to adequately explain the reported appearances of Jesus to eyewitnesses after his crucifixion, since such testimony concerned both his glorified body and his healed wounds.

It is no wonder that such a variant hypothesis has had very little following even among critics. The late dates of the sources and the lack of recognition by both Jesus' loved ones and his enemies alike, even at extremely close range, together with his glorified but scarred post-crucifixion appearances, combine to make this assertion quite unpalatable to scholars.

3. Lack of historical credibility

The third major objection to the thesis that Jesus was an international traveler after his crucifixion is that these theories lack historical credibility. Each of the theses is plagued with a lack of solid historical evidence. For instance, the Japanese legend not only rests on very questionable hearsay testimony but it was not even introduced into Japan until AD 500.[72] Certainly a gap of some 450 years should make us question the historical origin of this legend.

Concerning Joyce's thesis that Jesus died at the age of eighty while fighting the Romans at Masada, the historical basis is perhaps even more questionable. Joyce never knew the professor's true name, and even admits that he must rely on "hearsay" testimony. If that is not enough, the scroll has since vanished and no one knows the claimed whereabouts of either this document or the "professor" upon whose word the testimony rests! Interestingly, Joyce even wrote to Yigael Yadin, the well-known archaeologist who headed the Masada expedition. Yadin's response to Joyce's story was that

---

[72]Peterson, "Legend," p. 6A.

"anyone with a little knowledge of scrolls and conditions in which they were discovered at Masada would have immediately detected the nonsense in the story."[73] There can be little question that the story of the lost scroll cannot be used in any attempt to formulate the historical facts of the last years of Jesus' life.

In *Holy Blood, Holy Grail* we find a similar gap in the historical basis. The authors themselves characterize their *own* historical argument, before investigating the Christian sources, with the following description:

> Our hypothetical scenario . . . was also preposterous . . . much too sketchy . . . rested on far too flimsy a foundation . . . could not yet in itself be supported . . . too many holes . . . too many inconsistencies and anomalies, too many loose ends.[74]

After their research into Christian origins, does their evaluation change? While holding that their thesis was still probably true, the authors conclude, "We could not — and still cannot — prove the accuracy of our conclusion. It remains to some extent at least, a hypothesis."[75] As we will see below, their thesis also has numerous gaps in argumentation.

Historically, then, such theses lack the data needed for the conclusions. Very late documents, missing evidence and faulty historical reconstructions certainly do not prove one's case.

4. Illogical arguments

The fourth major problem with these theses is that, in addition to the lack of a historical basis, each exhibits decidedly illogical argumentation. The Japanese legend contains such inconsistencies as Jesus' brother dying in his place, the fact that Jesus' teachings reflect none of the Japanese philosophy that he supposedly learned during his "silent years"

---

[73]Joyce, *The Jesus Scroll*, p. 187; see also pp. 7-14.
[74]Baigent, Leigh and Lincoln, *Holy Blood*, p. 286.
[75]Ibid., p. 372.

spent in Japan, and the failure to acknowledge the Christian teachings of Francis Xavier. This Catholic priest visited Japan in the sixteenth century and probably accounts for much of the Christian influence in that country.[76] Even so, it is in the works of Joyce, Baigent, Leigh and Lincoln where we perceive more glaring gaps in logic.

For Joyce, the story does not stop with the admittedly hearsay evidence supplied by an anonymous "professor" who disappears along with all of the evidence for his claims, never to be heard from again. After asking where the scroll could have disappeared, Joyce postulates that there is one country in the world which would especially like to discover its contents — Russia! When he arrived in Delhi, India he remembered that the "professor" had also said he was going to Delhi. Therefore, Joyce felt that he had verified his thesis when he spotted a Russian plane at the airport, although he apparently never questioned the presence of planes from various other countries at such an international airport. Russia had to have sent the plane to pick up the "professor" and his valuable scroll![77]

To make matters worse, Joyce claims further evidence for his thesis in that a Russian official held a conference with the Vatican's Pope Paul in 1967. Although there was never a hint of what transpired at this meeting, Joyce is sure that they were talking about the "professor's" scroll! Russia was putting pressure on the Vatican, presumably with world revelation of the scroll hanging in the balances. And after all of this, Joyce states that the still unknown professor is probably a very respected scholar who is no longer free or perhaps even dead, thereby intimating that the Russians have him, so that his story will never be told![78]

Such illogic is also carried over into Joyce's treatment of the life of Jesus. This happens often, but we will recount just one example here. In Luke 8:1-3, we are told that several

---

[76]Peterson, "Legend," p. 6A.

[77]Joyce, *The Jesus Scroll*, pp. 158-159, 184.

[78]Ibid., pp. 159-160, 191.

women supported Jesus and his disciples financially. Joyce declares this to be "quite certain" evidence that Jesus was married.[79] Such a train of illogic hardly needs a comment, but it is certainly an example of how such hypotheses must really be strained to put together such a "case" for the life of Jesus. It is also typical of the assertions made in *Holy Blood, Holy Grail*, from which many examples could also be adduced.

It is held that since Jesus and his mother are called to a wedding in John 2:1-11 and since they play a major role, it must therefore automatically be Jesus' own wedding. Apparently no one can play a major role at anyone else's wedding, even if he is able to do miracles![80] In the account of the raising of Lazarus in John 11:1-46, it is asserted that, since Martha ran out to greet Jesus upon his arrival while Mary waited in the house until Jesus asked for her (vv. 20, 28), Mary must be Jesus' wife! The authors even admit a *non sequitur* argument by such reasoning.[81]

It is obvious that, oftentimes in such theses, conclusions are arrived at only by taking out of the Gospels and even adding to them what one would like to find. In this case, the authors even admit this procedure. After stating that they sifted through the Gospels searching for the specific points which they needed, they confessed that "we would be obliged to read between lines, fill in certain gaps, account for certain caesuras and ellipses. We would have to deal with omissions, with innuendos, with references that were, at best, oblique."[82] One instance of this arbitrary methodology occurs when they admit that they are utilizing such a procedure in order to find evidence for Jesus being married, which is obvious from the above examples on this subject. Another instance follows an attempt to make John the most historical of the four Gospels. The authors assert that modern scholarship has

---

[79]Ibid., pp. 78-79.

[80]Baigent, Leigh and Lincoln, *Holy Blood*, pp. 303-304.

[81]Ibid., pp. 307-308.

[82]Ibid., p. 103.

established this point, when such is simply not the case. But the authors' motives are exposed when they specifically acknowledge that they used John the most in an attempt to support their hypothesis![83] Thus, we again see examples of illogic being used to support a case for one's own desired results. One is reminded here of Louis Cassels' evaluation of such attempts to "explain away" the facts.

> The amazing thing about all these debunk-Jesus books is that they accept as much of the recorded Gospels as they find convenient, then ignore or repudiate other parts of the same document which contradict their notions.[84]

The trustworthiness of the Gospels, the failure of the swoon theory in all of its forms, the lack of a valid historical basis, and the decidedly illogical lines of argumentation demonstrate the failures of these theories. This is not even to mention their hopeless contradiction of one another as well.

Summary and Conclusion

There have been many popular attempts to discredit the Jesus of the Gospels. Even in the eighteenth and nineteenth centuries these attempts were prevalent. While they have been rejected almost unanimously by careful scholars, especially those who remember similar attempts disproven long ago, they still receive widespread attention among lay people. There have even been strictly fictional, novelistic attempts to deal with these subjects.[85]

It is because of this attention among the general populace that we have considered these popularistic "lives of Jesus" in this chapter. Accordingly, we investigated hypotheses

---

[83]Ibid.

[84]Louis Cassels, "Debunkers of Jesus Still Trying," *The Detroit News*, June 23, 1973, p. 7A.

[85]Templeton, *Act of God*; Irving Wallace, *The Word* (New York: Pocket, 1973); Og Mandino, *The Christ Commission* (New York: Bantam, 1981).

involving swoon, Qumran connections, perversions of Jesus' message, and theses involving Jesus as an international traveler. Each was refuted on its own grounds by a number of criticisms.

Louis Cassels responded rather harshly to such "debunking" attempts:

> You can count on it. Every few years, some "scholar" will stir up a short-lived sensation by publishing a book that says something outlandish about Jesus.
>
> The "scholar" usually has no standing as a Bible student, theologian, archaeologist, or anything else related to serious religious study.
>
> But that need not hold him back. If he has a job — any job — on a university faculty, his "findings" will be treated respectfully in the press as a "scholarly work."[86]

Although such satirical comments remind one of Schweitzer's similar remarks concerning the "imperfectly equipped freelances" who composed the "fictitious lives of Jesus" from 130 to 200 years ago,[87] these statements cannot fairly be applied to all of the writings in this chapter. Yet they do remind us of characteristics that are true of many. Accordingly, while all of the theses surveyed in this chapter are refuted by the facts, some of them are additionally to be viewed from the standpoint of fictitious attempts to avoid the Jesus of the Gospels.

---

[86]Cassels, "Debunkers," p. 7A.

[87]Schweitzer, *The Quest of the Historical Jesus*, p. 38.

5   The New Gnosticism

The year 1945 witnessed an amazing discovery at Nag Hammadi, about 300 miles south of Cairo in the Nile River region of Egypt. In the month of December, an Arab peasant accidently discovered 13 papyrus codices bound in leather. Though remaining obscure for years due to several bizarre occurrences, including murder, black market sales and the destruction of some of the findings, along with the normal amount of secrecy, 52 separate writings from those codices still exist today. Known as the Nag Hammadi Gnostic texts, these writings have grown increasingly important, especially since the appearance of the first English translation of the entire set of texts in 1977.[1]

There is general agreement that these Coptic translations are to be dated from about AD 350–400, based on the type of script and papyrus utilized. However, this is almost where the scholarly consensus on important conclusions ends. For example, it is also realized that the originals of these texts are to be dated much earlier, but how much so is a matter of sharp dispute. Further, some scholars assert that the Nag Hammadi texts contain almost nothing of significance for

---

[1]James M. Robinson, ed., *The Nag Hammadi Library*.

New Testament studies, while others think that the relevance is nothing short of colossal.

In this chapter, it will be necessary to be selective in the subtopics that will be addressed. Accordingly, we will state and evaluate several of the stronger claims on behalf of these Gnostic texts, since these are the ones that purport to most directly affect New Testament teachings about Jesus. Although there are many other areas we could investigate,[2] our criteria for discussion will be to center on assertions which challenge the orthodox understanding of the historicity of Jesus.

Challenges from the Gnostic Texts

One of the favorite theses advanced by some of those who make claims on behalf of the authority of the Gnostic texts is that, in some sense, these writings should be viewed on an equal footing with the canonical New Testament books. Perhaps the classical modern expression of such a contention was promoted by Walter Baur in his 1934 volume, *Orthodoxy and Heresy in Earliest Christianity*.[3]

Baur argued that second century Christendom witnessed a wide variety of theological viewpoints. Gnosticism existed in this milieu as an alternative to what was later recognized as the orthodox position. In fact, in some areas, Gnostic tendencies may have been the chief expressions of Christianity. However, out of this multiplicity, orthodoxy still emerged, but not necessarily because it was the original position of Jesus and his disciples.[4]

Such a theme reappears, in one form or another, in current discussions of this subject, as well. Frederik Wisse is

---

[2]Nonetheless, a number of these areas will be noted as we proceed.

[3]This work was originally published in German. An English translation, ed. by Robert Kraft and Gerhard Krodel, was issued by Fortress Press (Philadelphia) in 1971.

[4]Ibid., p. xxii, for example.

one of the most recent scholars to revive a contention quite similar to Baur's. He also insists that orthodoxy surfaced from the second century amalgam of views by asserting itself over the other positions involved in the conflict.[5]

More popularly but not as recently, A. Powell Davies also argued that orthodox Christianity existed in the midst of various other competing religious ideologies. After an intense struggle between such differing philosophies, orthodoxy triumphed in the third century AD.[6]

Thesis of Pagels

Elaine Pagels advanced a related thesis in her volume *The Gnostic Gospels*,[7] in which she brought some of the conclusions of various esoteric discussions to the attention of the general public. She holds that the second century church included a wide variety of options, since canonical, theological and ecclesiastical views had not yet been settled. Differing texts and traditions, both Gnostic and orthodox, circulated alongside each other.[8]

A struggle ensued, and orthodox beliefs prevailed. Thus, one of the several, competing options elevated itself above the others and became predominant. But, far from distinguishing itself as the superior historical and theological view, orthodoxy achieved victory largely on political and social grounds. Those who disagreed with these dogmatic assumptions were simply viewed as heretics.[9]

---

[5]Wisse's essay is included in Charles Hedrick and Robert Hodgson, eds., *Nag Hammadi, Gnosticism, and Early Christianity* (Peabody: Hendrickson, 1986). For an insightful critique, see James L. Jaquette's review in the *Journal of the Evangelical Theological Society*, Vol. 32, No. 1, March, 1989, pp. 120-122.

[6]A. Powell Davies, *The Meaning of the Dead Sea Scrolls* (New York: New American Library, 1956), especially p. 120.

[7]Elaine Pagels, *The Gnostic Gospels* (New York: Random House, 1979).

[8]Ibid., pp. xxii-xxiv.

[9]Ibid., pp. 29, 32, 56, 170-171, 179-181.

Pagels also raises other issues, such as the possible Gnostic interpretations of certain of Jesus' teachings, and the question of deciding between the conflicting itineraries of the orthodox and Gnostic traditions. She concludes that Gnosticism remains, even today, "a powerful alternative to what we know as orthodox Christian tradition." But, presumably, conclusions must be reached on more solid grounds than they were in the early centuries after Christ.[10]

Besides questions related to the milieu in which orthodox Christianity asserted itself, at least one other major issue needs to be introduced at this point. Earlier, we briefly mentioned differences among contemporary scholars with regard to the dating of the original Gnostic treatises. One particular case perhaps needs to be mentioned, both because of its crucial nature in the present discussions and as an actual example of the importance of these dating concerns. The case in point here concerns the *Gospel of Thomas*, which is chiefly characterized as a document which purports to record 114 secret sayings of Jesus, but with very little narrative about his life.

Classically dated from about AD 140–170, a major effort has been made by scholars who argue on behalf of the Gnostic tradition that *Thomas* ought to be viewed, at least in part, as a much earlier document. It is variously asserted that the tradition behind the book is more ancient than the actual writing or even that the composition of the book dates from the first century.

Thesis of Robinson and Koester

Perhaps the two scholars who most exemplify this tendency, thereby lending their considerable reputations to this position, are James M. Robinson and Helmut Koester. Robinson continues to pursue his quest for what he terms a "trajectory" from Jesus to Gnosticism by endeavoring to locate similarities between *Thomas* and Q ("*Quelle,*" the

---

[10]Ibid., pp. 12-13, 20, 84-90, 112-114, 177-178.

hypothesized source lying behind the synoptic Gospels), especially in regard to the genre of both texts. For him, such indicates the primitive tradition behind both.[11]

Koester appears to have steadily moved his dating for
Thomas in a backwards direction. In his introduction to
Thomas in *The Nag Hammadi Library*, Koester identifies the
composition as dating from before AD 200, but possibly being
as early as the first century.[12] Pagels, who was also involved in
the project, recalls Koester's position on this subject.[13]

A few years later, Koester stated his view that *Thomas* was
probably written during the first century in either Palestine
or Syria. His reasons for this early dating are the similarities
to Q, that the *Thomas* tradition is independent of and earlier
than that of the canonical Gospels, the location of the
Thomas tradition in Syria, and the Thomas-James (the brother
of Jesus) contrast in sayings 12 and 13.[14]

That such conclusions may present a challenge to the
orthodox understanding of Jesus might be indicated from
several considerations. Besides the question of dating, it is
also asserted that *Thomas* includes a number of new teachings
of Jesus not available in the canonical Gospel tradition, and
that there is "no trace of the kerygma of the cross and the
resurrection of Jesus" in *Thomas*, perhaps manifesting a
different tradition from that of orthodox Christian theology.[15] This last claim, in particular, demands a more detailed
response.

To be sure, a considerable number of influential critical
scholars have reacted strongly to theses such as those by
Pagels, Robinson, and Koester. It is generally thought that
the claims on behalf of the Gnostic tradition in the early

---

[11]Robinson's essay in Hedrick and Hodgson, *Nag Hammadi*, is a more
recent statement of his continuing emphasis on this subject.

[12]Helmut Koester in Robinson, *Nag Hammadi in English*, Vol. II, p. 117.

[13]Pagels, *Gnostic Gospels*, pp. xv-xvi.

[14]Koester in Robinson, *Nag Hammadi in English*, vol. II, pp. 150-154. On
Thomas as a sayings source, see vol. II, pp. 4, 47, 68, 180.

[15]Ibid., especially vol. II, pp. 152, 154.

church are very much overstated. We will turn now to an evaluation of several of these contentions.

A Critical Evaluation

As we have already said, we need to be selective in our treatment of these issues. Accordingly, we will propose to just briefly address four central questions, all of which impinge on our understanding of the historicity of Jesus.

These four topics for consideration include some very preliminary thoughts on two issues: the comparative dates of the Gnostic writings and the authority of the Gospels. This will be followed by a somewhat more detailed response to the two charges that the New Testament canon was in a state of flux until the late second century AD, and the general question of the downplaying of the gospel facts of the death and resurrection of Jesus in these writings. It should be noted that the employment of this strategy is designed not just to respond to these four critical areas, but the convergence of the critiques will hopefully provide an overall case against the Gnostic thesis outlined here.

1. Canonical Gospels earlier

First, from the perspective of the time factor alone, the four canonical Gospels are much earlier than their Gnostic counterparts. While the earliest Gnostic Gospels are perhaps dated from about AD 140–200 (see the comments below on the *Gospel of Thomas*), the canonical Gospels may be dated from AD 65–100, a difference of 75–100 years earlier on the average. Even though these Gnostic texts possibly include earlier material, the Gospels certainly include traditions that predate their writing.

So while Pagels and others would have us suppose that these various Gospels simply circulated together, inviting believers to espouse radically different beliefs,[16] the facts

---

[16]Pagels, *Gnostic Gospels*, p. xxiii.

indicate that these two groups of texts were not on an equal footing. The very fact that the canonical Gospels were written decades earlier is at least a preliminary indication that they could possibly also be more authoritative.

One scholar who agrees with this assessment is O.C. Edwards. Speaking in particular of Pagels' thesis, he asserts:

> It is precisely as history that I find her work most unsatisfactory. Nowhere, for instance, does she give the impression that the basic picture of Jesus given in the New Testament gospels did not arise contemporaneously with the Gnostic portrait, but antedated it by at least half a century. As historical reconstructions there is no way that the two can claim equal credentials.[17]

New Testament scholar Joseph A. Fitzmyer responds similarly: "Time and again, she is blind to the fact that she is ignoring a good century of Christian existence in which those 'Gnostic Christians' were simply not around."[18]

2. Canonical Gospels more authoritative

Second, beyond the matter of age alone, the canonical Gospels are both historically reliable and simply much closer to the authority of Jesus Himself. An issue here that some would say is as crucial as any other is the authorship of the Gospels. While we cannot pursue here a discussion of this question, the traditional authorship of each Gospel is still defended by outstanding scholars.[19]

But some intellectuals point out that authorship is not the main issue at all. If the Gospels are judged according to the

---

[17]O.C. Edwards, "A Surprising View of Gnosticism," *New Review of Books and Religion*, May, 1980, p. 27.

[18]Joseph A. Fitzmyer, "The Gnostic Gospels According to Pagels," *America*, February 16, 1980, p. 123.

[19]Cf. Drane, *Introducing the NT*, chapter 11. Guthrie presents detailed overviews of the present critical discussions (pp. 43-53 [Matthew], pp. 81-84 [Mark], pp. 113-125 [Luke], pp. 252-283 [John]). See Habermas, *Ancient Evidence for the Life of Jesus*, p. 63 (and endnotes) for a lengthy list of some contemporary scholars who accept the traditional authors.

standards of ancient historiography in terms of date and reliability on issues that can be compared to other known data, they measure well and ought to be accepted as good sources for historical information about Jesus.[20]

Perhaps it would be helpful to summarize the conclusion of New Testament critical scholar A. M. Hunter, who pointed out that there are several reasons why the Gospels are trustworthy sources.

(1) The earliest Christians were meticulous in preserving the tradition of Jesus' words and life.

(2) The Gospel writers were close to the eyewitnesses and pursued the facts about Jesus.

(3) There are indications that these authors were honest reporters.

(4) The overall composite of Jesus as presented in the four Gospels is essentially the same.[21]

Far from not being able to distinguish which teachings concerning Jesus are historical, the data strongly favors the New Testament Gospels.

3. NT canon decided early

Third, another major problem with the Gnostic thesis is the contention that the New Testament canon was in a state of flux until the late second century, allowing a variety of Gospels to circulate without any indication as to which ones were more authoritative. Pagels' brief and undifferentiated treatment is quite simplistic in that it gives virtually no indication of earlier developments.[22] Accordingly, critiques of her thesis have abounded.[23]

---

[20]Besides historians Michael Grant and A.N. Sherwin-White, whose views on the historical value of the Gospels we have studied in chapter 3, see R.T. France, *The Evidence for Jesus* (Downers Grove: InterVarsity, 1986), chapter 3, especially pp. 121-125; Blomberg, *Historical Reliability*, p. 161; Drane, *Introducing the NT*, chapter 12.

[21]A.M. Hunter, *Bible and Gospels*, pp. 32-37.

[22]Pagels, *Gnostic Gospels*, p. xxiii.

[23]Pheme Perkins, herself an "insider" in these studies who appreciates

Koester's approach is both typical and more sophisticated. While holding that the New Testament canon was "essentially created" at the end of the second century (by Irenaeus), he also informs his readers of the earlier recognition of important groupings of canonical texts. Yet, he still implies that certain apocryphal writings (including Gnostic documents) were also in general circulation, almost as alternative explanations to the early Christian tradition.[24]

Assessments such as Pagels' are misleading, at best, while Koester needs to heed some of the important ramifications of the data. Within the pages of the New Testament itself, the seeds of canonicity were already beginning to grow. Later, by the very early second century, there were several crucial indications that two blocks of books, in particular, were being recognized as authoritative. All of this occurred well before the written Gnostic tradition was established.

---

some of Pagels' work, still asserts that:

> Pagels either knows or cares too little about the theological diversity and development of "orthodox" Christian theology in the first three centuries to be fair to its defenders in their debates with the gnostics. She is frequently taken in by the stock rhetorical polemics of both sides, mistaking rhetoric for fact.

(See Pheme Perkins, "Popularizing the Past," *Commonweal*, 9 November, 1979, pp. 634-635.)

Other problems include Pagels' popularizing methodology, her constant imposition of political, sociological, and modern psychological factors upon ancient philosophical and theological questions, and the lack of her desired support for woman's rights in the Gnostic sources. (For details, see Edwards, p. 7; Fitzmyer, p. 122; Perkins, p. 635; Raymond E. Brown, "The Christians Who Lost Out," *The New York Times Book Review*, January 20, 1980, p. 3; Kathleen McVey, "Gnosticism, Feminism, and Elaine Pagels," *Theology Today*, vol. 37, January, 1981, pp. 498, 501.)

Lastly, Edwards charges that Pagels' volume is plagued by a reductionism for which no evidence is provided, but only her own word (p. 7). Perkins summarizes her critique this way:

> But the whole is so flawed by hasty generalization, over-interpretation of texts to fit a pre-determined scheme, and lack of sympathetic balance that this reviewer found herself constantly wishing that the whole could have been redone with more care (p. 635).

[24]Koester in Robinson, *Nag Hammadi*, vol. II, pp. 1-15.

Testimony of NT Itself

In 1 Timothy 5:18 two statements are termed "Scripture." The first is found in Deuteronomy 25:4, one of the Jews' most sacred Old Testament books. The second teaching is found in Luke 10:7 (compare Matt. 10:10), and recites the words of Jesus. By placing a text in Deuteronomy alongside a statement by Jesus, and referring to both of them as Scripture, we have an indication of the early realization that Jesus' teachings were to be viewed in some sense as being authoritative or canonical.

A major question here concerns whether citations such as the one in 1 Timothy 5:18 (as well as many others in the early church) make reference to the remembered *oral* teachings of Jesus (perhaps in early written form) or to the Gospels themselves. We will return to this issue later. We will just note here that we are at least presented with the possibility that it was the Gospel text in Luke itself which was being cited. If so, such could well be an implicit recognition of the principle that texts which authoritatively recount the life of Jesus could at least potentially be viewed as Scripture. But even if this is not the case, we will endeavor to indicate that Jesus' oral teachings had already attained a similarly authoritative status.

Additionally, 2 Peter 3:15-16 refers to Paul's epistles as Scripture. Such a text testifies to the existence of a certain Pauline corpus which was also recognized, at least by some, as being authoritative.

So very early, even before the last canonical New Testament book was written, at least two groupings were already being recognized and referred to as authoritative. These were the Gospels and/or the tradition of Jesus' oral teachings on the one hand and Paul's epistles on the other. Such conclusions are also supported by a number of other very early sources as well.[25]

---

[25]The division citations in our text follow J.B. Lightfoot, *The Apostolic Fathers* (Grand Rapids: Baker, 1971).

Testimony of Apostolic Fathers

In his *Epistle to the Corinthians*, usually dated about AD 95, Clement of Rome made an important reference to the "Gospel," which was the central message that the apostles had received from Jesus Christ himself and had passed on to their hearers (42). On other occasions, Clement cited various teachings of Jesus which are found in all three synoptic Gospels, introducing them as "the words of the Lord Jesus" and "His hallowed words" (13) or as "the words of Jesus our Lord" (46).

Here we have an early, first century reference either more generally to the teachings of Jesus or to the text of one or more of the canonical Gospels themselves, which were recognized in either case as the words of Jesus.

Ignatius, writing seven epistles around AD 110–115 on his way to Rome to suffer martyrdom, quoted the statement found in Luke 24:39 as the words of Jesus (*Smyrnaeans* 3). Polycarp wrote his *Epistle to the Philippians* about AD 115, shortly after Ignatius' letters, to which he makes reference (13). Polycarp also cites sayings found in all of the synoptic Gospels and, again, identifies them as the words of the Lord (2, 7).

The *Didache*, an ancient Christian manual, is usually dated somewhere between the end of the first century and the early second century AD. It frequently cites the words of Jesus as being authoritative, sometimes without reference to whose comments they are (1, 3, 16), once as the words of the Lord (9), and twice as the Gospel of the Lord (8, 15). In almost every case, the text contains teachings found in the synoptic Gospels (8, 15-16).

One interesting note is that several words from the Book of Acts are quoted in the *Didache* (4; cf. Acts 4:32), as are several examples from Paul's teachings (see below). The point in the former instance is that such would not be accounted for by any collection of Jesus' sayings. The most likely source is Acts itself.

The epistle of Barnabas, perhaps dated about AD 135, refers to Jesus' saying in Matthew 22:14 as "scripture" (4).

This is followed by a reference to Jesus' "Gospel" and a quotation of His words which is found in the synoptics (5).

From Papias' *Exposition of Oracles of the Lord*, written about AD 125–140, we obtain information which explicitly comments on the writing of the Gospels. Sadly, almost all of this work is no longer extant, with extracted fragments being all which remain. Yet, it is perhaps difficult to overemphasize the importance of the brief data which are still in existence.

Papias explains that Mark, as Peter's interpreter, accurately wrote his Gospel based on the teaching of this apostle, although not necessarily in chronological order. Then we are briefly told that Matthew wrote his account in Hebrew, with interested readers providing their own translations (III).

While anything which Papias may have said concerning the Gospels of Luke and John is not extant, a later manuscript summarizes Papias' testimony that John composed his Gospel while he was an elderly man (XIX). Incidently, Papias does testify that he received such material from those who learned directly from the Lord's apostles themselves (III).

To return to the significant issue of whether these early citations of Jesus' words are from a sayings tradition (either written or oral) or from the canonical Gospels themselves, at least two things need to be mentioned. Initially, while none of the quotations of Jesus are specifically said to be taken from the Gospels, this conclusion could still be successfully argued on several fronts.

The *Didache* excerpt from Acts (4) also does not identify the source, yet it is unlikely that it comes from any sayings source both because of its nature and in that it lacks those characteristics. Further, the citations from Paul (see below) are from his epistles, even though the specific books are not mentioned. Lastly, the passages from Papias about the authorship of Matthew, Mark, and John do not cite sayings from Jesus but definitely *do* acknowledge the Gospel sources.[26]

---

[26]Besides Papias' reference to the Gospel of John, allusions to this Gospel may be found in Clement's *Corinthians* (43), as well as Ignatius'

And it should be noted that our original goal was not so much to prove the source for the sayings, but to show that the Gospels were accepted as authoritative well before the end of the second century. This would certainly appear to be evident from this data, especially in that Papias also relates the importance of these Gospels — three times he explains that Mark made no errors in recording his material about Jesus (III). Such was evidently important to him.

But, additionally, *even if* most of the citations of Jesus' words are from a sayings source,[27] the earliest post-apostolic authors clearly refer to these statements as inspired and authoritative, on a par with that of the Old Testament. So once again, the chief point here is that the early Gnostic Gospels of the mid to late second century did not appear in a milieu where "anything goes." Rather, the sources for Jesus' life (see below) and teachings were clearly established and accepted. That the canonical Gospels are the texts which incorporate these teachings also says something about their authority.

So the facts certainly appear to indicate that the canonical Gospels were widely recognized as being authoritative well before the late second century. In addition to 1 Timothy 5:18, six major Christian sources refer to the teachings of Jesus alternatively as the Gospel, the words of Christ and Scripture between AD 95 and 140.

Thus, while the Gospels were one major corpus in the New Testament canon to be accepted as sacred, the other was Paul's epistles. Besides being called Scripture in 2 Peter 3:15-16, verses from Paul's epistles are referred to, often as inspired, in Clement's *Corinthians* (47), Ignatius' *Ephesians* (10) and *To Polycarp* (1, 5), as well as in Polycarp's *Philippians* (1, 3-4, 6, 12). In a few of these passages, Paul's letters as a whole are both discussed and referred to as Scripture.

Therefore, when the earliest Gnostic Gospels were being

Ephesians (5, 17). Later, the status of John is widely recognized by Justin Martyr (about AD 150), Tatian's *Fourfold Gospel* (about AD 170), and in the *Muratorian Canon* (about AD 180).

[27]See the discussion in the next section below.

written in the mid to late second century AD, at least the teachings of Jesus as presented in the canonical Gospels had already circulated for quite awhile and had been well established as Scripture. The same might be said for the Pauline corpus.

In fact, the Nag Hammadi Gnostic texts as a whole cite most of the canonical New Testament books and borrow often from some of these works. The *Gospel of Truth* and the *Gospel of Philip*, in particular, are examples of Gnostic writings which recognize most of the New Testament as authoritative.[28]

So, despite Pagels' complaint that history is written by the victors,[29] the four Gospels, in particular, were certainly not "forced" into the New Testament canon. Rather, there are fitting reasons why the biblical Gospels were the "victors" — the facts indicate that these writings are simply better-attested sources for the teachings of Jesus.

4. The death and resurrection of Jesus

Fourth, what about the status of the life of Jesus and his death and resurrection, in particular? Does the downplaying of these events in the *Gospel of Thomas* provide any challenge to the orthodox teaching of, say, the centrality of the gospel message?

Initially, it ought to be pointed out that the post-apostolic authors did not ignore the important aspects of the life of Jesus. Along with the emphasis on Jesus' teachings which we just surveyed, a number of (usually) brief passages concentrate on historical interests. In particular, the death and resurrection appear to be the *central* concern in these texts.[30]

---

[28]For a fairly popular treatment, see Andrew K. Helmbold, *The Nag Hammadi Gnostic Texts and the Bible* (Grand Rapids: Baker, 1967), pp. 88-89.

[29]Pagels, *Gnostic Gospels*, pp. 170-171.

[30]Even a briefly-discussed list of relevant passages would be quite lengthy. So it will simply be said here that the death and resurrection of Jesus are, without much doubt, the chief interest of these early historical passages on the life of Jesus, although other events are also mentioned frequently. For details, see Clement, *Corinthians* 42; Ignatius, *Trallians* 9; *Smyrnaeans* 1; 3; *Magnesians* 11; and *Barnabas* 5. For an early text on Jesus' miracles written by Quadratus about AD 125, see Eusebius, *Ecclesiastical*

With regard to the claim that Q and *Thomas* do not emphasize the death and resurrection of Jesus, there are several reasons why this does not change either the facticity or the importance of these events. (1) Both of these texts are sayings documents and by far the primary purpose is to list the purported teachings of Jesus, not his actions or events in his life.

(2) Neither of these records is without its own serious problems on other grounds. The growing number of critical scholars who think there are sufficient grounds to doubt the very existence of Q or related hypotheses are listed by William Farmer,[31] who also contends that "the existence of Q, the fount of all these speculations, is not proven and today is more hotly contested in gospel scholarship than at any other time in our century."[32]

On the other hand, Koester's reasons notwithstanding, it is generally concluded that *Thomas* was originally written in the mid second century. One reason for this conclusion is the majority view that *Thomas* relies on the gospel tradition in its citations. So, whether it preserves earlier traditions or not, it adds little to our knowledge of the life and teachings of Jesus.[33]

History IV:III. For examples of historical interests in Justin Martyr (about AD 150), see *First Apology* XXX, XXXII, XLVIII, L and *Dialogue With Trypho* LXXVII, XCVII, CVIII.

[31]For a handy summary of arguments for and against theses such as the priority of Mark and the existence of Q, see David Barrett Peabody, "In Retrospect and Prospect," *The Perkins School of Theology Journal*, Vol. XL, No. 2 (April, 1987), pp. 9-16. For a list of critical scholars who either advocate or lean toward other alternatives, see William R. Farmer, "Preface: Order Out of Chaos," *The Perkins School of Theology Journal*, Vol. XL, No. 2 (April, 1987), pp. 1-6.

[32]William R. Farmer, "The Church's Stake in the Question of 'Q'," *The Perkins School of Theology Journal*, Vol. XXXIX, No. 3 (July, 1986), pp. 9-19.

[33]See F.L. Cross and E.A. Livingstone, *The Oxford Dictionary of the Christian Church* (Oxford: Oxford Univ. Press, 1974), s.v. "Thomas, Gospel of," p. 1370. For a detailed summary, see Craig Blomberg, "Tradition and Redaction in the Parables of the Gospel of Thomas," *Gospel Perspectives*, vol. 5 (Sheffield: JSOT, 1985), pp. 177-205; Craig Evans, "Jesus and the Gnostic Literature," *Biblica*, vol. 62 (1981), pp. 406-412; France, *Evidence for Jesus*, pp. 75-78; Farmer, "Church's Stake," p. 14.

On this last point, Brown judges that "we learn not a single verifiable new fact about Jesus' ministry and only a few new sayings that might plausibly have been his."[34] Fitzmyer agrees, but in even stronger terms: "The Coptic texts of Nag Hammadi tell us little that is new . . . . It has been mystifying, indeed, why serious scholars continue to talk about the pertinence of this material to the study of the New Testament."[35]

Accordingly, any thesis that would pose Q and *Thomas* over against the New Testament tradition in favor of the death and resurrection of Jesus would have to argue from a tradition which is somewhat problematic from the outset. This is especially the case with regard to *Thomas*. The many obstacles caused Farmer to comment concerning the Robinson-Koester proposal: "We can only conclude that a hypothesis is being set forth for which there is very little evidence." So when Q theology is combined with *Thomas* and other Gnostic theses, Farmer responds that such is only "a grand vision. . . a romance"![36]

(3) The issue of whether Q includes or presupposes the knowledge of Jesus' death and resurrection is debated by scholars. Because of the nonexistence of this document, it is rather difficult to argue conclusively as to its content. Regardless, Fuller argues that, even without mentioning the resurrection, Q "presupposes it all the way through."[37]

But the purported sayings of Jesus contained in *Thomas* do acknowledge Jesus' death (34:25-27; 45:1-16), as well as encouraging believers to follow him in bearing their own crosses (42:27-28). Jesus' exaltation is depicted in the post-death illustration that asserts that the builders' rejected stone is the cornerstone (45:17-19). While the resurrection is not directly described, "the living Jesus" identified in the opening line of Thomas as the speaker who is imparting this information, is most likely the risen Jesus, causing Robert Grant to

---

[34]Brown, "The Christians Who Lost Out," p. 3.

[35]Fitzmyer, pp. 122-123.

[36]Farmer, "The Church's Stake," pp. 12, 14.

[37]Fuller, *Foundations*, p. 143.

explain that this is why so little attention is given to Jesus' life and death.[38]

(4) Last, the earliest creedal formulas in Christianity frequently recount the death and resurrection of Jesus. These confessions depict Christian doctrine in its earliest stages as it was transmitted orally, often recounting various details concerning these events and their importance. Although we cannot provide detailed arguments here, two examples that demand notice are 1 Corinthians 11:23-25 and 15:3ff.

The initial text depicts the Last Supper that Jesus shared with His disciples, explaining the significance of his death. Jeremias asserts that the tradition here comes from the earliest time in the early church, even going back to Jesus.[39] Additionally, 1 Corinthians 15:3ff. recounts the gospel facts of the death, burial, resurrection and appearances of Jesus Christ and is probably even earlier in its formulation. There are numerous other creedal statements in the New Testament that also report the subject of the death and resurrection of Jesus.[40] We will return to a detailed treatment of this topic in Part Two below.

The point to be made is that the report in 1 Corinthians 15:3ff. of the earliest eyewitnesses who themselves attested the appearances of the risen Jesus predates the Gnostic material. Further, it must be remembered that the Gnostic texts do not deny these facts; in reality, they affirm the resurrection of Jesus.[41] But Raymond Brown still reminds us that the

---

[38]*The Gospel of Thomas* 32:1; 42:13-18; 43:9-12; cf. Revelation 1:17-18. See Robert M. Grant, *Gnosticism and Early Christianity*, rev. ed. (New York: Harper and Row, 1966), pp. 183-184; cf. Blomberg, *Historical Reliability*, pp. 209, 212. Even the Jesus Seminar views this as a possible identification of "the living Jesus" in *Thomas*. (Robert W. Funk, Roy W. Hoover and the Jesus Seminar, *The Five Gospels: The Search for the Authentic Words of Jesus* [New York: Macmillan/Polebridge, 1993], p. 398.)

[39]Jeremias, *The Eucharistic Words of Jesus*, pp. 104-105.

[40]For some examples, see Luke 24:34; Rom. 1:3-4; 4:25; 10:9-10; Phil. 2:6-11; 1 Tim. 2:6; 6:13; 2 Tim. 2:8; 1 Pet. 3:18; cf. 1 Tim. 3:16.

[41]For some early Gnostic works that affirm the resurrection of Jesus, see *The Gospel of Truth* 20:25-34; 30:23, 27-33; *The Treatise on Resurrection* 45:14-28; 46:14-20; 48:4-19. We should note, however, the frequent Gnostic

earliest interest relative to the resurrection of Jesus is "an identifiable chain of witnesses," not Gnostic theology.[42] Farmer contends that any Gnostic scenario which implies that the death and resurrection of Jesus were unimportant for the earliest apostolic community "is like children making castles in a sandbox" in the sense that it is a "fanciful reconstruction" of the data.[43]

Summary and Conclusion

So what do those who appear to champion the Gnostic thesis think about the death and resurrection of Jesus? Perhaps surprisingly, there is apparently no attempt by Robinson or Koester to deny either historical event. Robinson, in fact, reminds us of a crucially important logical point: even if the death and resurrection of Jesus were absent from Q, it does not follow that the Q community was not aware of these occurrences.[44]

Further, Robinson argues elsewhere that the earliest accounts of the resurrection appearances depicted nonphysical visions of the radiant, spiritual body of Jesus. However, he argues that the mainstream Gnostic view preferred only the radiance apart from the body itself.[45] Although we wish to register disagreement over Robinson's disdain for physical appearances, we also need to point out that even a commitment to the Q and *Thomas* traditions do not at all necessitate a denial of Jesus' literal death and later appearances.

Koester clearly states the certainty of Jesus' death on the cross and then asserts that "We are on much firmer ground

---

denial of the resurrection of Jesus' **body**. In the texts above, such an idea is most evident in *The Treatise on Resurrection* 45:17-21.

[42]Brown, "The Christians Who Lost Out," p. 3.

[43]Farmer, "Church's Stake," p. 14.

[44]James M. Robinson, "The Sayings of Jesus: Q," *Drew Gateway*, Fall, 1983, p. 32.

[45]James M. Robinson, "Jesus from Easter to Valentinus," *Journal of Biblical Literature*, Vol. 101, 1982, pp. 6-17.

with respect to the appearances of the risen Jesus and their effect." And while he is not concerned to attempt to ascertain the nature of these experiences, Koester holds that their occurrence "cannot be questioned." He then explains that it was these appearances that account for the disciples' interest in missionary activity, in that:

> the resurrection changed sorrow and grief, or even hate and rejection, into joy, creativity, and faith. Though the resurrection revealed nothing new, it nonetheless made everything new for the first Christian believers.[46]

While we may guess that the assertion "the resurrection revealed nothing new" perhaps provides a hint about Koester's personal view, it must again be stated that the Q and Gnostic theses by no means require disbelieving either Jesus' death or his literal appearances. In other words, even those who may disbelieve apparently do not do so because of the Gnostic data. But it is also evident that the interest in Q and *Thomas*, with their relative silence on these subjects, still do not even keep Koester from concluding that the belief in Jesus' resurrection was *central* for the first believers.

In sum, we conclude our discussion by asserting that the general Gnostic trajectory fails, and for several reasons, some of which have not been mentioned here.[47] The Gnostic sources are too late, besides lacking evidence that they are based on eyewitness, authoritative authority.

---

[46]Koester in Robinson, *Nag Hammadi*, Volume II, pp. 84-86.

[47]Other problems with the Gnostic scenario take us beyond some of the immediate issues that are addressed in this chapter. While certain sayings of Jesus have been interpreted in different ways, this is definitely not the same as saying that Jesus' teachings support Gnosticism. His teachings about God, creation, the nature of the physical body, eternal life, the message of salvation and the necessity of taking His words to the entire world are some examples of the differences. (See Habermas, *Ancient Evidence for the Life of Jesus*, p. 64.) Pagels provides still more instances of contrasts between the teachings of Jesus and those of the Gnostics (*Gnostic Gospels*, pp. 177-178).

Another crucial area concerns the origin of Gnosticism. The predominant view is that it was derived from Christianity. Fitzmyer refers to

Furthermore, the New Testament canon was not formulated in an open forum where orthodox and Gnostic texts circulated on the same level. And while it may have been the late second century before canonical concerns were basically *solved*, the Gospel corpus (plus Acts) and the epistles of Paul had long before had an established tradition. In fact, somewhere during the time frame between the writing of some of the canonical books themselves until about 40 years after the close of the canon, these two collections of texts appear to be well-established as Scripture.

Last, there are a number of reasons why even the reliance on the Q and Gnostic traditions do not constitute grounds on which to deny the gospel facts of the death and resurrection of Jesus. Several responses were given to show that, at every turn, such a thesis is strongly opposed by the data.

Therefore, it must be concluded that the recent interest on the part of some scholars in this Gnostic scenario does not threaten the historicity of the life, teachings, death, or resurrection of Jesus. The majority of critical scholars have rejected such a conclusion and we have attempted to argue that there are certainly firm grounds for doing so.

Gnosticism as a "parasite" in this regard (p. 123). (See Robert Grant's *Gnosticism and Early Christianity*, as well as Edwin Yamauchi, *Pre-Christian Gnosticism: A Survey of the Proposed Evidences* [Grand Rapids: Eerdmans, 1973]).

Many other critiques on related topics are found in Ronald H. Nash, *Christianity and the Hellenistic World* (Grand Rapids: Zondervan, 1984).

6 The Jesus Seminar and the Historical Jesus

With an incredible amount of media fanfare, the Jesus Seminar has radically challenged the Gospel accounts of Jesus at their very foundation. This group of 74 scholars from various seminaries and universities met over a period of six years in order to produce a translation (called the Scholar's Version or SV) of the four canonical Gospels plus the *Gospel of Thomas*. After discussing more than 1500 purported sayings of Jesus, they cast their votes on each, judging the likelihood that the comment originated with Jesus. The degree of assurance was represented by coding the sayings texts in these five books with one of four colors. In the second phase of their work they are investigating the actions of Jesus, attempting to determine what Jesus actually did.[1]

It is clear that the overall conclusions of the Jesus Seminar are rather radical, even among contemporary critical scholars. Neither are they shy about announcing their theological disposition. One indication of this is their reaction to the supernatural in general and the orthodox view of Jesus, in particular:

---

[1]Robert W. Funk, Roy W. Hoover, and the Jesus Seminar, *The Five Gospels: The Search for the Authentic Words of Jesus* (New York: Macmillan Publishing Company and the Polebridge Press, 1993), Preface, pp. ix-x, xiii.

> The Christ of creed and dogma . . . can no longer command the assent of those who have seen the heavens through Galileo's telescope. The old deities and demons were swept from the skies by that remarkable glass. Copernicus, Kepler, and Galileo have dismantled the mythological abodes of the gods and Satan, and bequeathed us secular heavens.[2]

It is an understatement to say that the Jesus Seminar downplays the supernatural, especially in the life of Jesus. This chapter is an attempt to investigate and critique what these and related scholars assert concerning select aspects of the life of the historical Jesus, concentrating on their response to his death, burial, and resurrection, in particular.

Jesus' Miracles and Seminar Presuppositions[3]

The Jesus Seminar describes itself as taking a centrist position in the recent discussions on the historical Jesus. They stand between both the skeptics who deny the presence of historical reports in the Gospels and the fundamentalists who accept the total contents of these books.[4] Yet, it becomes obvious that this group is more closely aligned on the side of the skeptics when we review their composite work. One initial indication is the above quotation that severely restricts the supernatural, if not rejecting it outright, in favor of a modern scientific outlook. As another example, the Seminar reports that "Eighty-two percent of the words ascribed to Jesus in the Gospels were not actually spoken by him . . . ."[5]

The attitude of the Jesus Seminar towards science and the supernatural is reminiscent of a famous comment made by

---

[2]Ibid., p. 2.

[3]For an extended discussion of the material in this section (often in edited form) see Gary R. Habermas, "Did Jesus Perform Miracles?" in *Jesus Under Fire: Modern Scholarship Reinvents the Historical Jesus*, ed. by Michael Wilkins and J.P. Moreland (Grand Rapids: Zondervan, 1995), pp. 125-129.

[4]Funk, Hoover, and the Jesus Seminar, *Five Gospels*, pp. 2-5.

[5]Ibid., p. 5.

Rudolf Bultmann decades ago: "It is impossible to use elec-
tric light and the wireless and to avail ourselves of modern
medical and surgical discoveries, and at the same time to
believe in the New Testament world of spirits and miracles."[6]
Applying his conclusion to Jesus' resurrection, Bultmann asks
later: "But what of the resurrection? Is it not a mythical event
pure and simple? Obviously it is not an event of past
history . . . ."[7]

Some members of the Jesus Seminar, following other
more radical scholars, appear to echo views like those of
Bultmann. Regarding Jesus' miracles, Seminar Co-Founder
John Dominic Crossan asserts that Jesus "did not and could
not cure that disease or any other one . . . ."[8] He continues
later: "I do not think that anyone, anywhere, at any time
brings dead people back to life."[9] Jarl Fossum comments on
the same subject, including a derisive jab at conservatives:
"Or it can be asserted that Jesus really did raise the girl
from the dead — which would only reflect fundamentalist
naivete."[10]

Like Bultmann, the Jesus Seminar extends this same sort
of criticism to Jesus' resurrection. They assert: "Whenever
scholars detect detailed knowledge of postmortem events in
sayings and parables attributed to Jesus, they are inclined to
the view that the formulation of such sayings took place after
the fact."[11] But it appears from their work that they have
more than a mere "inclination" to rule out any post-death
details from Jesus' life. In fact, they rule out every saying
from the resurrection narratives. Later they provide insight
into their thinking: "By definition, words ascribed to Jesus

---

[6]Rudolf Bultmann, "New Testament and Mythology," p. 5.

[7]Ibid., p. 38.

[8]John Dominic Crossan, *Jesus: A Revolutionary Biography*, p. 82.

[9]Ibid., p. 95.

[10]Jarl Fossum, "Understanding Jesus' Miracles," *Bible Review*, Vol. X,
No. 2 (April 1994), p. 50. It should be noted that Fossum is **not** listed as a
Fellow of the Jesus Seminar.

[11]Funk, Hoover, and the Jesus Seminar, *Five Gospels*, p. 25.

after his death are not subject to historical verification."[12]

1. A priori *rejection of miracles*

One characteristic of Bultmann's rejection of the super-natural is that he failed to provide any actual reasons for his rejection; he simply assumed that such things do not happen. We have already seen in an earlier chapter how John Macquarrie, a leading commentator, specifically chides Bultmann for rejecting the resurrection due to "an entirely arbitrary dismissal . . . because of some prior assumption in his mind." Macquarrie then adds that "Bultmann does not take the trouble to examine what evidence could be adduced to show that the resurrection was an objective-historical event. He assumes that it is a myth."[13]

Bultmann's rejection of the resurrection really does appear to be arbitrary and *a priori*. He does not even think that we should be interested in the historical question at all.[14] Interestingly, the Jesus Seminar takes a similar route. We have already noted that they are honest enough to state at the outset their aversion to the supernatural, including the deity and resurrection of Jesus, preferring to think that the modern scientific worldview simply rules out such matters.

By way of explanation and justification, the Seminar schol-ars provide more than three dozen "rules of written evidence"[15] and often report that various sayings of Jesus are editorial summations. To be fair, we should not require that they always provide reasons for their comments. But the fact is they seldom attempt to provide *reasons* in order to justify their opinions. Rarely is there an attempt to verify their rules, except to say that certain things are accepted by scholars. Throughout, like Bultmann, their theological method is

---

[12]Ibid., p. 398.

[13]John Macquarrie, *An Existentialist Theology*, pp. 185-186.

[14]Bultmann, "New Testament and Mythology," p. 42.

[15]Funk, Hoover, and the Jesus Seminar, *Five Gospels*, pp. 19-35.

assumed and their conjectures can be thoughtfully challenged throughout. In short, we might say that these scholars exhibit a flare for the *a priori*.

For example, we are regularly told that since a certain passage fits the particular writer's motif, this indicates that the saying was not uttered by Jesus.[16] But how do we know this to be the case? Does the presence of a certain theme *require* that it did not originate with Jesus? Does not the critical method itself indicate that the writer may have presented the message, perhaps in his own style and words, *precisely because* it was the teaching of Jesus? We are certainly not required to imitate the Seminar leap from authorial motif to the subsequent invention of the message!

2. Genetic fallacy

Another point of logic concerns the Seminar's commission of the genetic fallacy, which occurs when one challenges the origin of an idea without actually addressing its facticity. In other words, if it is thought that merely attributing a Gospel report to the author's style, or to other ancient parallels, or to a pre-modern mindset thereby explains it away, this is a logical mistake.[17] These charges do not preclude historicity.

However, it is noteworthy that the Seminar scholars are not unanimous in their dismissal of the supernatural. While Crossan rejects the existence of demons,[18] Bruce Chilton perceptively observes that although rejecting the existence of demons sounds attractively rational, "it would seem to reduce

---

[16]Some instances are found in Ibid., pp. 199-200, 270, 399-400, 439, 468-469.

[17]After his above comment concerning "fundamentalist naivete," Fossum explains that "raising the dead was not considered impossible in the ancient world" (p. 50), apparently considering this to be an adequate explanation. But this is an instance of the genetic fallacy. For all we know, every ancient, miraculous report could be true, or some false and others true. This approach fails to disprove the Gospel accounts.

[18]Crossan, *Jesus: A Revolutionary Biography*, p. 85.

history to *a priori* notions of what is possible."[19] Again, while Crossan asserts that Jesus never really healed a disease or raised the dead,[20] Marcus Borg is not quite so sure. Much more guardedly, Borg thinks that we do not know whether Jesus resuscitated some who were actually dead.[21]

For our purposes, we will conclude at this point that it solves nothing to *state* one's views to be correct, regardless how vociferously the claim is made. However helpful it may be to report the conclusions of other scholars, neither does this solve the issue unless one also provides reasons why their views are correct. Additionally, to reject rival positions in an *a priori* manner is likewise illegitimate. Both believers and unbelievers could respond this way, revealing why these detrimental attempts need to be avoided. Such approaches are inadequate precisely because they fail to address the data. There is no substitute for a careful investigation of the possibilities.

The Death and Burial of Jesus

We have argued that the Jesus Seminar fails to adequately evidence its claims concerning its rejection of the supernatural, such as the miracles of Jesus. Before turning to their treatment of Jesus' resurrection, we will view the events that led to it.

Initially, it should be pointed out that the Seminar Fellows do not deny the death of Jesus. In keeping with the first phase of their research, they commented only on the words attributed to Jesus as he died on the cross.[22] Yet, no objections are raised concerning Jesus' death by crucifixion and

---

[19]B.D. Chilton, "Exorcism and History: Mark 1:21-28," *Gospel Perspectives*, Vol. 6, ed. by David Wenham and Craig Blomberg (Sheffield: JSOT, 1986), p. 263.

[20]Crossan, *Jesus: A Revolutionary Biography*, pp. 82, 95.

[21]Marcus J. Borg, *Jesus: A New Vision*, pp. 66-67, 70-71.

[22]Funk, Hoover, and the Jesus Seminar, *Five Gospels*, pp. 126, 268, 397, 464-465.

other member publications confirm the acceptance of at least the main outline of these events.

For example, Crossan affirms this event in the strongest terms: "That he was crucified is as sure as anything historical can ever be," and this event resulted in Jesus' death.[23] In an earlier volume he states: "I take it absolutely for granted that Jesus was crucified under Pontius Pilate." This is followed, interestingly enough, by reasons for this conclusion.[24] Borg agrees: "The most certain fact about the historical Jesus is his execution as a political rebel."[25]

But when it comes to Jesus' burial, Crossan takes a rather peculiar approach. He surmises that, consistent with crucifixion customs, Jesus was either left on the cross after his death to be torn apart by wild beasts or buried in a shallow grave where dogs would still have found the body. Thus, Jesus was not buried in Joseph's tomb and his body was most likely consumed by animals. In the end, he asserts that "by Easter Sunday morning, those who cared did not know where it was, and those who knew did not care. Why should even the soldiers themselves remember the death and disposal of a nobody?"[26]

Critique

But Crossan's approach is marred by numerous shortcomings. (1) All four Gospels agree on the basic burial scenario, which potentially provides even further confirmation if these texts are otherwise corroborated. (2) On the other hand, no early documents dispute these reports. One might ask Crossan for the *specific* data that support his thesis, especially from the first century. A challenge such as his cannot rest on

---

[23]Crossan, *Jesus: A Revolutionary Biography*, p. 145 along with pp. 154, 196, 201.

[24]Crossan, *The Historical Jesus:*, pp. 372-376.

[25]Borg, *Jesus*, p. 179; cf. pp. 178-184.

[26]Crossan, *Jesus: A Revolutionary Biography*, pp. 152-158, especially p. 158; also Crossan, *The Historical Jesus*, pp. 391-394, especially p. 394.

a surmisal, or even on a generalized practice among Jews.

Also, (3) are we to believe that the Jewish leaders, who had tried for so long to get rid of Jesus, would have paid no attention to his burial? Moreover, (4) Crossan's suggestion that the soldiers would merely have forgotten the location where they buried the body just a few days before is also preposterous. They should have remembered where they buried anyone. But contrary to Crossan's contention that Jesus was a "nobody," the interest occasioned by his preaching, his popularity, his trial, and his death would have insured both their work as well as their memory. After all, might they not be called upon later to evidence the death and burial of this famous insurrectionist?

Another major factor in favor of Jesus' burial and the empty tomb is that (5) both are actually admitted by the Jewish polemic against the Christian message. The response of the Jewish leaders is not only recorded in Matthew 28:11-15, but we are told by both Justin Martyr[27] and Tertullian[28] that this continued to be the Jewish message at least through the second century. It would be incredible that this would be their report instead of what Crossan thinks is the more likely scenario, if the latter had, indeed, occurred. Why was not this simpler thesis employed?

Of course, some may think that the Jewish report of the empty tomb is simply an invention of the early Christians. But such an assertion is question begging; it merely assumes what has not been proven. Once again, we ask for the evidence for such claims.

Continuing, certain evidences for the empty tomb also argue for a specific burial for Jesus. (6) From a very early date, the pre-Markan passion account points to an empty tomb.[29] And if the story was created later, (7) why would

---

[27]*Dialogue with Trypho*, 108.

[28]*On Spectacles*, 30.

[29]William Lane Craig dates this pre-Markan testimony, at the latest, to AD 37. See his essay, "The Empty Tomb of Jesus" in *Gospel Perspectives: Studies of History and Tradition in the Four Gospels*, vol. II, ed. by R.T. France and David Wenham (Sheffield: JSOT, 1981), pp. 182-183, 190-191.

women be cited as the initial witnesses, given the fact that they were not even allowed to give testimony in law courts? Such details argue for the traditional scenario.

Further, (8) Jesus' burial is supported by confessional statements in 1 Corinthians 15:3-4 and Acts 13:29.[30] These early, traditional reports confirm the ancient belief that he was buried in a tomb rather than in some unknown grave.

Lastly, (9) the apostles' early proclamation of the resurrection message in Jerusalem, the very city where Jesus died, was in direct opposition to the will of the Jewish leaders. This reality would have provided a catalyst to make sure that the burial details were known and that the grave was, in fact, empty.

In sum, the agreement of each of the Gospel texts, the lack of any early, contrary documentation, both the Jewish and Roman interest in Jesus' death, the Jewish polemic admitting the empty tomb, the pre-Markan narrative, the witness of the women, the early confessional statements, and the Jerusalem preaching all argue strongly against Crossan's challenge to the traditional burial of Jesus.[31] His allegation that absolutely no one either witnessed the burial by the soldiers or otherwise remembered it is simply unconvincing. Nothing even approaching strong evidence favors his hypothesis.

The Resurrection of Jesus

The Jesus Seminar fails to provide adequate evidence for either its general response to the supernatural or its particular skepticism towards the resurrection. But perhaps separate

---

[30]See the discussion in chapter 7 for the significance of these early kerygmatic reports.

[31]Another possible indication in favor of the traditional burial of Jesus is the Nazareth Decree, a first century marble slab that warns that grave robbing is punishable by death, which may be a response both to the Jewish charges, as well as the reports of Jesus' resurrection. Some think that the Shroud of Turin is at least an evidence of an individual burial for a crucifixion victim. For an overview of such reasons (including sources), see Gary R. Habermas, *Dealing with Doubt* (Chicago: Moody, 1990), pp. 43-45.

Seminar scholars offer a more careful response. Do we find additional critical approaches to this event? We will examine comments from Crossan and Borg in order to ascertain their thoughts on this subject.

John Dominic Crossan

Crossan probably spends the most time on this issue and does present a rather novel approach. He holds that the accounts of both Jesus' nature miracles and his resurrection appearances are *not* concerned with miraculous acts, but with authority structures in the early church. Taking Paul's famous account in 1 Corinthians 15:1-11, Crossan notes "that there are three types of recipients" of Jesus' "apparitions or revelations" consisting of: "three *specific leaders*," Peter, James, and Paul; "two *leadership groups*": the twelve and the apostles; and "one single *general community*" represented by the five hundred.[32]

Concerning these "three types of recipients," Crossan then makes two proposals. First, the post-resurrection phenomena are not about Jesus' appearances, but are "quite deliberate political dramatizations" showing the priority of one leader over another, or one group over the community as a whole. Second, the nature miracles (of which the resurrection is the greatest) likewise "serve the same function" and describe not Jesus' power but the "apostles' spiritual power over the community."[33]

Thus, Crossan interprets both the nature miracles and the resurrection narratives not as being indicative of any supernatural occurrences, but as a socio-political commentary on the early church leadership. The chief leaders held authority over the main groups, in turn directing the church community as a whole. These miracle texts, then, serve the purpose

---

[32]Crossan, *Jesus: A Revolutionary Biography*, p. 169. (The emphasis is Crossan's.)

[33]Ibid., pp. 169-170; Crossan, *The Historical Jesus*, p. 404. For other texts that carry on this theme, see *The Historical Jesus*, pp. 396-404; *Jesus: A Revolutionary Biography*, pp. 175, 181, 186, 190.

of being a powerful facilitator in establishing and maintaining the ecclesiastical hierarchy.

So what does all of this mean concerning the resurrection of Jesus? Crossan thinks that the New Testament accounts are not primarily concerned with the facticity of the appearances, but rather with "power and authority in the earliest Christian communities. That is what they were intended to be, and that is how we should read them."[34] In this sense, then, we ought not be inquiring about the miraculous element, and doing so is to trivialize the message. These accounts "tell us nothing whatsoever about the origins of Christian *faith* but quite a lot about the origins of Christian *authority*."[35]

Does this say anything about the facticity of the resurrection appearances? Even if recording the miraculous element is not the chief point of the New Testament narratives, Crossan is careful not to infer that the appearances never really happened. In fact, in speaking about Easter he expressly affirms: "Of course there may have been trances and visions." Then he adds that these sorts of things happen "in every religion" and so we should not be surprised.[36]

1. Inadequate basis

When considering Crossan's hypothesis, several critiques immediately come to mind. First, and in spite of some interesting contentions, Crossan has not established his sociopolitical schema as a central theme in the early church. Interpreting references in light of a secondary construction is far from proving it to be the original intent of the authors. His account remains an unverified hypothesis.

2. The resurrection and early church authority

Second, *even if* his theme of power, authority, and leader-

---

[34]Crossan, *Jesus: A Revolutionary Biography*, p. 186.

[35]Ibid., p. 190. (The emphasis is Crossan's.)

[36]Ibid.

ship is important to some extent,[37] his de-emphasis of the facticity of Jesus' resurrection simply does not follow. For Paul, it was not merely receiving "revelation from Christ"[38] that even made one an apostle in the first place, but specifically having seen the *resurrected* Jesus (1 Cor. 9:1; 15:8).

In fact, without this event, what is the *basis* of the claim to authority on behalf of the other two leaders specified by Crossan, namely Peter and James? In both of these cases, as well, the resurrection provided the *rationale* for their authority. It might be said that Peter's influence came at least in part from Jesus' appearance reported in the extremely early tradition in 1 Corinthians 15:5, and confirmed by another ancient confession in Luke 24:34. Numerous scholars have agreed, noting the link between Jesus' appearance and Peter's authority.[39]

But to say, as Crossan does, that the authority structure was the chief point of these narratives, with "nothing whatsoever"[40] being learned about Jesus' appearances and origin of the church is certainly mistaken. As Joachim Jeremias asserts, the "decisive event" here is that "*the Lord appears to Peter.*"[41] While Reginald Fuller also characterizes the appearances as hierarchical in the early church mission, agreeing to some extent with Crossan, he still insists on definable appearances.[42]

---

[37]I am not agreeing with his suggestion here. I simply think that, at this point, whether or not his socio-political theme is crucial to our central thesis is moot.

[38]Crossan, *The Historical Jesus*, p. 397.

[39]Joachim Jeremias, "Easter: The Earliest Tradition and the Earliest Interpretation," pp. 306-307; Reginald H. Fuller, *The Formation of the Resurrection Narratives* (New York: Macmillan, 1971), pp. 34-42; C.H. Dodd, "The Appearances of the Risen Christ: An Essay in Form-Criticism of the Gospels," *More New Testament Studies* (Grand Rapids: Eerdmans, 1968), pp. 125-126; Rudolf Bultmann, *Theology*, vol. I, p. 45. Bultmann also sees a probable parallel to 1 Cor. 15:5 and Luke 24:34 in Luke 22:31f.

[40]Crossan, *Jesus: A Revolutionary Biography*, p. 190; cf. pp. 169-170.

[41]Jeremias, "Easter: The Earliest Tradition and the Earliest Interpretation," p. 306. (The emphasis is Jeremias'.)

[42]Fuller, *Resurrection Narratives*, pp. 27-49.

The same is also true of James, in that the Lord likewise appeared to him (1 Cor. 15:7). Fuller concludes rather strikingly that even if the appearance to James was not recorded in the pages of the New Testament, "we should have to invent one in order to account for his post-resurrection conversion and rapid advance."[43] Thus, the texts insist and most scholars agree that it is unjustified to separate the appearances from the early church power structure.

3. Centrality of resurrection

Third, while the truth of the resurrection may precede and determine church authority, to attempt to circumscribe it almost totally within this latter, narrow parameter is certainly misplaced. In other words, the resurrection is absolutely *central* to the New Testament as a whole. It is related to far more than just socio-political factors in the early church, but this does not justify making any one of these other themes the chief focus, either.

Even a summary listing could take a separate chapter. For example, the resurrection is a sign for unbelievers (Matt. 12:38-40; 16:1-4) as well as a comfort for believers (John 11:23-26; Luke 24:36-39). It was an indispensable part of the gospel (Rom. 10:9; 1 Cor. 15:1-5) and the heart of early preaching (Acts 4:2; 4:33). It was the impetus for evangelism (Matt. 28:18-20; Luke 24:45-48) and the chief message in Paul's church planting methods (Acts 17:1-4).

Continuing, it provided daily power for the believer (Phil. 3:10; Rom. 8:11) and was the grounds for total commitment (1 Cor. 15:58). Believers would be raised like Jesus (1 John 3:2; Phil. 3:21) and the resurrection guarantees the reality of heaven (1 Pet. 1:3-5). And as we saw earlier in Paul, Acts also insists that one could not even be an apostle without having been a witness to this event (1:21-22).

An additional evidence for the resurrection and an especially powerful pointer to its centrality that is generally

---

[13]Ibid., p. 37.

ignored by members of the Jesus Seminar is the presence of early creedal traditions in the preaching of Acts. Yet there is strong evidence that the (especially Petrine) sermons record reliable accounts of the early messages on the death and resurrection of Jesus, including his appearances. Dodd also argues that these confessions are perhaps as early as Paul's creed in 1 Corinthians 15:3ff.[44]

4. Resurrection facts

Fourth, we still must deal with the data itself. Crossan admits that we have Paul's testimony concerning his personal experience, and that his report dates very early.[45] Then he concludes that "trances and visions" probably did occur, singling out Paul's experience as the chief example.[46] While this is not the place to argue for the historicity of these events, or their being caused by the risen Jesus,[47] we will simply note here that Crossan apparently does not intend to deny the reality of these experiences. Neither has he chosen to argue a naturalistic hypothesis. As such, they have to be adequately explained. And as we have argued, it is insufficient to attempt to pass them off as mere indications of early church power structures.

5. Other religious phenomena

Fifth, while Crossan does not deny the disciples' experiences, he further downplays their uniqueness by his remark that "trances or visions" are found in "every religion."[48] Such

---

[44]Of chief interest are Acts 2:14-39; 3:12-26; 4:8-12; 5:17-40; 10:34-43; 13:16-41. See Dodd, "Appearances," pp. 124, 131; C.H. Dodd, *The Apostolic Preaching and its Developments*, pp. 17-31 and chart after p. 96.

[45]Crossan, *The Historical Jesus*, p. 397; Crossan, *Jesus: A Revolutionary Biography*, pp. 165-166, 190.

[46]Crossan, *Jesus: A Revolutionary Biography*, p. 190.

[47]For an example of such arguments, see the excellent treatment by William Lane Craig, *Assessing the New Testament Evidence for the Historicity of the Resurrection of Jesus*.

[48]Crossan, *Jesus: A Revolutionary Biography*, p. 190.

a comparison is intriguing, since Crossan states earlier that the Gospel accounts of Jesus' appearances are *not* "entranced revelations." He declares that they "bear no marks of such phenomena."[49]

Regardless, whether such curiosities are taught in other belief systems is not the issue. Anyone can make claims. The real question is whether they can be *demonstrated*. I have argued elsewhere that such non-Christian claims are poorly evidenced.[50] If this is the case, they merely number among the myriads of unproven religious assertions. As such, they are not rivals to Jesus' resurrection.

In sum, Crossan fails to adequately explain or dismiss the resurrection of Jesus. His socio-political interpretation is unproven. Additionally, he fails to realize that even if his thesis is accurate, not only is it still an inadequate basis for his de-emphasis of the facticity of Jesus' resurrection, but his theme actually requires this event. Further, the resurrection is central not only to the early Christian authority structures, but to the New Testament as a whole. Yet this event cannot be reduced to any of these themes. Additionally, not only does Crossan admit the possibility of "visions," but his attempt to eliminate their uniqueness by noting the presence of such occurrences in other religions also fails.

Marcus Borg

On this topic also, Borg takes a more moderate approach than does Crossan, addressing the resurrection appearances of Jesus at more length, as well. Borg thinks that, while "the story of the historical Jesus ends with his death on a Friday in A.D. 30, the story of Jesus does not end there." According to Jesus' followers, "he appeared to them in a new way beginning on Easter Sunday."[51]

---

[49]Ibid., p. 169.

[50]On the absence of evidence for such phenomena, see Gary R. Habermas, "Resurrection Claims in Non-Christian Religions," *Religious Studies*, vol. 25 (1989), pp. 167-177.

[51]Borg, *Jesus*, p. 184.

However, "[w]e cannot know exactly what happened. According to the earliest accounts of Easter reported by his followers, Jesus 'appeared to them'" but "[w]e do not know what form those appearances took" since they are sometimes described as visionary and other times as corporeal. Did anything happen to Jesus' body? Borg states that, in historical terms, "we cannot say," maintaining that Jesus' resurrection was not a reanimation of his corpse but that "Jesus' followers continued to experience him as a living reality . . . ."[52] Presumably, Borg thinks that the truth lies somewhere in between these two positions.

In a more recent article that attempts to answer this question, Borg adds a few items. He continues to take seriously the claims that Jesus appeared, largely because such is the testimony of Paul, whom he considers the earliest New Testament author, the only eyewitness writer we have, and because this was the central event for him. Thus we must make sense of these occurrences. Yet, these are not "straightforward events" and could not have been photographed. Again, they signify the continuing presence of Jesus in "the lives of Christians as both companion and lord."[53]

We will look briefly at Borg's proposal by responding to his own question concerning the nature of Jesus' appearances. Although it is a crucially important issue, we will not be able to argue here the actual nature of these appearances,[54] since we are more interested at this point in their facticity. But obviously, these scholars struggle with the bodily nature of the appearances.

---

[52]Ibid., p. 185.

[53]Marcus J. Borg, "Thinking about Easter," *Bible Review*, vol. X, Number 2 (April 1994), pp. 15, 49.

[54]For details on what is nonetheless of fundamental importance, see Robert H. Gundry, *Soma in Biblical Theology: With Emphasis on Pauline Anthropology* (Grand Rapids: Zondervan, 1987), especially chapter 13; Craig, chapter 4; Norman L. Geisler, *The Battle for the Resurrection* (Nashville: Nelson,1989), especially chapters 7–8; Gary R. Habermas and J.P. Moreland, *Immortality* (Nashville: Nelson, 1992), chapter 9.

Critique

Borg accepts the historicity of a number of facts that, together, indicate that Jesus actually appeared to his followers after his resurrection. This is the case even if we were to examine only Paul's testimony, which is what Borg prefers. Borg is clear that Jesus really died and his followers reported that he had appeared to them afterwards. Paul was an early eyewitness to these occurrences. As a result, his life (as well as that of the other followers) was changed by what became his central message. They were convinced both that Jesus was alive and that he was their Lord.[55]

As we have said, Borg does not define or identify the nature of these appearances. Some of his language implies that he doubts their objective nature, especially when he seems to say that they are almost synonymous with the Christian conviction that Jesus is spiritually present with his followers. But on the other hand, he admits the crucial data for the early, eyewitness testimony to the appearances and seems to remain open to some unspecified type of manifestations.

It would seem that Borg has painted himself into a corner here. He realizes that the earliest, eyewitness data dictate, among other details, that Jesus appeared to Paul and many others after his death. Yet, he does not venture an alternative hypothesis such as hallucinations or other subjective conjectures. At any rate, such theses fail anyway.[56] So the chief question is this: how does Borg account for these admittedly real experiences, particularly when they happened to groups of people?

In short, even the minimal amount of information

---

[55]These affirmations are found in Borg, *Jesus*, pp. 184-185 and Borg, "Thinking about Easter," pp. 15, 49.

[56]Just some of the roadblocks to explaining Jesus' appearances as hallucinations (or as otherwise subjective incidents) include the private nature of such psychological phenomena, thereby precluding group citings such as the three reported by Paul in 1 Cor. 15:5-7, the negative mental states of the recipients, the variety of persons, times, and places involved, the extent of the disciples' transformations, the empty tomb, James' conversion, and Paul's experience on the way to Damascus.

supplied by Borg argues for objective appearances, while contrary suppositions are disproven. This conclusion is further reinforced by both the early, apostolic preaching in Acts, as well as the Gospel narratives.

Summary and Conclusion

The Jesus Seminar has made no secret about its contention that the orthodox conception of Jesus is outdated and ought to be rejected. Thus, supernatural events such as the Gospel reports of Jesus' miracles must at least be seriously questioned, and more likely repudiated.

Yet, seldom are any *reasons* given for such a stance. Mere theological assertion seems to be the order of the day. Appeals to peer pressure (in the name of the current state of modern scholarship) serve as the impetus and those who dare to disagree are sometimes painted as hopelessly backward. Nevertheless, it is certainly insufficient to simply state one's view or claim a critical consensus without adequate evidence.

Even worse, informal logical fallacies abound in statements by the Jesus Seminar. Comments about the "secular heavens" start to sound less like reasoned responses and more like *a priori* preaching. The lack of careful argumentation begs the question on behalf of the assertions that are made. Rejections of Gospel texts based on author's styles, ancient parallels, and a pre-modern temperament commit the genetic fallacy. Interestingly enough, some Seminar Fellows appear to recognize such dangers.[57] Unfortunately, this seems to be a minority acknowledgment.

The Jesus Seminar apparently offers no challenges to the basic fact of Jesus' death. But there are many reasons why Crossan's doubts concerning the traditional burial of Jesus cannot be substantiated. His surmisals are confronted by almost a dozen items of data.

When discussing the resurrection of Jesus, we have

---

[57]Chilton, "Exorcism," p. 263; Borg, *Jesus*, pp. 66-67, 70-71.

attempted to isolate a single issue: whether Jesus actually appeared to his followers. Both Crossan and Borg might prefer to question the New Testament texts, satisfied with what they think we *cannot* know. But we insisted that, when attempting to ascertain the truth of what happened after the death of Jesus, such is an insufficient approach. Rather than be satisfied with this negative tack, we maintain that the minimal amount of historical data is still sufficient to establish the literal nature of Jesus' appearances, whatever their actual form. These two scholars seem not to realize that their own writings establish a sufficient basis to confirm this truth.

Both Crossan and Borg admit at least the possibility of Jesus' appearances, with Borg being more open to them. Further, neither scholar attempts to explain away the core factual data by employing naturalistic, alternative hypotheses. The early, eyewitness data supplied by Paul and admitted by both Crossan and Borg are sufficient to show that Jesus did, indeed, appear to his followers after his death. Additional details concerning the other witnesses drawn from Paul's data, the Acts traditions, or even the Gospels, serve to greatly strengthen this conclusion.[58]

Although the Jesus Seminar has received much attention from its treatment of the historical Jesus, their conclusions must be apportioned to the data. As a result, their basic rejection of the supernatural events in Jesus' life is unwarranted.[59]

---

[58]Crossan and Borg are not the only members of the Jesus Seminar who have published important works on the resurrection of Jesus. For two such older examples that may be interpreted as providing *even more grounds* for the conclusions we have reached here, see James M. Robinson, "Jesus from Easter to Valentinus (or to the Apostles' Creed)," *Journal of Biblical Literature*, Vol. 101; No. 1 (1982), pp. 5-37; John Kloppenborg, "An Analysis of the Pre-Pauline Formula 1 Cor 15:3b-5 in Light of Some Recent Literature," *The Catholic Biblical Quarterly*, vol. 40 (1978), pp. 351-367.

[59]Several detailed critiques of the Jesus Seminar and related views have appeared in recent years. The interested reader might consult the following: Gregory A. Boyd, *Cynic Sage or Son of God? Recovering the Real Jesus in an Age of Revisionist Replies* (Wheaton: Victor, 1995); Wilkins and Moreland, eds., *Jesus Under Fire*; Ben Witherington III, *The Jesus Quest: The Third Search for the Jew of Nazareth* (Downers Grove: InterVarsity, 1995); N.T. Wright, *Who was Jesus?* (Grand Rapids: Eerdmans, 1992).

Part Two

Historical Data for the Life of Jesus

7 Primary Sources: Creeds and Facts

What facts did the earliest Christians report concerning Jesus in the initial years after his crucifixion? Of what did the earliest Christology consist before the composition of the New Testament? Is it possible to get back to eyewitness testimony and to historical facts with regard to Jesus? These are fascinating and very important questions, and one of the chief efforts of contemporary scholarship has been to address these issues. Such is also a major concern in this book.

In this chapter we will endeavor to investigate an area which many feel is the most promising means of describing the nature of Christian thought before the writing of the New Testament. This general subject concerns the existence of early Christian creeds which were first repeated verbally and later written in the books of the New Testament. Thus, in one sense, this material is not extrabiblical since we rely on the scriptural material for the creeds. At the same time, this data was formulated *before* the New Testament books, in which the creeds appear, were actually written. In short, these creeds were communicated verbally years before they were written and hence they preserve some of the earliest reports concerning Jesus from about AD 30–50. Therefore, in a real sense, the creeds preserve pre-New Testament material, and are our earliest sources for the life of Jesus.

This chapter also includes a listing of facts which are admitted by virtually all critical scholars who study this subject. In other words, critical theologians, historians and philosophers who have studied the New Testament have ascertained a number of facts from the life of Jesus by the critical examination of the biblical sources. The procedure in this chapter is first to examine some Christological creeds with regard to the information they relate concerning the life, death and resurrection of Jesus. This last subject will be the special concern in the second section of this chapter, as we investigate 1 Corinthians 15:3ff., which is perhaps the most important creed in the New Testament (at least for our purposes). This is followed by the presentation of the critically accepted facts, as mentioned above. Lastly, an examination of this data will follow.

Christological Creeds

In the early church there were multiple creedal formulas which corresponded to various circumstances in the Christian faith. The most common of these confessions were purely Christological in nature.[1] The two most common elements in these creeds concerned the death and resurrection of Jesus and his resulting deity.[2] Thus we note the major interest in the life and person of Jesus Christ.

The Life of Jesus Christ

The earliest Christians were confident that "Jesus Christ is come in the flesh," as proclaimed in the confession found in 1 John 4:2.[3] Seldom was belief in Jesus' incarnation expressed

---

[1]See Oscar Cullmann, *The Earliest Christian Confessions*, transl. by J.K.S. Reid (London: Lutterworth, 1949), pp. 35,38. This book is one of the classic works on this subject.

[2]Ibid., pp. 57-58, 63-64.

[3]Ibid., p. 32.

more clearly than in the "pre-Pauline hymn" of Philippians 2:6ff.,[4] which speaks of both Jesus' human and divine natures. His humble life on earth is clearly contrasted with his heavenly position "in the form of God" and his later exaltation and worship.

Another ancient creed which expresses a contrast between aspects of Jesus' life is 2 Timothy 2:8.[5] Here Jesus' birth in the lineage of David is contrasted with his resurrection from the dead, again showing the early Christian interest in linking Jesus to history.[6] Similarly, Romans 1:3-4 is also an ancient, pre-Pauline creed.[7] It juxtaposes the man Jesus "made of the seed of David according to the flesh" with the divine Jesus whose claims were vindicated by his rising from the dead.[8] For our present purposes, we need only note the early interest in Jesus' earthly, physical connections, as he was born of a descendant of David's family. As Moule relates, it was the same human Jesus who lived, died and was later vindicated.[9]

One early confessional creed is 1 Tim. 3:16[10] (sometimes referred to as a "Christ-hymn"[11]), which gives a brief recital of both the human and divine Jesus:

----

[4]Ibid., pp. 22-23, 28, 55, 57-62. Cf. Bultmann, *Theology of the New Testament*, vol. 1, pp. 27, 125, 131, 175, 298; Neufeld, *The Earliest Christian Confessions* (Grand Rapids: Eerdmans, 1964), pp. 9, 49, 57, 61; Fuller, *Foundations*, pp. 204-206, 221-225, 248; Pannenberg, *Jesus*, pp. 366-367.

[5]Bultmann, *Theology of the New Testament*, ibid., vol. 1, pp. 49, 81; Joachim Jeremias, *Eucharistic Words*, p. 102; Neufeld, ibid., p. 145, cf. p. 128.

[6]See Cullmann, *Confessions*, pp. 55, 58; C.F.D. Moule, *The Birth of the New Testament*, revised edition (New York: Harper and Row, 1982), p. 247; Neufeld, pp. 128-129, 133.

[7]Cullmann, ibid., p. 55; Bultmann, *Theology*, vol. 1, p. 27; II, p. 121; Pannenberg, *Jesus*, pp. 118, 283, 367; Neufeld, pp. 7, 50; cf. Dodd, *Apostolic Preaching*, p. 14.

[8]For example, see Bultmann, *Theology*, vol. 1, pp. 27, 50. Other such sources will be pursued later in this chapter.

[9]Moule, *Birth*, pp. 33-35.

[10]Jeremias, *Eucharistic Words*, p. 102; Neufeld, pp. 7, 9, 128.

[11]Jeremias, ibid., p. 132; cf. Bultmann, *Theology*, vol. 1, p. 176; 2, pp. 153, 156; Fuller, *Foundations*, pp. 214, 216, 227, 239.

> Great indeed, we confess, is the mystery of our religion:
>> He was manifested in the flesh,
>> vindicated in the Spirit, seen by angels,
>> preached among the nations,
>> believed on in the world,
>> taken up in glory (RSV).

Moule notes not only the early date of this creed but also its pattern of rhyme, which was probably utilized in worship and hymnody.[12] This statement also presents a contrast between Jesus' human birth "in the flesh" and his deity,[13] further mentioning his approval by the Spirit and the witness of the angels. He was preached among the nations of the world and believed by people before he was "taken up in glory."

Another early confession which may well reflect an event in Christ's life is Romans 10:9.[14] At present we are only concerned with the strong possibility that this may actually be a baptismal creed, cited by Christian candidates for baptism.[15] As such, it would be an indirect reference to Jesus' own baptism.

Although these early creeds are interested in theological elements of Christology, to be sure, they are also early reports of events in the life of Jesus. We are told *(1)* that Jesus was really born in human flesh (Phil. 2:6; 1 Tim. 3:16; 1 John 4:2) *(2)* of the lineage and family of David (Rom. 1:3-4; 2 Tim. 2:8). We find *(3)* an implication of his baptism (Rom. 10:9) and *(4)* that his word was preached, *(5)* resulting in persons believing his message (1 Tim. 3:16).

The Death and Resurrection of Jesus

Just prior to Jesus' trial and crucifixion, both the synoptic Gospels and Paul relate that Jesus had a private supper with

---

[12]Moule, *Birth*, pp. 33-35.

[13]Cullmann, *Confessions*, p. 41.

[14]Jeremias, *Eucharistic Words*, p. 112; Bultmann, *Theology*, vol. 1, pp. 81, 125; Neufeld, *Confessions*, pp. 43, 140.

[15]Bultmann, *Theology*, vol. 1, p. 312; Neufeld, *Confessions*, pp. 62, 68, 144.

his disciples. The Pauline account in 1 Corinthians 11:23ff. presents a fixed tradition which is probably based on material independent of the sources for the synoptic Gospels.[16] Jeremias notes that Paul's words "received" and "delivered" are not Paul's typical terms, but "represent the rabbinical technical terms" for passing on tradition.[17] Additionally, there are other non-Pauline phrases such as "he was betrayed," "when he had given thanks" and "my body" (11:23-24), which are further indications of the early nature of this report. In fact, Jeremias asserts that his material was formulated "in the very earliest period; at any rate before Paul . . . a pre-Pauline formula." Paul is actually pointing out "that the chain of tradition goes back unbroken to Jesus himself."[18]

It is widely held that this ancient tradition presents actual historical events which occurred on the evening of the so-called "last supper."[19] Such is even recognized by Bultmann.[20] As Martin Hengel explains, "Paul refers to a historical event with a specific date . . . ."[21] This tradition relates that Jesus did attend a dinner on the same evening as he was betrayed. He gives thanks to God before eating and afterward shared both bread and drink, which he referred to as the sacrifice of his body and blood for believers. Here we find insights not only to some of the events of the evening, but also to the actual words which may have been repeated at early Christian observances of the Last Supper.[22]

Another event just prior to Jesus' crucifixion is related by 1 Timothy 6:13, which is also an early tradition,[23] and

---

[16]Moule, *Birth*, p. 38; Jeremias, *Eucharistic Words*, pp. 101, 104-105.

[17]Jeremias, ibid., p. 101.

[18]Ibid., pp. 101, 104-105.

[19]Cullmann, *Confessions*, p. 64; Moule, *Birth*, pp. 38-39; Neufeld, *Confessions*, p. 52.

[20]Bultmann, *Theology*, vol. 1, p. 83.

[21]Martin Hengel, *The Atonement*, transl. by John Bowden (Philadelphia: Fortress, 1981), p. 53.

[22]Moule, *Birth*, p. 38.

[23]Bultmann, *Theology*, vol. 2, p. 121; Neufeld, *Confessions*, pp. 20, 31.

perhaps even a part of a more extensive oral Christian confession of faith.[24] This statement asserts that Jesus came before Pontius Pilate and made a good confession.[25] Neufeld points out that Jesus' testimony was probably his affirmative answer to Pilate's question as to whether he was the King of the Jews (see Mark 15:2).[26] At any rate, "Jesus did not deny his identity in the trials but made a good confession before the Jews and Pilate."[27]

We have already noted how some early Christian traditions presented a juxtaposition between the human and the divine Jesus. Several other early reports contrasted the seeming defeat suffered at the cross with the triumph of Jesus' resurrection. Earlier, Philippians 2:6ff. was mentioned as expressing this first comparison of the human Jesus who was to be exalted by God. More specifically, Philippians 2:8 additionally reports the humbling of Jesus as he died on the cross in direct contrast to this later exaltation. Another example is to be found in Romans 4:25, which Bultmann refers to as "a statement that had evidently existed before Paul and had been handed down to him."[28] The content of this tradition is that Jesus died for our sins and was afterward raised from the dead to secure the believer's justification. Similarly, 1 Peter 3:18 (cf. 1 Tim. 2:6) also contrasts Jesus' death for the sins of mankind (in spite of his own righteousness) with the resurrection as the means of bringing people to God.[29]

Early accounts of Jesus' resurrection are also preserved in Christian tradition. Next to 1 Corinthians 15:3ff., the most crucial texts for historical purposes are several early passages in the book of Acts (especially Peter's speeches).[30] The death

---

[24]See Cullmann, *Confessions*, pp. 25, 27.

[25]Ibid.; Bultmann, *Theology of the New Testament*, vol. 1, p. 82.

[26]Neufeld, *Confessions*, pp. 31, 63-64, 146.

[27]Ibid., p. 114; cf. pp. 132-133.

[28]Bultmann, *Theology*, vol. 1, p. 82.

[29]Cullmann, *Confessions*, pp. 41, 45, 53, 57-62, including the creedal nature of these two references.

[30]See especially Acts 2:14-39; 3:12-26; 4:8-12; 5:29-32; 10:34-43; cf. 13:16-41.

and resurrection of Jesus are the center of each sermon.[31] Critical research has shown that these texts reflect early, largely undeveloped theology, perhaps from the Jerusalem community. Drane explains it this way:

> The earliest evidence we have for the resurrection almost certainly goes back to the time immediately after the resurrection event is alleged to have taken place. This is the evidence contained in the early sermons in the Acts of the Apostles. . . . But there can be no doubt that in the first few chapters of Acts its author has preserved material from very early sources.
>
> Scholars have discovered that the language used in speaking about Jesus in these early speeches in Acts is quite different from that used at the time when the book was compiled in its final form.[32]

Many scholars have argued that in these early texts we have a clear summary of the earliest apostolic kerygma.[33]

Jeremias holds that Luke's brief mention of Jesus' resurrection appearance to Peter in Luke 24:34 is of even greater antiquity than is 1 Corinthians 15:5, which would make this an extremely early witness to these appearances.[34] Dodd and Bultmann also note the connections between the fact that Peter appears in the references in both Luke 24:34 and 1 Corinthians 15:5.[35] A previously mentioned tradition, 2 Timothy 2:8, presents another contrast by linking the Jesus who descended from David with the same person who was raised from the dead. Not only is Jesus' resurrection proclaimed as an event of history, but early creeds also assert that, on the basis of this event, Jesus' claims were justified. In particular, it is said that the resurrection revealed the uniqueness of Jesus' person.

---

[31]See Acts 2:22-23, 31; 3:15; 4:10; 5:30-31; 10:39-42; 13:28-29.

[32]Drane, *Introducing the NT*, p. 99.

[33]See the influential treatment by Dodd, *Apostolic Preaching*, pp. 17-31; cf. Craig's overview of the debate, pp. 36-38.

[34]Joachim Jeremias, "Easter: The Earliest Tradition and the Earliest Interpretation," p. 306.

[35]C.H. Dodd, "Risen Christ," p. 125; Bultmann, *Theology*, vol. 1, p. 45.

That Romans 1:3-4 is an ancient pre-Pauline creed is shown by the parallelism of the clauses,[36] which is especially seen in the contrast between Jesus as both the son of David and the Son of God.[37] The same Jesus who was born in space and time was raised from the dead.[38] This creed proclaims that Jesus was shown to be the Son of God, Christ (or Messiah) and Lord and vindicated as such by his resurrection from the dead.[39] Cullmann adds that redemption and Jesus' final exaltation were also included in this significant creedal affirmation.[40] Such an encompassing statement, including three major Christological titles and implying some actions of Jesus, reveals not only one of the earliest formulations of Christ's nature, but also conveys an apologetic motif in relating all this theology to the vindication provided by Jesus' resurrection (cf. Acts 2:22f.).

Another early creed which links the resurrection with the person and claims of Jesus is Romans 10:9-10.[41] In this passage, belief in this historical event is connected with confessing that Jesus is Lord. As a result one's salvation is secure.[42] Earlier it was pointed out that this may actually be a baptismal creed, whereby the candidate announced his belief in (and allegiance to) Jesus Christ.

Lastly, some creeds also confess Jesus' ascension to heaven and his resulting exaltation. Two examples of such early creeds were mentioned earlier with regard to the life of Jesus. In 1 Timothy 3:16, it is proclaimed that, after his incar-

---

[36]Cf. Neufeld, *Confessions*, pp. 7, 50; Pannenberg, *Jesus*, pp. 118, 283, 367; Dodd, *Apostolic Preaching*, p. 14; Bultmann, *Theology*, vol. 1, p. 27; vol. 2, p. 121; Fuller, *Foundations*, pp. 187, 189.

[37]Neufeld, *Confessions*, p. 50.

[38]Cullmann, *Confessions*, p. 55; Moule, *Birth*, p. 247.

[39]Cf. Moule, p. 247; Neufeld, *Confessions*, pp. 51-52; Pannenberg, *Jesus*, pp. 31, 133, 137, 147, 367; Bultmann, *Theology*, vol. 1, pp. 27, 50; Fuller, *Foundations*, pp. 180 (fn. 81), 187.

[40]Cullmann, *Confessions*, pp. 55, 57-62.

[41]Jeremias, *Eucharistic Words*, p. 112; Neufeld, *Confessions*, pp. 43, 140, 143; Bultmann, *Theology*, vol. 1, pp. 81, 125.

[42]See Dodd, *Apostolic Preaching*, p. 11.

nation, Jesus was "taken up in glory." In Philippians 2:6f. it is related that after Jesus humbled himself as a man, he was highly exalted and is to be worshiped by all persons (2:9-11).[43] This latter passage is taken from Isaiah 45:23 where God the Father is receiving such praise and glory.

Before proceeding to the extended examination of 1 Corinthians 15:3ff. it will be advantageous to briefly summarize the facts reported in various other creeds concerning the death and resurrection of Jesus. A few earlier events of Jesus' life are mentioned, all from the creeds in Acts: (6) Jesus was born in the lineage of David (13:23; also Rom. 1:3; 2 Tim. 2:8), and (7) came from the town of Nazareth (2:22; 4:10; 5:38). (8) John preceded Jesus' ministry (10:37; 13:24-25), (9) which began in Galilee, (10) afterwards expanding throughout Judea (10:37). (11) Jesus performed miracles (2:22; 10:38) and (12) fulfilled numerous Old Testament prophecies (2:25-31; 3:21-25; 4:11; 10:43; 13:27-37).

We are further informed by the creed in 1 Corinthians 11:23ff. that (13) Jesus attended a dinner (14) on the evening of his betrayal. (15) He gave thanks before the meal and (16) shared both bread and drink, (17) which, he declared, represented his imminent atoning sacrifice for sin.

(18) Later, Jesus stood before Pilate (Acts 3:13; 13:28) and (19) made a good confession, which very possibly concerned his identity as the King of the Jews (1 Tim. 6:13). (20) Afterwards, Jesus was killed (Acts 3:13-15; 13:27-29) (21) for mankind's sins (1 Pet. 3:18; Rom. 4:25; 1 Tim. 2:6), (22) in spite of his righteous life (1 Pet. 3:18). (23) Crucifixion was specified as the mode of death (Acts 2:23; 2:36; 4:10; 5:30; 10:39), being performed (24) in the city of Jerusalem (Acts 13:27; cf. 10:39), (25) by wicked men (Acts 2:23). (26) Then he was buried (Acts 13:29).

(27) After his death he was resurrected (Acts 2:24, 31-32; 3:15, 26; 4:10; 5:30; 10:40; 13:30-37; 2 Tim. 2:8), (28) on the third day (Acts 10:40) and (29) appeared to his followers (Acts 13:31), even (30) eating with them (Acts 10:40-41). (31) His

---

[43]Cullmann, *Confessions,* pp. 55, 57-62.

disciples were witnesses of these events (Acts 2:32; 3:15; 5:32; 10:39, 41; 13:31). *(32)* After his resurrection, Jesus ascended to heaven and was glorified and exalted (Acts 2:33; 3:21; 5:31; 1 Tim. 3:16; Phil. 2:6f.).

(33) The risen Jesus instructed that salvation be preached in his name (Acts 2:38-39; 3:19-23; 4:11-12; 5:32; 10:42-43; 13:26, 38-41). *(34)* This event showed God's approval of Jesus, by validating his person and message (Acts 2:22-24, 36; 3:13-15; 10:42; 13:32-33; Rom. 1:3-4; 10:9-10).

The person of Jesus Christ

Regarding his person, Jesus is called *(35)* the Son of God (Acts 13:33; Rom. 1:3-4), *(36)* Lord (Luke 24:34; Acts 2:36; 10:36; Rom. 1:4; 10:9; Phil. 2:11), *(37)* Christ or Messiah (Acts 2:36, 38; 3:18, 20; 4:10; 10:36; Rom. 1:4; Phil. 2:11; 2 Tim. 2:8), *(38)* Savior (Acts 5:31; 13:23), *(39)* Prince (Acts 5:31) and *(40)* the Holy and Righteous One (Acts 3:14; cf. 2:27; 13:35). *(41)* It is even said that, regarding his essential nature, he is God (Phil. 2:6).

1 Corinthians 15:3ff.

While the subject of early Christian creeds is a fascinating area of research, some may wonder on what grounds the facts of the creeds themselves may be established. One approach to this question is to validate the New Testament documents as reliable sources and then argue to the creeds as trustworthy testimony. Although we have provided much of the grounds for such a response in the above chapters, and while this writer believes that such an answer is an approach that has much to commend it, we are again reminded that the task we have set up for ourselves is to pursue *independent* evidence for such claims. Therefore, because of this particular goal, we will endeavor to provide special evidence for the death and resurrection of Jesus by referring to what is perhaps the most important single creed in the New Testament.

In 1 Corinthians 15:3-4, Paul states:

> For I delivered to you as of first importance what I also received, that Christ died for our sins in accordance with the scriptures, that he was buried, that he was raised on the third day in accordance with the scriptures (RSV).

As the passage continues, Paul records appearances of the resurrected Christ to Peter, to the "twelve" disciples, to over 500 persons at one time, to James, to all of the apostles and then to Paul himself (vv. 5-8).

That this confession is an early Christian, pre-Pauline creed is recognized by virtually all critical scholars across a very wide theological spectrum.[44] There are several indications that reveal this conclusion.

First, Paul's words "delivered" and "received" are technical terms for passing on tradition. As such, we have Paul's statement that this material was not his own, but received from another source.[45]

Second, a number of words in this creed are non-Pauline, again indicating another origin of this material.[46] Jeremias, a

---

[44]See Reginald Fuller, *Resurrection Narratives*, p. 10; Oscar Cullmann, *The Early Church: Studies in Early Christian History and Theology*, ed. by A.J.B. Higgins (Philadelphia: Westminster, 1966), p. 64; Pannenberg, *Jesus*, p. 90; Wilckens, *Resurrection*, p. 2; Hengel, *The Atonement*, pp. 36-38, 40; Bultmann, *Theology*, vol. 1, pp. 45, 80, 82, 293; Willi Marxsen, *The Resurrection of Jesus of Nazareth*, transl. by Margaret Kohl (Philadelphia: Fortress, 1970), pp. 80, 86; Hans Conzelmann, *1 Corinthians*, transl. by James W. Leitch (Philadelphia: Fortress, 1969), p. 251; Hans-Ruedi Weber, *The Cross*, transl. by Elke Jessett (Grand Rapids: Eerdmans, 1978), p. 58; Dodd, "Risen Christ," pp. 124-125; A.M. Hunter, *Bible and Gospel*, p. 108; Raymond E. Brown, *The Virginal Conception and Bodily Resurrection of Jesus* (New York: Paulist Press, 1973), pp. 81, 92; Norman Perrin, *The Resurrection According to Matthew, Mark and Luke* (Philadelphia: Fortress, 1977), p. 79; George E. Ladd, *I Believe in the Resurrection of Jesus* (Grand Rapids: Eerdmans, 1975), p. 104; Neufeld, *Confessions*, p. 47.

[45]Fuller, *Resurrection Narratives*, p. 10; Wilckens, *Resurrection*, p. 2; Bultmann, *Theology*, vol. 1, p. 293; Dodd, *Apostolic Preaching*, pp. 13-14; "Risen Christ," p. 125; Neufeld, *Confessions*, p. 27; Brown, *Bodily Resurrection*, p. 81.

[46]Cullmann, *Early Church*, p. 64; Fuller, *Resurrection Narratives*, p. 10; Marxsen, *Resurrection*, p. 80; Weber, *The Cross*, p. 59.

leading authority on this issue, notes such non-Pauline phrases as (1) "for our sins" (v. 3); (2) "according to the scriptures" (vv. 3-4); (3) "he has been raised" (v. 4); (4) the "third day" (v. 4); (5) "he was seen" (vv. 5-8); and (6) "the twelve" (v. 5).[47]

Third, it is likely that the creed is organized in a stylized, parallel form, thereby providing a further indication of the oral and confessional nature of this material.[48]

Fourth, there are indications that there may be a Semitic source, such as the use of the Aramaic "Cephas" for Peter (v. 5), hence pointing to an earlier source before Paul's Greek translation.[49]

Fifth, other indications of ancient Hebrew narration include the triple usage of "and that" along with the two references to the Scripture being filfilled.[50]

How early is this creed? Numerous critical theologians have endeavored to answer this important question, with very striking results. Ulrich Wilckens asserts that this creed "indubitably goes back to the oldest phase of all in the history of primitive Christianity."[51] Joachim Jeremias calls it "the earliest tradition of all."[52] Concerning a more exact time, it is very popular to date this creed in the mid AD 30s. More specifically, numerous critical theologians date it from three to eight years after Jesus' crucifixion.[53]

---

[47]Jeremias, *Eucharistic Words*, pp. 101-102.

[48]See especially Fuller, *Resurrection Narratives*, pp. 11-12; Weber, *The Cross*, p. 59; Jeremias, *Eucharistic Words*, pp. 102-103.

[49]Jeremias, in particular, provides a list of such Semitisms (*Eucharistic Words*, pp. 102-103). See also Pannenberg, *Jesus*, p. 90; Fuller, *Resurrection Narratives*, p. 11; *Foundations*, p. 160; Weber, *The Cross*, p. 59.

[50]Lapide, *Resurrection*, p. 98.

[51]Wilckens, *Resurrection*, p. 2.

[52]Jeremias, "Easter," p. 306.

[53]For a sample of some of those who hold to these specific dates for this creed, see Hans Grass, *Ostergeschen und Osterberichte*, Second Edition (Göttingen: Vandenhoeck und Ruprecht, 1962), p. 96; Leonard Goppelt, "The Easter Kerygma in the New Testament," *The Easter Message Today* transl. by Salvator Attanasio and Darrell Likens Guder (New York: Nelson, 1964), p. 36; Thomas Sheehan, *First Coming: How the Kingdom of God Became Christianity* (New York: Random House, 1986), pp. 110, 118; Cullmann,

How would Paul have received this creed? A number of scholars have arrived at the same scenario. Dating Jesus' crucifixion around AD 30, Paul's conversion would have occurred shortly afterwards, about AD 33–35. Three years after his conversion (AD 36–38) he visited Jerusalem and specifically met with Peter and James (Gal. 1:18-19). It is therefore reasoned that the gospel of the death and resurrection of Jesus would in all likelihood be the normal center of discussion,[54] and that the presence of both Peter and James in the list of appearances (1 Cor. 15:5,7) indicates the probability that Paul received this creed from these apostles when he visited them in Jerusalem.[55] Another possibility is that Paul received this material in Damascus immediately after his conversion, which would make it even three years earlier, but the presence of the Semitisms in the creed, as mentioned above, in addition to the two proper names, favor Jerusalem as the location where Paul first received it.

A Jerusalem location would date Paul's reception of the creed at about five to seven years after the crucifixion. But we can actually proceed back two stages earlier. Since the tradition would actually have been formulated before Paul first heard it, the creed itself would be dated even earlier. Additionally, the independent beliefs themselves, which later composed the formalized creed, would then date back to the actual historical events. Therefore, we are dealing with material

---

The Early Church, pp. 65-66; Pannenberg, *Jesus*, p. 90; Dodd, *Apostolic Preaching*, p. 16; Hunter, *Jesus*, p. 100; Brown, *Bodily Resurrection*, p. 81; Fuller, *Foundations*, pp. 142, 161; *Resurrection Narratives*, pp. 10, 14, 28, 48; Ladd, *I Believe*, p. 105. O'Collins points out that, as far as he is aware, no scholars date this creed later than the AD 40s. Even with such a date in the 40s, the general conclusions which we draw here, especially concerning the early and eyewitness testimony for the resurrection, still follow. See Gerald O'Collins, *What Are They Saying About the Resurrection?* (New York: Paulist Press, 1978), p. 112.

[54]It is interesting that when Paul returned to Jerusalem 14 years later, again meeting with Peter and James, the gospel was specifically mentioned as the center of the discussion (Gal. 2:1-10).

[55]See note 53 above, since each of these scholars also adopts this general framework. Grass favors the Damascus location (p. 96), while Sheehan does not give the locale in his immediate context.

that proceeds *directly* from the events in question and this creed is thus crucial in our discussion of the death and resurrection of Jesus.

Not only are these facts reported *early*, but they are reported directly by the *eyewitnesses* themselves. Paul states that he specifically checked out his message with the apostles (Gal. 2:1-10) and he probably received this creed directly from these eyewitnesses themselves (Gal. 1:18-19), as already noted. As a direct result, not only had Paul personally seen the risen Christ (1 Cor. 15:8-9), but his testimony concerning the facts of the gospel agreed with that of the apostolic eyewitnesses (vv. 11, 14, 15).[56] Thus, Paul's factual account was the same as that of the other apostles, in spite of the fact that Paul distinguished himself from the others.[57]

As a result of this early and eyewitness testimony, the Christian teachings concerning the death, burial and resurrection of Jesus are open to historical testing. As German historian Hans von Campenhausen attests concerning 1 Corinthians 15:3ff., "This account meets all the demands of historical reliability that could possibly be made of such a text."[58] A.M. Hunter states that "The passage therefore preserves uniquely early and verifiable testimony. It meets every reasonable demand of historical reliability."[59]

Now we begin to perceive the immense importance of this creed in terms of both facts and faith. Initially, it reveals some crucial facts concerning the gospel of the deity, death, burial and resurrection of Jesus. It also shows that Paul was very close to these facts.[60] As Dodd asserts concerning this creed:

---

[56]See Cullmann, *The Early Church*, pp. 65-66; cf. p. 73; Jeremias, *Eucharistic Words*, p. 106; Hengel, *The Atonement*, p. 38; Dodd, *Apostolic Preaching*, pp. 16-17.

[57]Cullmann, *Confessions*, pp. 72-73.

[58]Hans von Campenhausen, "The Events of Easter and the Empty Tomb," in *Tradition and Life in the Church* (Philadelphia: Fortress, 1968), p. 44, as quoted by Ladd, *I Believe*, p. 105.

[59]Hunter, *Jesus*, p. 100.

[60]Cullmann, *The Early Church*, p. 64; Jeremias, *Eucharistic Words*, p. 96; Pannenberg, *Jesus*, p. 90; Dodd, *Apostolic Preaching*, p. 17.

Thus Paul's preaching presents a special stream of Christian tradition which was derived from the mainstream at a point very near to its source. . . . anyone who should maintain that the primitive Christian gospel was fundamentally different from that which we have found in Paul must bear the burden of proof.[61]

This factual witness to the death and resurrection of Jesus also became an apologetic for Christian belief.[62] The belief that the same Jesus who was dead and buried was raised again (1 Cor. 15:3-4) also strongly implies the empty tomb, especially in the context of Jewish thought.[63] On the other hand, this creed is also referred to by some as the most important single formulation of faith in the early church.[64]

The importance of the creed in 1 Corinthians 15:3ff. can hardly be overestimated. No longer can it be charged that there is no demonstrable early, eyewitness testimony for the resurrection or for the other most important tenets of Christianity, for this creed provides just such evidential data concerning the facts of the gospel, which are the very center of the Christian faith. It links the events themselves with those who actually participated in time and space. As such this creed yields a strong factual basis for Christianity through the early and eyewitness reports of the death, burial, and resurrection of Jesus, as will be shown in more detail in the next section of this chapter.

We said earlier that the naturalistic theories fail to account for this data. Additionally, the evidence demonstrates that these witnesses actually did see the risen Jesus, as they claimed.

---

[61]Dodd, *Apostolic Preaching*, p. 16.

[62]Bultmann, *Theology*, vol. 1, p. 295; Neufeld, *Confessions*, pp. 66-67, 146.

[63]Cullmann, *Earliest Confessions*, p. 32; Wolfhart Pannenberg, "A Dialogue on Christ's Resurrection," in *Christianity Today*, 12/14, April 12, 1968, pp. 9-11.

[64]Weber, *The Cross*, p. 58; Hengel, *The Atonement*, p. 37.

The Known Historical Facts

Because of the testimony of these early Christian creeds, as well as other data, even contemporary critical scholars recognize a certain amount of historical facts surrounding the death, burial and resurrection of Jesus. In other words, even treating the New Testament as nothing more than a book of ancient literature, critics have deduced numerous historical facts concerning Jesus' life. In particular, 1 Corinthians 15:3ff. has played a significant part in this reconstruction.

There are a minimum number of facts agreed upon by practically all critical scholars, whatever their school of thought. At least *twelve* separate facts are considered to be knowable history.

(1) Jesus died by crucifixion and (2) was buried. (3) Jesus' death caused the disciples to despair and lose hope, believing that his life was ended. (4) Although not as widely accepted, many scholars hold that the tomb in which Jesus was buried was discovered to be empty just a few days later.

Critical scholars further agree that (5) the disciples had experiences which they believed were literal appearances of the risen Jesus. Because of these experiences, (6) the disciples were transformed from doubters who were afraid to identify themselves with Jesus to bold proclaimers of his death and resurrection. (7) This message was the center of preaching in the early church and (8) was especially proclaimed in Jerusalem, where Jesus died and was buried shortly before.

As a result of this preaching, (9) the church was born and grew, (10) with Sunday as the primary day of worship. (11) James, who had been a skeptic, was converted to the faith when he also believed that he saw the resurrected Jesus. (12) A few years later, Paul was converted by an experience which he, likewise, believed to be an appearance of the risen Jesus.

These facts are crucial for our contemporary investigation of Jesus' resurrection. With the exception of the empty tomb, virtually all critical scholars who deal with this issue agree that these are the minimum of known historical facts surrounding this event. As such, any conclusion concerning the historicity of the resurrection should properly account for these facts. An additional vital (and major) function of these known historical facts will be explained in the next section below.

These known historical facts have a twofold part in our case for the resurrection which is developed in this section. First, they answer the various theories which have been proposed in order to account for Jesus' resurrection on naturalistic grounds. These hypotheses, chiefly popularized by liberal scholars in the nineteenth century, are rarely held today by critics, especially since they failed to account for the historical facts surrounding this event (such as those just mentioned above). Several reasons for this rejection could be enumerated.

Each naturalistic theory is beset by many major objections that invalidate it as a viable hypothesis. Combinations of these improbable theories likewise fail, again on factual grounds.[65] Three other historical reasons also illustrate this initial major point. David Hume's essay against miracles, as well as more recent updates, are invalid rejections of the possibility of miraculous events, thereby eliminating such reasoning as the traditional backdrop for these alternative theses.[66] Nineteenth century liberal scholars themselves destroyed each alternative theory individually,[67] while twentieth century critical scholars of various schools of thought have rejected these theories wholesale.[68] In conclusion,

---

[65]For details, see, in particular, Gary R. Habermas, *The Resurrection of Jesus: A Rational Inquiry* (Ann Arbor: University Microfilms, 1976), pp. 114-171; Orr, *The Resurrection of Jesus*, chapters VIII and IX in particular.

[66]Numerous excellent critiques of Hume and more recent updates have appeared, exposing the invalidity of such attempts. For example, see C.S. Lewis, *Miracles* (New York: Macmillan, 1961); Richard Swinburne, *The Concept of Miracle*; Werner Schaaffs, *Theology, Physics and Miracles*, transl. by Richard L. Renfield (Washington, DC: Canon Press, 1974); Gary R. Habermas, "Skepticism: Hume" in Norman L. Geisler, ed., *Biblical Errancy: An Analysis of its Philosophical Roots* (Grand Rapids: Zondervan, 1981).

[67]For details, including a listing of primary sources from these nineteenth century rejections of each other's views, see Habermas, *The Resurrection of Jesus: A Rational Inquiry*, pp. 286-293.

[68]For examples, see Karl Barth, *Church Dogmatics*, vol. 4, part 1, p. 340; Raymond E. Brown, "The Resurrection and Biblical Criticism," especially

naturalistic alternative hypotheses have thereby been shown to be unable to account for these facts concerning Jesus' resurrection.

This leads to the second major argument for the resurrection based on the known historical facts. Not only do the naturalistic theories fail due to these historical facts, but these same facts also establish numerous positive evidences that corroborate the historical and literal nature of this event. Nine such evidences will be listed here, all of which have been taken from our list of accepted historical facts listed above. Thus, the factual basis for these nine evidences is admitted by virtually all scholars. However, because of the limitations of this chapter, these nine will simply be stated with very little elaboration.

The key evidence for Jesus' resurrection is [1] the *disciples' experiences*, which they believed to be literal appearances of the risen Jesus, since these experiences cannot be explained by naturalistic theories (as just shown) and because they are attested as both early and eyewitness sources, as pointed out above. Other positive evidences include [2] the *transformation of the disciples into bold witnesses*, [3] the *empty tomb* and [4] the fact that the resurrection of Jesus was the very *center of the apostolic message*, all of which require adequate explanations. It was also found that the disciples proclaimed this message in Jerusalem itself, where it is related that in repeated confrontations with the authorities, [5] the *Jewish leaders could not disprove their message* (Acts 1-5). Additionally, [6] the very existence and growth of the *church*, [7] featuring *Sunday* as the primary day of worship demand historical causes, as well.

Two additional major facts arguing for the historicity of the resurrection are that two skeptics, [8] *James*, the brother of Jesus, and [9] *Paul*, became believers after having experiences which they also believed were appearances of the risen Jesus. Fuller concludes that even if the appearance to James had not been recorded by Paul (1 Cor. 15:7), such an occurrence

---

p. 233; Pannenberg, *Jesus*, pp. 88-97; Wilckens, *Resurrection*, pp. 117-119; Günther Bornkamm, *Jesus of Nazareth*, pp. 181-185.

would still have to be postulated anyway in order to account for both James' conversion and his subsequent promotion to a position of authority in the early church.[69] The same could be said even more emphatically concerning Paul.[70]

When combined with the failure of the naturalistic theories, this minimum of nine evidences provides a strong case for the historicity of Jesus' resurrection. This is especially so in that each of these evidences was based on a known historical fact.[71] In particular, when the early and eyewitness experiences of the disciples, James and Paul, are considered along with their corresponding transformations,[72] the historical resurrection becomes the best explanation for the facts, especially since the naturalistic theories failed.

Four Key Historical Facts

Earlier, twelve facts were enumerated as knowable history, accepted as such by almost all scholars. It is this writer's conviction that even by utilizing only four of these accepted facts, a sufficient case can be made for the historicity of the resurrection, which will strengthen the earlier apologetic.[73]

---

[69]Fuller, *Resurrection Narratives*, p. 37. See also Wilckens, *Resurrection*, p. 113.

[70]Fuller, ibid., pp. 37, 46-47.

[71]As mentioned above, some would not include the empty tomb as a known fact, but it is accepted by many scholars as historical. For an excellent defense of this fact, see Edward Lynn Bode, *The First Easter Morning*, *Analecta Biblica* 45 (Rome: Biblical Institute, 1970), pp. 155-175; William Lane Craig, "The Empty Tomb of Jesus," pp. 173-200; Robert H. Stein, "Was the Tomb Really Empty?" in the *Journal of the Evangelical Theological Society* 20 (1977), pp. 23-29.

[72]This does not even include the experience of the more than 500 persons who also claimed to have seen the risen Jesus, concerning whom Paul asserted that most were still alive and could be questioned.

[73]The advantage of using only four of the facts is that, with such a small number, there is even wider support for these facts among critical scholars. Additionally, these four reveal how strong the case for the resurrection is, in actuality. But it should be noted that the case for the resurrection does not rest on these four facts alone. In fact, there is no particular reason to use only four, except to make a point concerning their strong attestation.

The four facts to be used here are [1] Jesus' death due to crucifixion, [5] the subsequent experiences that the disciples were convinced were literal appearances of the risen Jesus, [6] the corresponding transformation of the disciples, and [12] Paul's conversion appearance, that he also believed was an appearance of the risen Jesus. These four "core" facts are even more widely accepted as knowable history than the rest of the twelve, being accepted by virtually all critical scholars.[74]

Each of these four facts is established by means of normal historical methodology (see Appendix 1). The *death* of Jesus due to crucifixion is evidenced not only by 1 Corinthians 15:3, but is further corroborated by the nature of crucifixion (including Yohanan's skeleton, which we examine in the next chapter), medical testimony concerning Jesus' heart wound, and Strauss' famous critique of the swoon theory. Other New Testament creeds (like Phil. 2:8; 1 Cor. 11:23-26), as well as certain non-Christian and early non-New Testament Christian sources (see chapters below) are also helpful.

The fact of the disciples' *experiences* that they believed to be appearances of the risen Jesus, is corroborated chiefly by the early and eyewitness testimony of 1 Corinthians 15:3ff. Other creeds (like Luke 24:34), and especially contemporary research on early confessions in the book of Acts,[75] are particularly valuable. Non-biblical references will also be discussed below.

Since naturalistic theories have failed and the evidence so strongly confirms these early creeds, the earliest Christian experiences (both to groups and to individuals) are generally considered by critical scholars to be as firmly established as

---

[74]For a sampling of critical theologians who accept these four core facts, see Fuller, *Resurrection Narratives* especially pp. 27-49; Bultmann, *Theology*, vol. 1, pp. 44-45; Tillich, *Systematic Theology*, vol. 2, pp. 153-158; Bornkamm, *Jesus*, pp. 179-186; Wilckens, *Resurrection*, pp. 112-113; Pannenberg, *Jesus*, pp. 88-106; Moltmann, *Theology of Hope*, especially pp. 197-202; Hunter, *Jesus*, pp. 98-103; Perrin, *Resurrection*, pp. 78-84; Brown, *Bodily Resurrection*, especially pp. 81-92; Paul VanBuren, *The Secular Meaning of the Gospel* (New York: Macmillan, 1963), pp. 126-134.

[75]See especially Acts 1:1-11; 2:32; 3:15; 5:30-32; 10:39-43; 13:30-31.

almost any fact in the life of Jesus. In short, it is admitted by virtually all that the disciples had real experiences that caused them to believe that Jesus was raised from the dead.[76] Fuller even boldly states that these are "indisputable facts . . . upon which both believer and unbeliever may agree"![77]

The *transformation* of the disciples as a result of these experiences is confirmed by the material immediately following this early creed (1 Cor. 15:9-11), which reports the ministry of the eyewitnesses. Again, the entire New Testament also verifies this conclusion, as does the testimony of the early church authors, including the reports of the disciples dying for their faith as martyrs.[78]

Lastly, *Paul's conversion* due to an experience that he also believed to be an appearance of the risen Jesus, is both recorded by him personally in 1 Corinthians 9:1 and 15:8-10, and reported three times in Acts (9:1-9; 22:5-11; 26:12-18). Naturalistic theses also fail to apply to Paul.[79]

Therefore, these four core facts are established on strong, historical grounds. They are generally accepted not only by critical theologians but also by historians and philosophers who study this subject.[80]

Of these four core facts, the nature of the disciples' experiences is the most crucial. As historian Michael Grant asserts, historical investigation actually proves that the earliest eyewitnesses were convinced that they had seen the risen Jesus.[81] Carl Braaten adds that other skeptical historians also agree with this conclusion:

---

[76]Compare the testimony of historian Michael Grant (*Jesus: An Historian's Review*, p. 176) with that of theologian Rudolf Bultmann (*Theology*, vol. 1, p. 45), who agree at this point with scholarship as a whole.

[77]Fuller, *Foundations*, p. 142.

[78]See Eusebius, Book II: IX, XXIII; XXV.

[79]See Habermas and Moreland, *Immortality*, pp. 245-246, endnote 67.

[80]See note 74 above. See also Grant, *Jesus: An Historian's Review*, especially pp. 175-178; W.T. Jones, *The Medieval Mind* (New York: Harcourt, Brace, Jovanovich, 1969), pp. 34-35; Carl Braaten, *History and Hermeneutic* (Philadelphia: Westminster, 1966), p. 78.

[81]Grant, ibid., p. 176.

> Even the more sceptical historians agree that for primitive Christianity . . . the resurrection of Jesus from the dead was a real event in history, the very foundation of faith, and not a mythical idea arising out of the creative imagination of believers.[82]

One major advantage of these core facts is that, not only are they critically accepted as knowable history, but they directly concern the nature of the disciples' experiences. As such, these four historical facts are able, on a lesser scale, to both disprove the naturalistic theories and to provide major positive evidences which relate the probability of Jesus' literal resurrection.[83] A few examples will now point out these claims.

First, using only these four historical facts, the naturalistic theories can be disproven. For instance, the swoon theory is ruled out by the facts concerning Jesus' death and by Paul's conversion. The disciples' experiences disprove the hallucination and other subjective theories both because such phenomena are not collective or contagious, being observed by one person alone, and because of the wide variety of time and place factors involved. The psychological preconditions for hallucinations were also lacking in these men. Paul's experience also rules out these theories because he certainly would not be in the proper theological frame of mind.

That it was the disciples and other early eyewitnesses who had these experiences likewise rules out legend or myth theories, since the original teaching concerning the resurrection is therefore based on the early testimony of real eyewitnesses and not on later legends (as shown by the creed in 1 Corinthians 15:3ff.). Paul's experience likewise cannot be explained by legends, since such could not account for his conversion from skepticism. Lastly, the stolen body and fraud theories are disproven by the disciples' experiences and by their transformation, both because this change shows that the disciples

---

[82]Braaten, *History*, p. 78.

[83]See Gary R. Habermas, *The Resurrection of Jesus: An Apologetic*, chapter I for this argument in expanded form, including support for these facts.

really believed that Jesus rose from the dead and because of the probability that such liars would not become martyrs. Similarly, Paul would not have been convinced by such fraud.[84]

Second, these four core facts also provide the major positive evidences for Jesus' literal resurrection appearances, such as the disciples' early and eyewitness experiences that have not been explained away naturalistically, their transformation into men who were willing to die for their faith and Paul's experience and corresponding transformation. Thus, these core historical facts provide positive evidences which further verify the disciples' claims concerning Jesus' literal resurrection, especially in that these arguments have not been accounted for naturalistically.[85]

Since these core historical facts (and the earlier accepted facts in general) have been *established by critical and historical procedures*, contemporary scholars cannot reject the evidence simply by referring to "discrepancies" in the New Testament texts or to its general "unreliability." Not only are such critical claims refuted by evidence discussed in other chapters,

---

[84]Expansions of these critiques and many additional refutations gathered from the larger list of known historical facts above cannot be presented here. For a more complete treatment of these and other such alternative theories, see Habermas, *The Resurrection of Jesus: A Rational Inquiry*, pp. 114-171.

[85]The additional known facts also provide other significant arguments for this event, such as the other evidences listed there.

Perhaps an illustration utilizing a court case will be helpful. We will postulate that more than a dozen eyewitnesses clearly observed some events that involved seeing a person perform a series of acts on various occasions. This testimony both came immediately after the occurrences themselves and the eyewitnesses were firm in their claims, as evidenced at numerous points. Further, the opposing lawyer and his assistants could not disprove the testimony even after literally years of research, in spite of their interest in doing so. No lying, collusion or other fraud, hallucinations, or any other means of fakery or misconception could be established. Admittedly, quite a strong case would be made that this person in question was, in fact, seen by these persons at those places and times. But even more revealing, a limited but demonstrable case could be built based only on the facts that their opponents admitted to be true. Thus the argument could be based on the antagonistic testimony alone. *(more)*

but it has been concluded that the resurrection can be historically demonstrated *even when the minimum amount of historical facts are utilized.* Neither can it be concluded merely that "something" occurred which is indescribable due to naturalistic premises, or to the character of history or because of the "cloudiness" or "legendary character" of the New Testament texts. Neither can it be said that Jesus rose spiritually, but not literally. Again, these and other such views are refuted in that the *facts admitted by virtually all scholars as knowable history are adequate* to historically demonstrate the literal resurrection of Jesus according to probability.

In short, instead of stating what they believe we *cannot* know concerning the gospel accounts, critical scholars would do well to concentrate on what even they admit *can* be known about the texts at this point. Although Jesus was not photographed in his resurrection body for the benefit of the disciples, the factual basis is enough to show that Jesus' resurrection is by far the best historical explanation. While critical doubts may be present with regard to other issues in the New Testament, the accepted facts are sufficient in themselves to show that Jesus rose from the dead in a new, spiritual body. As detailed in Appendix I, historical inquiry can yield certainty. The resurrection has remained established in the face of criticism for almost 2000 years. The various types of evidence for this event are outstanding, surpassing that of the great majority of ancient events. Sidestepping or rejecting the evidence *a priori* is invalid, as we have seen. There is, indeed,

---

Theoretically, would the jury be satisfied if the opposing lawyer pleaded that "Maybe the witnesses did not really see the person for some unknown reason in spite of the evidence" or "It's not really important whether they saw him or not"? Clearly these would be inappropriate responses because the testimony reveals that the eyewitnesses did, in fact, literally see the person.

However, evidence for Jesus' resurrection is actually superior to this. To be sure, as with the court case, people must make a decision about this event, but unlike the court case, their decision does not determine the issue. The historical fact is established on the evidence alone and not by any decision. And it is here that the evidence for the resurrection reveals that the earliest eyewitnesses did see the risen Jesus, as well as the literal nature of these appearances. Critical attempts fail at this point.

historical proof for this event.[86] Jesus did rise from the dead in real history.

Synopsis of Creeds and Facts

In this chapter we have investigated probably the strongest single category of evidence for the death and resurrection of Jesus. The data supplied by oral creeds that circulated before the actual composition of the New Testament and, often corresponding to these creeds, the facts that critical scholars admit as knowable history, together provide a formidable basis for knowledge about Jesus.

From these sources we find reports of some incidents of Jesus' life but especially numerous details concerning his death and resurrection. Jesus was a real flesh and blood person (Phil. 2:6; 1 Tim. 3:16; 1 John 4:2) who was physically born in the lineage of David (Acts 13:23; Rom. 1:3-4; 2 Tim. 2:8) and came from the town of Nazareth (Acts 2:22; 4:10; 5:38). John preceded Jesus (Acts 10:37; 13:24-25), and it is implied that Jesus was baptized (Rom. 10:9). Jesus' ministry began in Galilee, and was extended throughout Judea (Acts 10:37). Jesus both performed miracles (Acts 2:22; 10:38) and fulfilled many Old Testament prophecies (2:25-31; 3:21-25; 4:11; 10:43; 13:27-37). He preached his message among men, resulting in people believing his testimony (1 Tim. 3:16).

On the night Jesus was betrayed, he first attended a dinner, where he prayed and gave thanks before the meal. Afterward, Jesus passed around both bread and drink, which he referred to as the sacrifice of his body and blood for sin (1 Cor. 11:23ff.). Later, Jesus appeared before Pilate (Acts 3:13; 13:28), where he made a good confession, which very possibly concerned his identity as the Messiah (1 Tim. 6:13).

---

[86]It should be mentioned here that the New Testament asserts that the believer is given an assurance of this event (as well as other truths of God) by the witness of the Holy Spirit (Rom. 8:16; 1 John 5:9-13). Believers need not rely on investigations of critical hermeneutical methodology, as was done here. Such processes can confirm what is already certified, however, or answer the questions of skeptics.

In spite of the fact that Jesus was a righteous man (1 Pet. 3:18), he died for the sins of others (1 Pet. 3:18; Rom. 4:25; 1 Tim. 2:6). He was killed (Acts 3:13-15; 13:27-29; 1 Cor. 15:3; Phil. 2:8) by crucifixion (Acts 2:23; 2:36; 4:10; 5:30; 10:39), dying in the city of Jerusalem (Acts 13:27; cf. 10:39), at the hands of wicked men (Acts 2:23). Afterwards, he was buried (Acts 13:29; 1 Cor. 15:4). These events caused the disciples to doubt and despair.

On the third day after the crucifixion (Acts 10:40), the tomb was empty (1 Cor. 15:4, implied) and Jesus was raised from the dead (Acts 2:24, 31-32; 3:15, 26; 4:10; 5:30; 10:40; 13:30-37; 2 Tim. 2:8). Jesus appeared to numerous eyewitnesses (Luke 24:34; Acts 13:31; 1 Cor. 15:4ff.), even eating with them (Acts 10:40-41). Two of these persons — namely James (1 Cor. 15:7) and Paul (1 Cor. 15:8-9) — were formerly skeptics before they met the risen Jesus. The disciples were witnesses of the appearances (Acts 2:32; 3:15; 5:32; 10:39, 41; 13:31), which were reported at a very early date (Acts 10:40-41; 13:31; 1 Cor. 15:4-8). After his resurrection, Jesus ascended to heaven where he was glorified and exalted (Acts 2:33; 3:21; 5:31; 1 Tim. 3:16; Phil. 2:6f.).

The disciples were transformed by these experiences (cf. 1 Tim. 3:16) and made the gospel the very center of their early preaching (1 Cor. 15:1-4). In fact, it was the risen Jesus who taught that salvation was to be preached in his name (Acts 2:38-39; 3:19-23; 4:11-12; 5:32; 10:42-43; 13:26, 38-41). The resurrection was the chief validation of Jesus' person and message (Acts 2:22-24, 36; 3:13-15; 10:42; 13:32-33; Rom. 1:3-4; 10:9-10). The apostolic preaching initially centered in Jerusalem, the same place where Jesus had been killed. Here the church was born and grew, with Sunday as the chief day of worship.

In the early Christian preaching, Jesus was given numerous titles: Son of God (Acts 13:33; Rom. 1:3-4), Lord (Luke 24:34; Acts 2:36; 10:36; Rom. 1:4; 10:9; Phil. 2:11), Christ or Messiah (Acts 2:36, 38; 3:18, 20; 4:10; 10:36; Rom. 1:4; Phil. 2:11; 2 Tim. 2:8), Savior (Acts 5:31; 13:23), Prince (Acts 5:31) and the Holy and Righteous One (Acts 3:14; cf. 2:27; 13:35). Concerning his essential nature, he was even called God (Phil. 2:6).

Most of these facts are reported in early Christian creeds and actually predate the writing of the New Testament. Others are virtually unanimously accepted by critical scholars, usually because of these creeds and other early historical data. It should be pointed out that these latter, critical facts were not accepted in this chapter simply because the critics also accept them, but because they are established by the facts, such as by the creeds that we investigated in this chapter and by the work of careful historical methodology.[87] Thus, critical scholars should not object to this data, since it is both validated by their methods and accepted by their cohorts.

Summary and Conclusion

This chapter has presented perhaps our strongest category of evidence, especially for the death and resurrection of Jesus. Admittedly, the amount of material concerning the life and ministry of Jesus before his death was not overwhelming. However, when we enter the "passion week" of Jesus' life prior to his crucifixion and afterwards, the situation changes drastically.

The strength of the testimony for Jesus' death and resurrection comes from several facets of the evidence. First, the material in this chapter was quite *early*. These early Christian traditions predate the writing of the New Testament and hence give us our earliest look at data dealing with the life of Jesus. In the case of 1 Corinthians 15:3ff. and the Acts creeds (along with a few other examples), this material dates within

---

[87]See Grant, *Jesus: An Historian's Review*, for an example of a critical historical work which uncovers other such early data (in addition to the creeds) concerning the life of Jesus. Again, Grant also recognizes the four core facts (pp. 175-178). See Sherwin-White's *Roman Society and Roman Law in the New Testament* for an instance of another ancient historian who also uses critical methodology and applies it to the trial of Jesus and of the journeys of Paul, in particular. Interestingly, Sherwin-White finds that the appropriate New Testament texts are very trustworthy at these points (see pp. 186-193), as we indicated especially in chapter 3 above.

a few years of the actual events. This is not disputed by the critical community.

Second, these creeds present *eyewitness* testimony for the facts that they report. Again, 1 Corinthians 15:3ff. and the Acts traditions are the keys in that they link us with the apostles, both singly and in groups, primarily through the testimonies of the two eyewitnesses Paul and Peter. An additional example is Luke 24:34, which may also date to the earliest church and Peter.

Third, additional evidences for Jesus' resurrection include strong considerations like the empty tomb, the disciples' radical transformations and willingness to die for the truth of the gospel, which was their central message, along with the conversions of skeptics Paul and James. These and other considerations must be explained.

Fourth, alternative hypotheses that seek to explain away the resurrection in natural terms have failed to adequately account for the known historical facts. Not only is this conclusion dictated by the data themselves, but critical scholars have even admitted this failure. Few researchers have favored any of these theses in recent times.

Fifth, the accepted facts, and the *minimal facts* in particular, are not only established historically but are recognized by virtually all critical scholars as well. The advantages are that these facts provide a strong basis for belief in the death and resurrection of Jesus and, at the same time, should not be rejected since they are recognized on strictly historical grounds. The facts that almost all scholars accept provide a strong basis for belief in Jesus' literal resurrection from the dead, especially in the absence of viable naturalistic theories.

On this basis, then, we may conclude that the early Christian creeds and accepted historical facts prove the historicity of the death and resurrection of Jesus. These data are sufficient both to disprove the alternative theories, and to present strong evidences for these events (such as the early and eyewitness testimony), all on the grounds of known history. Critical doubts in other areas cannot disprove and change these basic facts.

8 Archaeological Sources

As pointed out in Appendix 1, historical methodology includes the use of non-written as well as written sources. Archaeology is able to provide much information about the past, in that it can both confirm and shed new light on known data, as well as establish evidence on its own.

In this chapter we will attempt to point out some archaeological evidence that either corroborates or helps establish historical facts in the life of Jesus. To be sure, the amount of material here is not as abundant as are the other avenues in studying the life of Jesus. Still, the examples we use will continue to build a case for what can be known of Jesus from extrabiblical sources.

Luke's Census

In Luke 2:1-5 we read that Caesar Augustus decreed that the Roman Empire should be taxed and that everyone had to return to his own city to pay taxes. So Joseph and Mary returned to Bethlehem and there Jesus was born.

Several questions have been raised in the context of this taxation.[1] Even if such a taxation actually did occur, would

---

[1]See Bruce, *Christian Origins*, p. 192, for example.

every person have to return to his home? Was Quirinius really the governor of Syria at this time (as in v. 2)? Archaeology has had a bearing on the answers to these questions.

It has been established that the taking of a census was quite common at about the time of Christ. An ancient Latin inscription called the *Titulus Venetus* indicates that a census took place in Syria and Judea about AD 5-6 and that this was typical of those held throughout the Roman Empire from the time of Augustus (23 BC–AD 14) until at least the third century AD. Indications are that this census took place every fourteen years. Other such evidence indicates that these procedures were widespread.[2] Concerning persons returning to their home city for the taxation-census, an Egyptian papyrus dating from AD 104 reports just such a practice. This rule was enforced, as well.[3]

The question concerning Quirinius also involves the date of the census described in Luke 2. It is known that Quirinius was made governor of Syria by Augustus in AD 6. Archaeologist Sir William Ramsay discovered several inscriptions that indicated that Quirinius was governor of Syria on two occasions, the first time several years prior to this date.[4] Within the cycle of taxation-censuses mentioned above, an earlier taxation would be dated from 10–4 BC.[5] Another possibility is Bruce's suggestion that the Greek in Luke 2:2 is equally translatable as "This enrollment (census) was before that made when Quirinius was governor of Syria."[6] This would mean that Luke was dating the taxation-census before

---

[2]Ibid., pp. 193-194.

[3]Ibid., p. 194.

[4]Robert Boyd, *Tells, Tombs, and Treasure* (Grand Rapids: Baker, 1969), p. 175.

[5]Cf. Bruce, *Christian Origins*, pp. 193-194 with Boyd, *Tells*, p. 175. Bruce prefers the date 10-9 BC for the empire-wide census, with that which took place in Judea occurring a few years later. Boyd places the date of the earlier census at 6-5 BC, which coincides closely with the accepted dates for Jesus' birth.

[6]Bruce, *Christian Origins*, p. 192.

Quirinius took over the governorship of Syria. Either possibility answers the question raised above.[7]

Therefore, while some questions have been raised concerning the events recorded in Luke 2:1-5, archaeology has provided some unexpected and supportive answers. Additionally, while supplying the background behind these events, archaeology also assists us in establishing several facts. *(1)* A taxation-census was a fairly common procedure in the Roman Empire and it did occur in Judea, in particular. *(2)* Persons were required to return to their home city in order to fulfill the requirements of the process. *(3)* These procedures were apparently employed during the reign of Augustus (37 BC–AD 14), placing it well within the general time frame of Jesus' birth. *(4)* The date of the specific taxation recounted by Luke could very possibly have been 6–5 BC, which would also be of service in attempting to find a more exact date for Jesus' death.

Yohanan — Crucifixion Victim

Most of this chapter pertains to archaeological evidence that bears on the issues of Jesus' death and resurrection. The first example of this concerns an important discovery made in June, 1968, that provides some important information about the nature of crucifixion as it was exercised in first century AD Palestine. While a portion of Jerusalem was being prepared for the erection of new apartment buildings, an ancient Jewish burial site was uncovered. Located about one mile north of the Old Damascus Gate, this site yielded the remains of some thirty-five Jews that were buried in fifteen stone ossuaries, used for the reburial of human skeletons some time after the original interment.

Upon investigation, archaeologist Vasilius Tzaferis found that these Jews had probably died about AD 70 in the Jewish

---

[7]While ruling out the two-date approach to the governorship of Quirinius, Sherwin-White basically vindicates Luke's account, while still finding more problems than does Bruce (pp. 162-171).

uprising against Rome. Several of the skeletons gave evidence of having suffered violent deaths, such as being burned, starved, or beaten to death. One person had been killed by an arrow.[8]

In terms of our study, the most important discovery at this site was the skeleton of a man named Yohanan Ben Ha'galgol, whose name was written in Aramaic on the stone ossuary. Further study by Hebrew University pathologist Dr. N. Haas revealed some preliminary data regarding Yohanan's skeleton. Yohanan was about five feet seven inches in height, was about twenty-four to twenty-eight years old, had a cleft palate and was a victim of crucifixion. Still piercing his feet was a large nail about seven inches long that had been driven sideways through his heel bones, which indicates the direction in which the feet and legs were twisted in order to be attached to the cross. The nail pierced an acacia beam on the cross, which was anchored in the ground. Small pieces of wood still attached to the spike indicated that the beam itself was olive wood. The end of the nail was bent backwards toward the head due either to a knot in the wood or to purposeful bending.

An examination disclosed the fact that nails had also been driven between the radius and ulna bones in the lower arm. The radius bone was both scratched and actually worn smooth. This latter result was apparently due to repeated friction caused by the crucifixion victim pulling himself upward in order to breathe, followed by sinking back down again. As the weight of the body was repeatedly moved in order to free the pectoral and intercostal muscles, which inhibit breathing in the "down" position, the radius was worn.

Additionally, Haas discovered that Yohanan's lower leg bones were broken. The left tibia and fibula bones and the right tibia bone were apparently crushed by a common blow, with the legs being sawed off at a later time. This is quite

---

[8]Vasilius Tzaferis, "Jewish Tombs At and Near Giv'at ha-Mivtar," *Israel Exploration Journal* 20 (1970), pp. 38-59.

consistent with the dreaded Roman *crucifragium* spoken of in John 19:31-32 as being normal procedure for crucifixion victims. Death was hastened because the victim was not able to push himself up on the cross in order to breathe, which brought death in a comparatively short period of time.[9]

However, Haas' study has been seriously criticized by some researchers, who dispute his findings at a number of points. J. Zias and E. Sekeles published their study that argues, among other findings, that there was insufficient evidence to indicate either a cleft palate, that nails pierced the forearms, or that the ankles were broken during the process of crucifixion.[10]

The crucifixion process recorded in the Gospels has been at least partially corroborated by this discovery, with the extent of confirmation depending on the correct view of the data. Archaeology provides us with at least some facts that have a bearing on the death of Jesus. *(1)* Victims were often nailed to crosses through the feet or heels and through the wrist or lower arm area. Whether or not the latter was the case with Yohanan, it is the normal way of Roman crucifixion.[11] *(2)* The vast majority of medical researchers agree that the positioning of the body required the victim to move upward and downward in order to alternatively breathe and rest.[12] *(3)* Smashing the leg bones was used in cases where a hasty death was desired.[13]

---

[9]N. Haas, "Anthropological Observations on the Skeletal Remains from Giv'at ha-Mivtar," *Israel Exploration Journal* 20 (1970), pp. 38-59.

[10]J. Zias and E. Sekeles, "The Crucified Man from Giv'at ha-Mivtar: A Reappraisal," *Israel Exploration Journal*, 35 (1985), pp. 22-27; cf. the list of objections in Joe Zias and James H. Charlesworth, "Crucifixion: Archaeology, Jesus, and the Dead Sea Scrolls," in Charlesworth, ed., *Dead Sea Scrolls*, pp. 279-280.

[11] See especially Martin Hengel, *Crucifixion* (Philadelphia: Fortress, 1977), pp. 25, 31-32 in particular.

[12]See the discussion of the Swoon Theory (along with the listed sources) in Chapter 4.

[13]On the administering of the *coup de grace* in these executions, see Hengel, *The Atonement*, p. 70.

The Nazareth Decree

In 1878 a marble slab measuring approximately fifteen by twenty-four inches was discovered at Nazareth, describing itself as an "ordinance of Caesar." The message was a strict prohibition against the disturbing of graves. Scholars generally agree that it was issued by Claudius between AD 41–54. The inscription was written in Greek, translated as follows:

> Ordinance of Caesar. It is my pleasure that graves and tombs remain perpetually undisturbed for those who have made them for the cult of their ancestors or children or members of their house. If, however, anyone charges that another has either demolished them, or has in any other way extracted the buried, or has maliciously transferred them to other places in order to wrong them, or has displaced the sealing on other stones, against such a one I order that a trial be instituted, as in respect of the gods, so in regard to the cult of mortals. For it shall be much more obligatory to honor the buried. Let it be absolutely forbidden for anyone to disturb them. In case of violation I desire that the offender be sentenced to capital punishment on charge of violation of sepulchre.[14]

As noted by Maier, all previous Roman indictments of this nature prescribe only a fine for the offender, but this order demands capital punishment. Why should such a strong penalty be levied in Palestine?[15]

Although the exact reasoning is not known for sure, scholars have frequently suggested that such an order straight from the emperor can best be explained by the likelihood that Claudius investigated some of the beliefs of Christians after the riots that erupted around the Roman Empire during his reign, events associated with the spread of Christianity (see Acts 17:1-9, for example). Such an investigation would be especially likely in the case of Claudius because of these riots in Rome in AD 49, which caused the emperor to expel

---

[14]See P. Maier, *First Easter*, p. 119.

[15]Ibid., pp. 119-120.

the Jews from the city. Suetonius remarks that the troubles were instigated by Christ.[16]

Upon examination, Claudius could well have discovered the Christian teaching that Jesus had risen from the dead and may also have heard the Jewish report that the disciples stole the body. This possibility is made more significant due to the Nazareth Decree's mention of those who would disturb tombs that had been sealed. This is certainly reminiscent of Matthew 27:66, where we are told that the Jews were careful to seal the tomb of Jesus after permission was secured from Pilate. The Nazareth Decree could be a reaction both to the Christian teaching that Jesus was raised and the Jewish contention that the body was stolen.[17]

From this decree we may glean certain historical facts, irrespective of the exact occasion for the indictment. *(1)* Apparently there were reports in Palestine that caused the emperor (probably Claudius) to issue this stern warning against disturbing or robbing graves. *(2)* Jewish burial sometimes included sealing the sepulchre, as well as the use of stones. *(3)* The offense of grave robbing had now become a capital offense and was punishable by death.

Shroud of Turin

The Shroud of Turin, Italy, is a linen cloth measuring 14'3" long by 3'7" wide. Historically proclaimed to be the actual burial garment of Jesus, the linen contains a double, head-to-head image of a crucified man reposed in death, that reveals both the obverse and reverse of the body.

With a known history stretching back to at least the fourteenth century, there are a number of important factors that indicate that the shroud is much more ancient, including a number of historical references that extend back several centuries. In the definitive work on the possible history of

---

[16]Suetonius, Claudius, 25; cf. Acts 18:2.

[17]See Bruce, *Christian Origins*, p. 196; Maier, *First Easter*, pp. 119-120; Boyd, *Tells*, p. 185.

the shroud, Ian Wilson postulates that the cloth left Palestine about AD 30 and proceeded to the ancient kingdom of Edessa, to Constantinople, to France, to Switzerland, and finally to Italy.[18]

In addition to the historical data, there are also a number of scientific reasons indicating that the shroud could be dated very early. Samples of pollen discovered on the cloth point to an origin in Palestine possibly as far back as the first century, while analyses of the cloth and weave discovered that the shroud is compatible with first century cloth.

However, more important indicators of the age of the shroud have also emerged. Some researchers have asserted that sophisticated methods such as photographic enhancement and computer analysis are able to identify one of the coins placed over the eyes of the man in the shroud as a lepton of Pontius Pilate, minted between AD 29-32. Such an identification would be a crucial determination of age.[19]

Biblical questions concerning the type of burial depicted on the shroud have failed to discover any discrepancies with the New Testament texts. Wrapping a body lengthwise and positioning it as shown on the shroud is corroborated by both recently discovered Qumran burial practices and by the *Code of Jewish Law* ("Laws of Mourning"). Further studies have revealed that the head napkin was first rolled up and then wrapped around the head, as reported by the Gospel of John (11:44; 20:5-7), the Jewish Mishnah (*Shabbath* 23:5) and the "Laws of Mourning."

While some believe that the body of the man wrapped in the shroud was not washed, the "Laws of Mourning" point out that there are conditions when washing is not appropriate, such as when a person suffered capital punishment or a violent death. The use of several strips of linen in John is also confirmed on the shroud, since pieces of linen were apparently used there, as well.

---

[18]See Ian Wilson, *The Shroud of Turin* (New York: Doubleday, 1978).

[19]For these details, see Kenneth E. Stevenson and Gary R. Habermas, *Verdict on the Shroud* (Ann Arbor: Servant, 1981), especially chapter 2.

One additional point concerns Jesus' burial, as it is recorded in the Gospels. Since it is related that Jesus underwent a hasty burial with the women planning to return later to finish the process (Luke 23:54–24:4; Mark 15:42; 16:1-3), we have another explanation of possible "oddities" in his burial procedure.[20]

One characteristic of the Shroud of Turin that separates it from other such religious remains is that it was the subject of an intense (and ongoing) scientific investigation. In October, 1978, a team of well-qualified scientists applied a large battery of non-destructive tests to the shroud.[21] The three most important issues to be answered concerned the nature of the apparent bloodstains, the composition of the image, and its cause. In particular, it was determined that the bloodstains were real blood and that the shroud was probably not a fake. The image was not caused by paint, dye, powder, or any other foreign substance being added to the cloth. The image on the shroud is composed of oxidized, dehydrated, and conjugated fibrils of cloth, similar to the effects of a scorch, but an exact cause of the image was not proven. Additional characteristics of the image, such as its three-dimensional, superficial and non-directional nature, have become quite an enigma to the scientists.[22]

The description of the man who was apparently buried in the shroud has also been enlightening. The scientific team pathologist and other medical doctors determined that the man was crucified and was dead, with his body in a state of rigor mortis. The man's injuries were the same as the Gospel reports of Jesus' crucifixion. The most interesting facet of

---

[20]Ibid., Chapter 4.

[21]For an authoritative description of some of the proposed tests to be performed on the shroud, see Kenneth E. Stevenson, Editor, *Proceedings of the 1977 United States Conference on the Shroud of Turin* (Bronx: Holy Shroud Guild, 1977).

[22]See Stevenson and Habermas, *Verdict*, chapters 5-6 and Appendix A. See also John Heller, *Report on the Shroud of Turin* (Boston: Houghton Mifflin, 1983), especially chapters 12-14.

this study is that many unnatural things were done to Jesus and these same types of things appeared on the shroud.

Both men suffered a series of punctures throughout the scalp from many sharp objects, a seriously bruised face, a horrible whipping (over 100 wounds from this beating have been counted on the shroud), abrasions on both shoulders from a rough, heavy object, and contusions on both knees. Both men had the more normal wounds associated with crucifixion; namely, punctured feet and wrists. Strangely, both men escaped having their ankles broken, as was normal, but both had post-mortem chest wounds instead, from which blood and watery fluid flowed. Both men were buried hastily in fine linen and were buried individually.[23]

Indications that the man buried in the shroud could be Jesus come from the correspondence between the two. They agree even down to the small details in about one dozen areas that were not normal crucifixion procedures. The chances are seemingly minimal that two men would have so many agreements, especially in points of abnormal circumstances. Also, no areas of contradiction apparently exist. It should additionally be remembered that the shroud has been kept for hundreds of years as the actual burial garment of Jesus, long before such scientific testing could be done. While this last point by no means demonstrates the shroud's authenticity in any sense, it does show further a possible relationship between Jesus and the man buried in the shroud.[24]

Naturalistic attempts to account for such phenomena as the three-dimensional, superficial and non-directional image, plus additional details such as its resolute and unsaturated nature, have failed to produce a viable alternative theory that explains all of the data. The scientists reported that they were unable to discover any known natural causes that could account for the shroud's image. In scientific terms, the image is a "mystery."[25]

---

[23]Stevenson and Habermas, *Verdict*, chapters 3, 10.

[24]For details concerning this correspondence that cannot be presented in this book, see ibid., chapter 9.

[25]Heller, *Report*, p. 218.

Perhaps even more amazing, the shroud contains no bodily decomposition, indicating that the body exited the cloth after a comparatively short interment. Furthermore, according to the scientific team pathologist, the body was probably not unwrapped, as indicated by the fact that many of the bloodstains were intact (including the blood clots), since such action would have disturbed the bloodstains. Even more interesting is the possibility that the image was caused by some sort of light or heat scorch that emanated from a dead body in the state of rigor mortis.[26] In short, the converging scientific facts show that the body left the cloth by some as yet unknown means. Since the man buried in the shroud is possibly Jesus, we also have some possible empirical evidence for his resurrection.[27]

But all of these conclusions were seriously challenged in the fall of 1988. Small portions taken from the shroud material were sent to three different laboratories in England, Switzerland and the United States. After the tests were concluded, it was claimed that the shroud had been carbon dated to the late Middle Ages.

Admittedly, this was a serious objection to the possibility that the shroud was the burial garment of Jesus. If the material did, in fact, originate in the Middle Ages, it could be some kind of fake or perhaps even an actual burial cloth that belonged to another crucifixion victim besides Jesus. In the latter case, it could still provide excellent information about death by crucifixion, but other claims that rely on this being Jesus' cloth would, obviously, be mistaken.

---

[26]These conclusions do not necessarily represent the views of any other researchers. See Stevenson and Habermas, *Verdict*, chapter 11. For a more detailed and intricate argument concerning the shroud as evidence for the resurrection, see also Gary R. Habermas, "The Shroud of Turin: A Rejoinder to Basinger and Basinger," *Journal of the Evangelical Theological Society* 25 (1982), pp. 219-227.

[27]A stern disclaimer is definitely in order here. Whether the shroud is or is not the true burial sheet of Jesus, it is absolutely crucial that we not be involved with any sort of worship or veneration of this cloth. God's warning against worshiping *any* object still stands, along with the serious judgment pronounced against those who disobey (Exod. 20:4-6, for example). We need to totally oppose any such activities.

However, many scholars challenged the 1988 tests, strictly on scientific grounds, charging that serious problems occurred. For example, various cloth samples with known dates were pretested by a number of major laboratories, but achieved incorrect dates of up to many centuries! With regard to the shroud sampling itself, the material was not taken from three different locations, but came from the same portion of the material, known as "Raes Corner." Although this is the most contaminated section of the famous cloth, there was an absence of controlled recognition and removal of contaminants.

Further, the lack of peer review before the testing began bothered some researchers. Additionally, there was evidently no blind testing as reports indicated would be the case. For one thing, the non-shroud control specimens were reportedly marked with their dates, further distinguishing them from the shroud samples.

But perhaps most damaging of all to the carbon dating tests, a secret dating of shroud fibers in 1982 differed from the 1988 tests by centuries, and even suggested a date that could, with the plus-minus factor, date the cloth to the first century AD! Last, a few scientists have even remarked that if the shroud image was caused by Jesus' resurrection, the sort of molecular change that results from scorch could actually have made the cloth appear younger, due to neutron flux.

As a result, the 1988 carbon testing appears to be less authoritative than one might originally think. At least it is not a closed case. This is especially so when all three cloth samples were taken from a single area on the shroud, which may have been affected in any of several ways.

Even beyond all of this, it is also crucial to realize that virtually all of the other shroud data stand in opposition to the medieval dating. Contrary results come from studies such as the pollen research, the possibility of the Pontius Pilate coins over the eyes, textile evaluations, and the historical trail the shroud may have taken across Europe. So here we have one body of scientific results clashing with another. Which should be favored over the other? More than one opinion has been expressed, to be sure. Further testing and peer review will hopefully follow and may be helpful. We can only conclude that a medieval date has not, at present, been proven.[28]

In spite of the questions we have lodged, it must be admitted that the 1988 carbon dating is still a serious objection to the shroud being the burial garment of Jesus. Yet, the testing problems, plus other considerations like those above, tend to offset the force of the results. Still, we must be clear that, even if the shroud did not belong to Jesus, nothing in Christianity is affected. Even though it reports the discovery of Jesus' graveclothes, the New Testament never claims that the shroud is genuine.

If the Shroud of Turin is Jesus' garment, we have highly evidential data for the death and probably even the resurrection of Jesus. Since there is strong evidence against the shroud being a fake, even if it wrapped the body of another victim of crucifixion, it can still provide important and reliable details concerning Jesus' demise. As such, several facts can be learned, most of which, it should be carefully noted, do not depend on the identification of the man buried in the shroud.

(1) Once again we learn of the normal wounds associated with crucifixion such as the pre-cross beating, the pierced wrists and feet, as well as lesser details like the knee contusions (presumably from falling) and the shoulder abrasions (perhaps from carrying part of the cross).

(2) We also learn of several abnormal points of crucifixion procedure that the man in the shroud had in common with Jesus. Such include: the scalp wounds caused by sharp objects, the absence of broken ankles, the post-mortem chest wound, and the flow of blood plus watery fluid.

---

[28]For many of these objections to the 1988 carbon dating, see, for example, Paul C. Maloney, "Is the Shroud of Turin Really Medieval?" and "The Carbon Date for the Shroud of Turin: The Position Statement of the Association of Scientists and Scholars International for the Shroud of Turin, Ltd.," in *The Assist Newsletter*, vol. 1, no. 1 (1989), pp. 1, 5-8. Cf. Kenneth E. Stevenson and Gary R. Habermas, *The Shroud and the Controversy: Science, Skepticism, and the Search for Authenticity* (Nashville: Nelson, 1990), chapters 3-4, Appendix A.

(3) Afterward, an individual but hasty burial in fine linen for one convicted as a "criminal" is also rather odd.

(4) There is strong evidence that the man in the shroud had to move up and down in order to breathe. The blood from each wrist proceeded down each arm and formed a V-shaped blood flow, which is one evidence that suggests that two major bodily positions were taken on the cross.

(5) There is evidence that the man buried in the shroud was very possibly raised from the dead, such as the absence of decomposition, an apparent lack of unwrapping the body, and a probable scorch from a dead body. If the man in the shroud is Jesus, as indicated by the similarities in dissimilar areas pointed out in (2), then (4) becomes possible evidence for Jesus' resurrection.

Other Archaeological Data

A few additional finds bear on the historicity of Jesus, if only indirectly. The existence of the pools of Bethesda and Siloam "can be identified with certainty" due to archaeological discoveries.[29] Although the very existence of these two pools does not prove anything in Jesus' life, it is still interesting that the Gospel of John associates one of Jesus' healing miracles with each site (John 5:1-9; 9:1-41).

One other note concerns the historical existence of Pontius Pilate. Coins have been discovered, minted to honor Pilate's rule, dated AD 30–31.[30] Additionally, an inscription containing his name was discovered at Caesarea.[31] Again, this does not prove anything specifically concerning Jesus. However, the historical connection between Pilate and the crucifixion of Jesus is well established by such ancient historians as Tacitus and Josephus.[32]

-----

[29]Bruce, *Christian Origins*, p. 188.

[30]Boyd, *Tells*, p. 183.

[31]Ibid.

[32]Tacitus, *Annals*, 15.44; Josephus, *Antiquities*, 18:3.

Synopsis of Archaeological Sources

From these archaeological sources we learn numerous facts that are beneficial in a study of Christ's life, especially with regard to his death and possibly his resurrection. But unless the shroud is Jesus' burial cloth, the sources chiefly provide background information that helps verify the Gospel accounts.

Concerning the taxation-census reported in Luke 2, data from archaeological discoveries reveal several facts. Such processes were fairly common in the ancient Roman Empire, involving persons traveling to their own cities. This taxation-census began during Augustus' reign (37 BC–AD 14) and continued to the third century AD, often at fourteen year intervals. One such taxation-census was apparently enacted at approximately the same time as Jesus' birth.

With regard to crucifixion, much depends on one's conclusions concerning Yohanan and the Shroud of Turin. If they can be taken at face value, we learn that victims had their wrists and feet nailed to the cross (shroud; cf. Yohanan), and were apparently made to carry part of the cross to the crucifixion site, which often resulted in falls (shroud). Normal crucifixion procedure usually involved breaking the victim's legs (Yohanan). The shroud corresponds to Jesus' death by numerous agreements in points of abnormal crucifixion procedure, such as the crown of thorns, the severe whipping, the absence of broken ankles, the post-mortem chest wound and the flow of blood and watery fluid. Other "odd" similarities in the burial include an individual burial for a crucified person, yet a hasty burial in fine linen. We also learn much about medical factors, such as the cause of death being closely related to asphyxiation, as the victim pushed up and down in order to breathe (shroud; cf. Yohanan).

The Jewish burial process sometimes involved a sealed tomb, and usually the presence of a large stone. There were apparently reports in Palestine that caused the emperor to issue an exceptionally strong warning against grave robbing, which was punishable by death (Nazareth Decree).

If the Shroud of Turin is Jesus' burial garment, then we have strong evidence for the resurrection, derived from the information on the cloth. In particular, the lack of bodily decomposition, indicative of a rather hasty bodily departure, the apparent lack of unwrapping, and the probable presence of an image caused by a scorch from a dead body, all reveal the probability of Jesus' resurrection.

Conclusion

While archaeological evidence numerically includes only a comparatively few examples, we still find some helpful items that can provide insight into several aspects of the life of Jesus. As France points out, this subject contributes indirect material, usually of a background nature, that helps to confirm what we know about him.[32]

The skeleton of Yohanan is quite valuable in relating some of the details of crucifixion, including both mechanical and medical factors. The Nazareth Decree provides some insight into Jewish burial. As long as it is not a fake, the Shroud of Turin is an excellent witness to most of the details involved in the processes of crucifixion and burial. If it is the burial garment of Jesus, these facts of crucifixion and burial apply directly to him. Additionally, the shroud would then supply some strong evidence for the resurrection.

---

[33]France, *The Evidence for Jesus*, pp. 141-142.

9 Ancient Non-Christian Sources

Continuing our historical investigation into the early sources for the life, death and resurrection of Jesus, we turn next to the ancient non-Christian sources. We will move, successively, from ancient historians, to government officials, to other Jewish and Gentile sources, to early Gnostic sources and then to lost works that speak of Jesus.

Ancient Historians

Tacitus

Cornelius Tacitus (ca. AD 55–120) was a Roman historian who lived through the reigns of over a half dozen Roman emperors. He has been called the "greatest historian" of ancient Rome, an individual generally acknowledged among scholars for his moral "integrity and essential goodness."[1]

Tacitus is best known for two works — the *Annals* and the *Histories*. The former is thought to have included eighteen books and the latter to have included twelve, for a total of

---

[1]Moses Hadas, "Introduction" to *The Complete Works of Tacitus* (New York: Random House, 1942), pp. IX, XIII-XIV.

thirty.[2] The *Annals* cover the period from Augustus' death in AD 14 to that of Nero in AD 68, while the *Histories* begin after Nero's death and proceed to that of Domitian in AD 96.

Tacitus recorded at least one reference to Christ and two to early Christianity, one in each of his major works. The most important one is that found in the *Annals*, written about AD 115. The following was recounted concerning the great fire in Rome during the reign of Nero:

> Consequently, to get rid of the report, Nero fastened the guilt and inflicted the most exquisite tortures on a class hated for their abominations, called Christians by the populace. Christus, from whom the name had its origin, suffered the extreme penalty during the reign of Tiberius at the hands of one of our procurators, Pontius Pilatus, and a most mischievous superstition, thus checked for the moment, again broke out not only in Judaea, the first source of the evil, but even in Rome, where all things hideous and shameful from every part of the world find their centre and become popular. Accordingly, an arrest was first made of all who pleaded guilty; then, upon their information, an immense multitude was convicted, not so much of the crime of firing the city, as of hatred against mankind. Mockery of every sort was added to their deaths. Covered with the skins of beasts, they were torn by dogs and perished, or were nailed to crosses, or were doomed to the flames and burnt, to serve as a nightly illumination, when daylight had expired.
>
> Nero offered his gardens for the spectacle, and was exhibiting a show in the circus, while he mingled with the people in the dress of a charioteer or stood aloft on a car. Hence, even for criminals who deserved extreme and exemplary punishment, there arose a feeling of compassion; for it was not, as it seemed, for the public good, but to glut one man's cruelty, that they were being destroyed.[3]

From this report we can learn several facts, both explicit and implicit, concerning Christ and the Christians who lived in

---

[2]An alternate theory is that the *Annals* included sixteen books and the *Histories*, fourteen books, also for a total of thirty (cf. Hadas, p. XII).

[3]Tacitus, 15.44.

Rome in the AD 60s. Chronologically, we may ascertain the following information.

(1) Christians were named for their founder, Christus (from the Latin), *(2)* who was put to death by the Roman procurator Pontius Pilatus (also Latin), *(3)* during the reign of emperor Tiberius (AD 14–37). *(4)* His death ended the "superstition" for a short time, *(5)* but it broke out again, *(6)* especially in Judaea, where the teaching had its origin.

(7) His followers carried his doctrine to Rome. *(8)* When the great fire destroyed a large part of the city during the reign of Nero (AD 54–68), the emperor placed the blame on the Christians who lived in Rome. *(9)* Tacitus reports that this group was hated for their abominations. *(10)* These Christians were arrested after pleading guilty, *(11)* and many were convicted for "hatred for mankind." *(12)* They were mocked and *(13)* then tortured, including being "nailed to crosses" or burnt to death. *(14)* Because of these actions, the people had compassion on the Christians. *(15)* Tacitus therefore concluded that such punishments were not for the public good but were simply "to glut one man's cruelty."[4]

Several facts here are of interest. As F.F. Bruce has noted, Tacitus had to receive his information from some source and this may have been an official record. It may even have been contained in one of Pilate's reports to the emperor, to which Tacitus would probably have had access because of his standing with the government.[5] Of course, we cannot be sure at this point, but a couple of early writers do claim to know the contents of such a report, as we will perceive later.

Also of interest is the historical context for Jesus' death, as he is linked with both Pilate and Tiberius. Additionally, J.N.D. Anderson sees implications in Tacitus' quote concerning Jesus' resurrection.

It is scarcely fanciful to suggest that when he adds that "A most mischievous superstition, thus checked for the moment, again broke out" he is bearing indirect and unconscious

---

[4]Ibid.

[5]F.F. Bruce, *Christian Origins*, p. 23.

testimony to the conviction of the early church that the Christ who had been crucified had risen from the grave.[6]

Although we must be careful not to press this implication too far, the possibility remains that Tacitus may have indirectly referred to the Christians' belief in Jesus' resurrection, since his teachings "again broke out" after his death.

Also interesting is the mode of torture employed against the early Christians. Besides burning, a number were crucified by being "nailed to crosses." Not only is this the method used with Jesus, but tradition reports that Nero was responsible for crucifying Peter as well, but upside down. The compassion aroused in the Roman people is also noteworthy.

The second reference to Jesus in the writings of Tacitus is found in the *Histories*. While the specific reference is lost, as is most of this book, the reference is preserved by Sulpicus Severus.[7] He informs us that Tacitus wrote of the burning of the Jerusalem temple by the Romans in AD 70, an event which destroyed the city. The Christians are mentioned as a group that were connected with these events. All we can gather from this reference is that Tacitus was also aware of the existence of Christians other than in the context of their presence in Rome. Granted, the facts that Tacitus (and most other extrabiblical sources) report about Jesus are well known in our present culture. Yet we find significance in the surprising confirmation for the life of Jesus.

Suetonius

Another Roman historian who also makes one reference to Jesus and one to Christians is Gaius Suetonius Tranquillas. Little is known about him except that he was the chief secretary of Emperor Hadrian (AD 117–138) and that he had access to the imperial records.[8] The first reference occurs in

---

[6]J.N.D. Anderson, *Christianity: The Witness of History* (London: Tyndale, 1969), p. 19.

[7]Chronicles 2:30.6.

[8]Robert Graves, "Introduction" to Suetonius' *The Twelve Caesars*, transl. by Robert Graves (Baltimore: Penguin, 1957), p. 7.

the section on emperor Claudius (AD 41–54). Writing about the same time as Tacitus,[9] Suetonius remarked concerning Claudius:

> Because the Jews at Rome caused continuous disturbances at the instigation of Chrestus, he expelled them from the city.[10]

The translator notes that "Chrestus" is a variant spelling of "Christ," as noted by other commentators as well,[11] and is virtually the same as Tacitus' Latin spelling.

Suetonius refers to a wave of riots which broke out in a large Jewish community in Rome during the year AD 49. As a result, the Jews were banished from the city. Incidentally, this statement has an interesting corroboration in Acts 18:2, which relates that Paul met a Jewish couple from Pontus named Aquila and his wife Priscilla, who had recently left Italy because Claudius had demanded that all Jews leave Rome.

The second reference from Suetonius is again to the Christians who were tortured by emperor Nero:

> After the great fire at Rome . . . . Punishments were also inflicted on the Christians, a sect professing a new and mischievous religious belief.[12]

Few facts are derived from the two references by Suetonius. The first relates **(1)** to the expulsion of Jews from Rome, but also makes the claim **(2)** that it was Christ who caused the Jews to make the uproar in Rome, apparently by his teachings. The second reference is quite similar to the longer statement by Tacitus, **(3)** including the use of the word "mischievous" to describe the group's beliefs and **(4)** the term "Christians" to identify this group as followers of the teachings of Christ.

---

[9]François Amiot, "Jesus A Historical Person," in Daniel-Rops, ed., *Sources*, p. 8.

[10]Suetonius, *Claudius*, 25.

[11]Graves, *The Twelve Caesars*, p. 197; Bruce, *Christian Origins*, p. 21; Amiot, "Jesus," p. 8.

[12]Suetonius, *Nero*, 16.

Josephus

Jewish historian Flavius Josephus was born in AD 37 or 38 and died in AD 97. He was born into a priestly family and became a Pharisee at the age of nineteen. After surviving a battle against the Romans, he served commander Vespasian in Jerusalem. After the destruction of Jerusalem in AD 70, he moved to Rome, where he became the court historian for emperor Vespasian.[13]

The *Antiquities*, one of Josephus' major works, provides some valuable but disputed evidence concerning Jesus. Written around AD 90–95, it is earlier than the testimonies of the Roman historians. Josephus speaks about many persons and events of first century Palestine and makes two references to Jesus. The first is very brief and is in the context of a reference to James, "the brother of Jesus, who was called Christ."[14] Here we find a close connection between Jesus and James and the belief on the part of some that Jesus was the Messiah.

The second reference is easily the most important and the most debated, since some of the words appear to be due to Christian interpolation. For instance, a portion of the quotation reports:

> Now there was about this time Jesus, a wise man, if it be lawful to call him a man. For he was one who wrought surprising feats. . . . He was (the) Christ . . . he appeared to them alive again the third day, as the divine prophets had foretold these and ten thousand other wonderful things concerning him.[15]

Since Josephus was a Jew, it is unlikely that he would have written about Jesus in this way. Origen informs us that Josephus did not believe Jesus to be the Messiah,[16] yet

---

[13]Daniel-Rops, "Silence of Jesus' Contemporaries," pp. 19-21; Bruce, *The New Testament Documents*, pp. 102-103.

[14]Josephus, *Antiquities* 20:9. The edition of Josephus used here is *The Works of Josephus*, transl. by William Whiston (Philadelphia: David McKay, n.d.).

[15]Josephus, *Antiquities* 18:3.

[16]Origen, *Contra Celsum* 1:47.

Eusebius quotes the debated passage including the words above.[17] Therefore, probably the majority of commentators believe that at least a portion of the citation (the distinctly "Christian" words, in particular) is a Christian interpolation. Yet, other scholars have also supported the original ending.[18] A mediating position taken by many holds that the passage itself is written by Josephus with the questionable words either deleted or modified. So the major question here concerns the actual words of Josephus.

There are good indications that the majority of the text is genuine. There is no textual evidence against it, and, conversely, there is very good manuscript evidence for this statement about Jesus, thus making it difficult to ignore. Additionally, leading scholars on the works of Josephus have testified that this portion is written in the style of this Jewish historian.[19] Thus we conclude that there are good reasons for accepting this version of Josephus' statement about Jesus, with modification of the questionable words. In fact, it is possible that these modifications can even be accurately ascertained.

In 1972 Professor Schlomo Pines of the Hebrew University in Jerusalem released the results of a study on an Arabic manuscript containing Josephus' statement about Jesus. It includes a different and briefer rendering of the entire passage, including changes in the key words listed above:

> At this time there was a wise man who was called Jesus. His conduct was good and (he) was known to be virtuous. And many people from among the Jews and the other nations became his disciples. Pilate condemned him to be crucified and to die. But those who had become his disciples did not abandon his discipleship. They reported that he had appeared to them three days after his crucifixion, and that he was alive;

---

[17]Eusebius, *Ecclesiastical History*, 1:XI.

[18]Daniel-Rops, "Silence of Jesus' Contemporaries," p. 21.

[19]Ibid.; Anderson, *Christianity*, p. 20; Bruce, *The New Testament Documents*, p. 108. Cf. also Bruce, p. 109 for the views of British historian H. St. John Thackery and Jewish scholar Joseph Klausner.

accordingly he was perhaps the Messiah, concerning whom the prophets have recounted wonders.[20]

Of the three disputed portions, none remains unchanged. The initial problematic statement "if it be lawful to call him a man" has been dropped completely, recounting only that Jesus was a wise man. The words "he was a doer of wonderful works" have also been deleted. Instead of the words "He was (the) Christ" we find "he was perhaps the messiah." The phrase "he appeared to them the third day" now reads "they (the disciples) reported that he had appeared to them," which is an entirely true statement which was voiced by the first century eyewitnesses. Lastly, the statement that "the divine prophets had foretold these and ten thousand other wonderful things concerning him" has been drastically reduced to "concerning whom the prophets have recounted wonders," which concerns the messiah and possibly not even Jesus, according to Josephus. Therefore, while some words are completely deleted, others are qualified by "perhaps" and "reported."

There are some good reasons why the Arabic version may indeed be the original words of Josephus before any Christian interpolations. As Schlomo Pines and David Flusser, of the Hebrew University, have stated, it is quite plausible that none of the arguments against Josephus writing the original words even applies to the Arabic text, especially since the latter would have had less chance of being censored by the church. In addition, Flusser notes that an earmark of authenticity comes from the fact that the Arabic version omits the accusation that the Jews were to blame for Jesus' death, which is included in the original reading.[21]

After an investigation of the question, Charlesworth explains his view that Josephus' original version is "both an interpolation and a redaction."[22] But he provides three

---

[20]Charlesworth, *Jesus Within Judaism*, p. 95.

[21]David Flusser, "New Evidence on Jesus' Life Reported," *The New York Times*, February 12, 1972, pp. 1, 24.

[22]Charlesworth, ibid., p. 93.

reasons why Josephus still wrote most of the passage: some of the words are very difficult to assign to a Christian writer, the passage fits both grammatically and historically, and the brief reference to Jesus in *Antiquities* 20 seems to presuppose an earlier mention.[23]

Charlesworth concludes that the Arabic rescension is basically accurate, even if there are still a few subtle Christian alterations. He concludes about this passage with some strong words: "We can now be as certain as historical research will presently allow that Josephus did refer to Jesus," providing "corroboration of the gospel account."[24]

We conclude that Josephus did write about Jesus, not only in the brief statement concerning James, but also in this longer account. The evidence points to his composition of this latter passage with the deletion and modification of a number of key phrases which were probably interpolated by Christian sources.

What historical facts can be ascertained from the deleted and altered portions of Josephus' statement such as those changes made in the Arabic version? *(1)* Jesus was known as a wise and virtuous man, one recognized for his good conduct. *(2)* He had many disciples, both Jews and Gentiles. *(3)* Pilate condemned him to die, *(4)* with crucifixion explicitly being mentioned as the mode. *(5)* The disciples reported that Jesus had risen from the dead and *(6)* that he had appeared to them on the third day after his crucifixion. *(7)* Consequently, the disciples continued to proclaim his teachings. *(8)* Perhaps Jesus was the Messiah concerning whom the Old Testament prophets spoke and predicted wonders. We would add here two facts from Josephus' earlier quotation as well. *(9)* Jesus was the brother of James and *(10)* was called the messiah by some.[25]

There is nothing really sensational in such a list of facts from a Jewish historian. Jesus' ethical conduct, his following,

---

[23]Ibid., pp. 93–94.

[24]Ibid., pp. 96–97.

[25]Bruce presents a somewhat similar list of facts. See *The New Testament Documents*, p. 112.

and his crucifixion by the command of Pilate are what we would expect a historian to mention. Even the account of the disciples reporting Jesus' resurrection appearances (if it is allowed), has an especially authentic ring to it. Josephus, like many historians today, would simply be repeating the claims, which were probably fairly well known in first century Palestine. That the disciples would then spread his teachings would be a natural consequence.

Josephus presented an important account of several major facts about Jesus and the origins of Christianity. In spite of some question as to the exact wording, we can view his statements as providing probable attestation, in particular, of some items in Jesus' public ministry, his death by crucifixion, the disciples' report of his resurrection appearances, and their subsequent teaching of Jesus' message.

Thallus

The death of Jesus may have been mentioned in an ancient history composed many years before Tacitus, Suetonius, or Josephus ever wrote and probably even prior to the Gospels. Circa AD 52, Thallus wrote a history of the Eastern Mediterranean world from the Trojan War to his own time.[26] This work itself has been lost and only fragments of it exist in the citations of others. One such scholar who knew and spoke of it was Julius Africanus, who wrote about AD 221. It is debated whether Thallus was the same person referred to by Josephus as a wealthy Samaritan, who was made a freedman by Emperor Tiberius and who loaned money to Herod Agrippa I.[27]

In speaking of Jesus' crucifixion and the darkness that covered the land during this event, Africanus found a reference in the writings of Thallus that dealt with this cosmic report. Africanus asserts:

---

[26]Bruce, *Christian Origins*, pp. 29-30.

[27]Ibid.; Anderson, *Witness of History*, p. 19.

On the whole world there pressed a most fearful darkness; and the rocks were rent by an earthquake, and many places in Judea and other districts were thrown down. This darkness Thallus, in the third book of his *History*, calls, as appears to me without reason, an eclipse of the sun.[28]

Julius Africanus objected to Thallus' rationalization concerning the darkness that fell on the land at the time of the crucifixion because an eclipse could not take place during the time of the full moon, as was the case during the Jewish Passover season.[29] But Wells raises a fair question about this testimony. Africanus only implies that Thallus linked the darkness to Jesus' crucifixion, but we are not specifically told if Jesus is mentioned in Thallus' original history at all.[30]

If this brief statement by Thallus refers to Jesus' crucifixion we can ascertain that **(1)** the Christian gospel, or at least an account of the crucifixion, was known in the Mediterranean region by the middle of the first century AD. This brings to mind the presence of Christian teachings in Rome mentioned by Tacitus and by Suetonius. **(2)** There was a widespread darkness in the land, implied to have taken place during Jesus' crucifixion. **(3)** Unbelievers offered rationalistic explanations for certain Christian teachings or for supernatural claims not long after their initial proclamation, a point to which we will return below.

Government Officials

Pliny the Younger

A Roman author and administrator who served as the governor of Bithynia in Asia Minor, Pliny the Younger was

---

[28]Julius Africanus, *Extant Writings*, XVIII in the *Ante–Nicene Fathers*, ed. by Alexander Roberts and James Donaldson (Grand Rapids: Eerdmans, 1973), vol. VI, p. 130.

[29]See the discussion below on the Talmud (*Sanhedrin* 43a).

[30]Wells, *Did Jesus Exist?*, pp. 12–13. Wells' overall thesis is examined in detail in Chapter 2.

the nephew and adopted son of a natural historian known as Pliny the Elder. The younger Pliny is best known for his letters, and Bruce refers to him as "one of the world's great letter writers, whose letters . . . have attained the status of literary classics."[31]

Ten books of Pliny's correspondence are extant today. The tenth book, written around AD 112, speaks about Christianity in the province of Bithynia and also provides some facts about Jesus.[32] Pliny found that the Christian influence was so strong that the pagan temples had been nearly deserted, pagan festivals severely decreased and the sacrificial animals had few buyers. Because of the inflexibility of the Christians and the emperor's prohibition against political association, governor Pliny took action against the Christians. Yet, because he was unsure how to deal with believers, if there should be any distinctions in treatment or if repentance made any difference, he wrote to Emperor Trajan to explain his approach.

Pliny dealt personally with the Christians who were turned over to him. He interrogated them, inquiring if they were believers. If they answered in the affirmative he asked them two more times, under the threat of death. If they continued firm in their belief, he ordered them to be executed. Sometimes the punishment included torture to obtain desired information, as in the case of two female slaves who were deaconesses in the church. If the person was a Roman citizen, they were sent to the emperor in Rome for trial. If they denied being Christians or had disavowed their faith in the past, they "repeated after me an invocation to the Gods, and offered adoration . . . to your [Trajan's] image." Afterwards they "finally cursed Christ." Pliny explained that his purpose in all this was that "multitudes may be reclaimed from error."[33]

---

[31]Bruce, *Christian Origins*, p. 24.

[32]Pliny, *Letters*, transl. by William Melmoth, rev. by W.M.L. Hutchinson (Cambridge: Harvard Univ. Press, 1935), vol. II, X:96.

[33]Ibid.

Since Pliny's letter is rather lengthy, we will quote the portion which pertains directly to an account of early Christian worship of Christ:

> They (the Christians) were in the habit of meeting on a certain fixed day before it was light, when they sang in alternate verses a hymn to Christ, as to a god, and bound themselves by a solemn oath, not to any wicked deeds, but never to commit any fraud, theft or adultery, never to falsify their word, nor deny a trust when they should be called upon to deliver it up; after which it was their custom to separate, and then reassemble to partake of food — but food of an ordinary and innocent kind.[34]

At this point Pliny adds that Christianity attracted persons of all societal ranks, all ages, both sexes and from both the city and the country.

From Pliny's letter we find several more facts about Jesus and early Christianity. **(1)** Christ was worshiped as deity by early believers. **(2)** Pliny refers late in his letter to the teachings of Jesus and his followers as "excessive superstition" and "contagious superstition," which is reminiscent of the words of both Tacitus and Suetonius. **(3)** Jesus' ethical teachings are reflected in the oath taken by Christians never to be guilty of a number of sins mentioned in the letter. **(4)** We find a probable reference to Christ's institution of communion and the Christian celebration of the "love feast" in Pliny's remark about their regathering to partake of ordinary food. The reference here alludes to the accusation on the part of non-Christians that believers were suspected of ritual murder and drinking of blood during these meetings, again confirming our view that communion is the subject to which Pliny is referring. **(5)** There is also a possible reference to Sunday worship in Pliny's statement that Christians met "on a certain day."

Concerning early Christianity, **(6)** we see Pliny's method of dealing with believers, from their identification, to their

---

[34]Ibid.

interrogation, to their execution. For those who denied being Christians, worship of the gods and the emperor gained them their freedom. *(7)* Interestingly, Pliny reports that true believers could not be forced to worship the gods or the emperor. *(8)* Christian worship involved a pre-dawn service, *(9)* which included singing hymns. The early time probably facilitated a normal working day. *(10)* These Christians apparently formed a typical cross-section of society in Bithynia, since they were of all classes, ages, localities and of both sexes. *(11)* There were recognized positions in the church, as illustrated by the mention of the two female deaconesses who were tortured for information. While Pliny does not relate many facts about Jesus, he does provide a look at a very early example of Christian worship. Believers were meeting regularly and worshiping Jesus.

Emperor Trajan

Pliny's inquiry received a reply which is published along with his letters, although Emperor Trajan's response is much shorter:

> The method you have pursued, my dear Pliny, in sifting the cases of those denounced to you as Christians is extremely proper. It is not possible to lay down any general rule which can be applied as the fixed standard in all cases of this nature. No search should be made for these people; when they are denounced and found guilty they must be punished; with the restriction, however, that when the party denies himself to be a Christian, and shall give proof that he is not (that is, by adoring our Gods) he shall be pardoned on the ground of repentance, even though he may have formerly incurred suspicion. Informations without the accuser's name subscribed must not be admitted in evidence against anyone, as it is introducing a very dangerous precedent, and by no means agreeable to the spirit of the age.[35]

---

[35]Ibid., X:97.

Trajan responds that Pliny was generally correct in his actions. If confessed Christians persist in their faith, they must be punished. However, three restrictions are placed on Pliny.

(1) Christians should not be sought out or tracked down.

(2) Repentance coupled with worship of the gods sufficed to clear a person. Pliny expressed doubts as to whether a person should be punished in spite of repentance and only recounts the pardoning of persons who had willingly given up their beliefs prior to questioning.

(3) Pliny was not to honor any lists of Christians which were given to him if the accuser did not name himself.

These conditions imposed by emperor Trajan give us some insight into early official Roman views about Christianity. While persecution was certainly an issue and many Christians died without committing any actual crimes, it is interesting that, contrary to popular opinion, the first century was not the worst period of persecution for believers. Trajan's restrictions on Pliny at least indicate that it was not a wholesale slaughter. Nonetheless, the persecution was real and many died for their faith.

Emperor Hadrian

The existence of trials for Christians, such as the ones held in the time of Pliny, is confirmed by another historical reference to Christians. Serenius Granianus, proconsul of Asia, wrote to emperor Hadrian (AD 117–138), also in reference to the treatment of believers. Hadrian replied to Minucius Fundanus, the successor as Asian proconsul and issued a statement against those who would accuse Christians falsely or without due process. In the letter, preserved by third century church historian Eusebius, Hadrian asserts:

> I do not wish, therefore, that the matter should be passed by without examination, so that these men may neither be harassed, nor opportunity of malicious proceedings be offered to informers. If, therefore, the provincials can clearly evince their charges against the Christians, so as to answer

before the tribunal, let them pursue this course only, but not by mere petitions, and mere outcries against the Christians. For it is far more proper, if any one would bring an accusation, that you should examine it.[36]

Hadrian explains that, if Christians are found guilty, after an examination, they should be judged "according to the heinousness of the crime." Yet, if the accusers were only slandering the believers, then those who inaccurately made the charges were to be punished.[37]

From Hadrian's letter we again ascertain: [1] that Christians were frequently reported as lawbreakers in Asia and were punished in various ways. [2] Like Trajan, Hadrian also encouraged a certain amount of temperance, and ordered that Christians not be harassed. [3] If Christians were indeed guilty, as indicated by careful examination, punishments could well be in order. [4] However, no undocumented charges were to be brought against believers and those engaged in such were to be punished themselves.

Other Jewish Sources

The Talmud

The Jews handed down a large amount of oral tradition from generation to generation. This material was organized according to subject matter by Rabbi Akiba before his death in AD 135. His work was then revised by his student, Rabbi Meir. The project was completed about AD 200 by Rabbi Judah and is known as the Mishnah. Ancient commentary on the Mishnah was called the Gemaras. The combination of the Mishnah and the Gemaras form the Talmud.[38]

It would be expected that the most reliable information about Jesus from the Talmud would come from the earliest

---

[36]Eusebius, *Ecclesiastical History*, IV:IX.

[37]Ibid.

[38]Bruce, *Christian Origins*, pp. 54-55.

period of compilation — AD 70 to 200, known as the Tannaitic period. A very significant quotation is found in *Sanhedrin* 43a, dating from just this early period:

> On the eve of the Passover Yeshu was hanged. For forty days before the execution took place, a herald went forth and cried, "He is going forth to be stoned because he has practiced sorcery and enticed Israel to apostasy. Any one who can say anything in his favour, let him come forward and plead on his behalf." But since nothing was brought forward in his favour he was hanged on the eve of the Passover![39]

Here we have another brief account of the death of Jesus. These two references to Jesus being "hanged" certainly provide an interesting term to describe his death. But it should be noted that the New Testament speaks of crucifixion in the same way. Jesus is said to have been "hanged" (Greek *kremamenos* in Gal. 3:13), as were the two males killed at the same time (Greek *kremasthentōn* in Luke 23:39). While the term "crucified" is a much more common reference to this event,[40] "hanged" is a variant expression of the same fate.

From this passage in the Talmud we learn about **(1)** the fact of Jesus' death by crucifixion and **(2)** the time of this event, which is mentioned twice as occurring on the eve of the Jewish Passover. We are surprisingly told **(3)** that for forty days beforehand it was publicly announced that Jesus would be stoned. While not specifically recorded in the New Testament, such is certainly consistent with both Jewish practice and with the report that this had also been threatened on at least two other occasions (John 8:58-59; 10:31-33, 39). It is related **(4)** that Jesus was judged by the Jews to be guilty of "sorcery" and spiritual apostasy in leading Israel astray by his teaching. **(5)** It is also stated that since no witnesses came forward to defend him, he was killed.

---

[39]This quotation was taken from the reading in *The Babylonian Talmud*, transl. by I. Epstein (London: Soncino, 1935), vol. III, *Sanhedrin* 43a, p. 281.

[40]Greek *stauros*, as in such references as Matt. 27:31; Mark 15:13, 14, 20, 27, etc.

It is interesting that there is no explanation as to why Jesus was crucified ("hanged") when stoning was the prescribed punishment. It is likely that the Roman involvement provided the "change of plans," without specifically being mentioned here.

Another early reference in the Talmud speaks of five of Jesus' disciples and recounts their standing before judges who make individual decisions about each one, deciding that they should be executed. However, no actual deaths are recorded.[41] From this second portion we can ascertain only (6) the fact that Jesus had some disciples and (7) that some among the Jews felt that these men were also guilty of actions which warranted execution.

There are various other references to Jesus in the Talmud, although most are from later periods of formulation and are of questionable historical value. For instance, one reference indicates that Jesus was treated differently from others who led the people astray, for he was connected with royalty.[42] The first portion of this statement is very possibly an indication of the fact that Jesus was crucified instead of being stoned. The second part could be referring to Jesus being born of the lineage of David, or it could actually be a criticism of the Christian belief that Jesus was the Messiah. Another possible reference to Jesus states that he was either thirty-three or thirty-four years old when he died.[43] Many other allusions and possible connections could be mentioned, such as derision of the Christian doctrine of the virgin birth[44] and references to Mary, Jesus' mother,[45] but these depend on questions of identification of pseudonyms and other such issues.

Because of the questionable nature and dates of these latter Talmudic references, we will utilize only the two earlier

---

[41]*Sanhedrin* 43a.

[42]Ibid., where this reference is apparently a third century addition to the earlier material in this section of the Talmud.

[43]*Sanhedrin* 106b.

[44]For instance, *Yeb.* IV:3, 49a.

[45]*Hagigah* 4b; *Sanhedrin* 106a.

passages from the Tannaitic period in our study. While the latter references are interesting and may reflect older traditions, we cannot be sure.

Toledoth Jesu

This anti-Christian document not only refers to Jesus, but gives an interesting account of what happened to Jesus' body after his death. It relates that his disciples planned to steal his body. However, a gardener named Juda discovered their plans and dug a new grave in his garden. Then he removed Jesus' body from Joseph's tomb and placed it in his own newly dug grave. The disciples came to the original tomb, found Jesus' body gone and proclaimed him risen. The Jewish leaders also proceeded to Joseph's tomb and found it empty. Juda then took them to his grave and dug up the body of Jesus. The Jewish leaders were greatly relieved and wanted to take the body. Juda replied that he would sell them the body of Jesus and did so for thirty pieces of silver. The Jewish priests then dragged Jesus' body through the streets of Jerusalem.[46]

It is true that the *Toledoth Jesu* was not compiled until the fifth century AD, although it does reflect early Jewish tradition. Even though Jewish scholars scorn the reliability of this source,[47] the teaching that the disciples were the ones who removed the dead body of Jesus persisted in the early centuries after Jesus' death. As reported in Matthew 28:11-15, this saying was still popular when the Gospel was written, probably between AD 70–85. Additionally, Justin Martyr, writing about AD 150, states that the Jewish leaders had even sent specially trained men around the Mediterranean, even to Rome, to further this teaching,[48] which is confirmed by Tertullian about AD 200.[49] In other words, even if the

---

[46]Maier, *First Easter*, pp. 117-118.

[47]Ibid., pp. 118-119.

[48]Justin Martyr, *Dialogue with Trypho*, 108.

[49]Tertullian, *On Spectacles*, 30.

Toledoth Jesu itself is too late or untrustworthy a source, in spite of its early material, the idea that the tomb was empty because the body was moved or stolen was common in early church history, as witnessed by other sources.

Other Gentile Sources

Lucian

A second century Greek satirist, Lucian spoke rather derisively of Jesus and early Christians. His point was to criticize Christians for being such gullible people that, with very little warrant, they would approve charlatans who pose as teachers, thereby supporting these persons even to the point of making them wealthy. In the process of his critique he relates some important facts concerning Jesus and Christians:

> The Christians, you know, worship a *man* to this day — the distinguished personage who introduced their novel rites, and was crucified on that account. . . . You see, these misguided creatures start with the general conviction that they are immortal for all time, which explains the contempt of death and voluntary self-devotion which are so common among them; and then it was impressed on them by their original lawgiver that they are all brothers, from the moment that they are converted, and deny the gods of Greece, and worship the crucified sage, and live after his laws. All this they take quite on faith, with the result that they despise all worldly goods alike, regarding them merely as common property.[50]

From the material supplied by Lucian we may derive the following data concerning Jesus and early Christians. **(1)** We are told that Jesus was worshiped by Christians. **(2)** It is also related that Jesus introduced new teachings in Palestine (the location is given in another unquoted portion of Section II) and **(3)** that he was crucified because of these teachings. Jesus

---

[50]Lucian, *The Death of Peregrine*, 11-13, in *The Works of Lucian of Samosata*, transl. by H.W. Fowler and F.G. Fowler, 4 vols. (Oxford: Clarendon, 1949), vol. 4.

taught his followers certain doctrines, such as *(4)* all believers are brothers, *(5)* from the moment that conversion takes place and *(6)* after the false gods are denied (such as those of Greece). Additionally, these teachings included *(7)* worshiping Jesus and *(8)* living according to his laws. *(9)* Lucian refers to Jesus as a "sage," which, especially in a Greek context, would be to compare him to the Greek philosophers and wise men.

Concerning Christians, we are told *(10)* that they are followers of Jesus who *(11)* believe themselves to be immortal. Lucian explains that this latter belief accounts for their contempt of death. *(12)* Christians accepted Jesus' teachings by faith and *(13)* practiced their faith by their disregard for material possessions, as revealed by the holding of common property among believers.

The portion of Lucian not quoted presents some additional facts. *(14)* The Christians had "sacred writings" which were frequently read. *(15)* When something affected their community, "they spare no trouble, no expense." *(16)* However, Lucian notes that Christians were easily taken advantage of by unscrupulous individuals.[51] From Lucian, then, we learn a number of important facts about Jesus and early Christian beliefs. Many of these are not reported by other extra-New Testament beliefs.

Mara Bar-Serapion

The British Museum owns the manuscript of a letter written sometime between the late first and third centuries AD. Its author was a Syrian named Mara Bar-Serapion, who was writing from prison to motivate his son Serapion to emulate wise teachers of the past:[52]

> What advantage did the Athenians gain from putting Socrates to death? Famine and plague came upon them as a judgment for their crime. What advantage did the men of Samos gain from burning Pythagoras? In a moment their land was covered

---

[51]These additional facts are found in Lucian, ibid., 12-13.

[52]Bruce, *Christian Origins*, p. 30.

with sand. What advantage did the Jews gain from executing their wise King? It was just after that that their kingdom was abolished. God justly avenged these three wise men: the Athenians died of hunger; the Samians were overwhelmed by the sea; the Jews, ruined and driven from their land, live in complete dispersion. But Socrates did not die for good; he lived on in the statue of Hera. Nor did the wise King die for good; he lived on in the teaching which he had given.[53]

From this passage we learn *(1)* that Jesus was considered to be a wise and virtuous man. *(2)* He is addressed twice as the Jews' King, possibly a reference to Jesus' own teachings about himself, to that of his followers or even to the wording on the *titulus* placed over Jesus' head on the cross. *(3)* Jesus was executed unjustly by the Jews, who paid for their misdeeds by suffering judgment soon afterward, probably at least as reference to the fall of Jerusalem to the Roman armies. *(4)* Jesus lived on in the teachings of the early Christians, which is an indication that Mara Bar-Serapion was almost certainly not a Christian. Rather, he follows Lucian and others in the popular comparison of Jesus to philosophers and other wise men in the ancient world.

As Bruce notes, some of Mara Bar-Serapion's material concerning Athens and Samos is quite inaccurate.[54] Yet the statements about Jesus do not appear to be flawed and thus add to our extra-New Testament data about him.

Gnostic Sources

This category of extra-New Testament sources is different from all the others in that these works often at least make the claim to be Christian. Although scholars still debate the question of the origin of Gnosticism, it is generally said to have flourished mainly from the second to the fourth centuries

---

[53]British Museum, Syriac Manuscript, Additional 14,658. For this text, see Bruce, *Christian Origins*, p. 31.

[54]Bruce, ibid.

AD. It is from four, second century documents that we get the material for this section. While it is possible that there are other Gnostic sources as old or older than the four used here, these have the advantage both of being better established and of claiming to relate facts concerning the historical Jesus, many of which are not reported in the Gospels.

However, it must be admitted that this group of writers was still more influenced by the New Testament writings than the others in this chapter. Yet, although many of the ideas in these four books are Christian, Gnosticism in many of its forms and teachings was pronounced heretical and viewed as such by the church. Hence we are discussing such material in this chapter.

The Gospel of Truth

This book was possibly written by the Gnostic teacher Valentinus, which would date its writing around AD 135–160. If not, it was probably at least from this school of thought and still dated in the second century AD.[55] Unlike some Gnostic works, *The Gospel of Truth* addresses the subject of the historicity of Jesus in several short passages. It does not hesitate to affirm that the Son of God came in the flesh. The author asserts that "the Word came into the midst . . . it became a body."[56] Later he states:

> For when they had seen him and had heard him, he granted them to taste him and to smell him and to touch the beloved Son. When he had appeared instructing them about the Father . . . . For he came by means of fleshly appearance.[57]

---

[55]For scholarly views on this question of authorship, see Hans Jonas, *The Gnostic Religion* (Boston: Beacon, 1963), p. 40; Robert M. Grant, *Gnosticism and Early Christianity*, pp. 5, 128-134; George W. MacRae, "Introduction," *The Gospel of Truth* in James M. Robinson, ed., *The Nag Hammadi Library*, p. 37.

[56]*The Gospel of Truth* 26:4-8. The edition used here is Robinson. Ibid.

[57]Ibid., 30:27-33; 31:4-6.

From these two quotations this book indicates *(1)* that Jesus was the Son of God, the Word and *(2)* that he became a man and took on an actual human body which could be perceived by all five senses. *(3)* We are also told that he instructed his listeners about his Father.

According to *The Gospel of Truth*, Jesus also died and was raised from the dead:

> Jesus was patient in accepting sufferings . . . since he knows that his death is life for many . . . he was nailed to a tree; he published the edict of the Father on the cross. . . . He draws himself down to death through life . . . eternal clothes him. Having stripped himself of the perishable rags, he put on imperishability, which no one can possibly take away from him.[58]

Here and later (18:23) the author states *(4)* that Jesus was persecuted and suffered and *(5)* that he was "nailed to a tree," obviously referring to his crucifixion. *(6)* We are also told of the belief that it was Jesus' death that brought salvation "for many," which is referred to as the imparting of Light to those who would receive it (30:37; 31:12-20). It is also asserted *(7)* that Jesus was raised in an eternal body which no one can harm or take from him.

The theological overtones in *The Gospel of Truth* (as well as in other Gnostic writings) present an obvious contrast to the ancient secular works inspected above. Yet, even allowing for such theological motivation, these early Gnostic sources still present us with some important insights into the historical life and teachings of Jesus.

The Apocryphon of John

Grant asserts that this work is closely related to the thought of the Gnostic teacher Saturninus, who taught around AD 120–130.[59] *The Apocryphon of John* was modified as

---

[58]Ibid., 20:11-14, 25-34.

[59]Grant, *Gnosticism and Early Christianity*, p. 109.

it was passed on and was known in several versions. Irenaeus made use of one of these versions as a source for his treatment of Gnosticism, *Against Heresies*, written ca. AD 185. Thus, by this time, at least the major teachings of *The Apocryphon of John* were in existence.[60]

In a largely mythical treatise involving esoteric matters of Gnostic theology, this book does purport to open with a historical incident. We are told:

> It happened [one day]when Jo[hn, the brother] of James,— who are the sons of Ze[bed]ee—went up and came to the temple, that a [Ph]arisee named Arimanius approached him and said to him, "[Where] is your master whom you followed?" And he [said] to him, "He has gone to the place from which he came." The Pharisee said to him, "[This Nazarene] deceived you (pl.) with deception and filled [your ears with lies] and closed [your hearts and turned you] from the traditions [of your fathers]."[61]

This passage relates **(1)** that John the disciple, in response to a question from Arimanius the Pharisee, stated that Jesus had returned to heaven, a possible reference to the Ascension. **(2)** The Pharisee responded by telling John that Jesus had deceived his followers with his teachings, which is reminiscent of the Talmud's statements about Jesus. Whether such an encounter between John and Arimanius actually occurred or not, such is apparently a typical view of Jesus' teachings from the standpoint of the Jewish leaders.

The Gospel of Thomas

This book describes itself in the opening statement as "the secret sayings which the living Jesus spoke."[62] Grant notes that this collection of teachings thereby purports to be the words

---

[60]Ibid., pp. 109-112; Jonas, *Gnostic Religion* 40, 199-205; Frederick Wisse, "Introduction" in James Robinson, *The Nag Hammadi Library*, p. 98; Walter Baur, *Orthodoxy and Heresy in Earliest Christianity*, p. 49.

[61]*The Apocryphon of John* 1:5-17.

[62]*The Gospel of Thomas* 32:10-11.

of the risen Jesus, thus accounting for the almost complete absence of statements concerning his birth, life and death.[63]

The text is usually dated from around AD 140–200, although it reflects thought of even earlier periods.[64] As such it could present some accurate facts concerning Jesus.

In an incident similar to Jesus' question at Caesarea Philippi,[65] reported in the synoptic Gospels, *The Gospel of Thomas* also presents Jesus asking his disciples, "Compare me to someone and tell Me whom I am like." They respond by describing him as an angel, a philosopher and as an indescribable personage.[66] In a later passage the disciples refer to Jesus as the consummation of the prophets (42:13-18).

Jesus is said to have partially answered his own question on several occasions. He describes himself as the Son of Man (47:34–48:4), which is also the name most commonly reported in the Gospels. On other occasions he speaks of himself in more lofty terms. To Salome, Jesus states "I am He who existed from the Undivided. I was given some of the things of My father."[67] Elsewhere he speaks of himself as the Son in *The Gospel of Thomas*.[68] In another instance Jesus speaks in more specifically Gnostic terminology:

> Jesus said, "It is I who am the light which is above them all. It is I who am the All. From Me did the All come forth, and unto Me did the All extend. Split a piece of wood, and I am there. Lift up the stone, and you will find Me there."[69]

In these passages which concern the identity of Jesus, we are told **(1)** that Jesus asked his disciples for their view. **(2)** Their responses were varied, with the comparison of Jesus to a

---

[63]See Grant, *Gnosticism and Early Christianity*, pp. 183-184.

[64]Helmut Koester, "Introduction" in James Robinson, *The Nag Hammadi Library*, p. 117; Baur, p. 310; Pagels, *Gnostic Gospels*, XV-XVI.

[65]See Mark 8:27-30; Matt. 16:13-17; Luke 9:18-21.

[66]*The Gospel of Thomas* 34:30–35:4.

[67]Ibid., 43:28-30.

[68]Ibid., 44:34-35; 45:11-15; 49:21-26.

[69]Ibid., 46:23-28.

philosopher being especially reminiscent of the references by Lucian and Mara Bar-Serapion. Jesus then identified himself as *(3)* the Son of Man, *(4)* the Son of His Father and *(5)* as the All of the Universe.

The Gospel of Thomas also records a parable concerning the death of Jesus (45:1-16) and relates his subsequent exaltation (45:17-19). Again, Jesus is identified as "living" or as the "Living One," a reference to his post-resurrection life (see Rev. 1:17-18).[70] These references relate *(6)* the death of Jesus and *(7)* his exaltation as a result of his resurrection from the dead.

The foregoing references in *The Gospel of Thomas* require further comment. Initially, they often appear to be dependent on Gospel testimony, especially in the question of Jesus' identity and in the parable of the vineyard. Additionally, the overly obvious Gnostic tendencies, such as those found in the identification of Jesus with the "Undivided" and with the "All," including monistic tendencies, certainly cast doubt on the reliability of these reports.[71]

The Treatise On Resurrection

This book is addressed to an individual named Rheginos by an unknown author. Some have postulated that Valentinus is the author, but most scholars object to this hypothesis. The ideas are somewhat Valentinian, which could point to the presence of earlier ideas, but it is probably better to date the work itself from the late second century AD.[72]

For the author of *The Treatise on Resurrection*, Jesus became a human being but was still divine:

> The Lord . . . existed in flesh and . . . revealed himself as Son of God . . . Now the Son of God, Rheginos, was Son of Man.

---

[70]Ibid., 32:10-11; 43:9-12; cf. 42:13-36.

[71]See chapter 5, where such Gnostic tendencies are evaluated in comparison to the canonical Gospels.

[72]Malcolm L. Peel, "Introduction" in James Robinson, *The Nag Hammadi Library*, p. 50.

> He embraced them both, possessing the humanity and the
> divinity, so that on the one hand he might vanquish death
> through his being Son of God, and that on the other through
> the Son of Man the restoration to the Pleroma might occur;
> because he was originally from above, a seed of the Truth,
> before this structure (of the cosmos) had come into being.[73]

In this passage we find much Gnostic terminology in addition
to the teachings **(1)** that Jesus became flesh as the Son of Man
in spite of **(2)** his true divinity as the Son of God who
conquers death.

So Jesus came to this world in the flesh of a man, died and
rose again:

> For we have known the Son of Man, and we have believed
> that he rose from among the dead. This is he of whom we say,
> "He became the destruction of death, as he is a great one in
> whom they believe." Great are those who believe.[74]

In less esoteric language we are told **(3)** that Jesus died, **(4)** rose
again and **(5)** thereby destroyed death for those who believe
in him.

We are told of Jesus' resurrection in other passages as well:

> The Savior swallowed up death. . . . He transformed [himself]
> into an imperishable Aeon and raised himself up, having swal-
> lowed the visible by the invisible, and he gave us the way of
> our immortality.[75]

> Do not think the resurrection is an illusion. It is no illusion,
> but it is truth. Indeed, it is more fitting to say that the world is
> an illusion, rather than the resurrection which has come into
> being through our Lord the Savior, Jesus Christ.[76]

These two quotations even present an interesting contrast on
the subject of Jesus' death and resurrection. While the first

---

[73]*The Treatise on Resurrection* 44:13-36.

[74]Ibid., 46:14-21; cf. 44:27-29.

[75]Ibid., 45:14-23.

[76]Ibid., 48:10-19.

statement is mixed with Gnostic terminology, the second assures believers that the resurrection was not an illusion, which reminds us of some Gnostic tendencies to deny the actual, physical death of Christ.[77]

Since Jesus has been raised the author counseled Rheginos that "already you have the resurrection . . . why not consider yourself as risen and (already) brought to this?" Thus he is encouraged not to "continue as if you are to die."[78] The resurrection of Jesus thereby provides practical considerations in causing the believer to realize that he already has eternal life presently and should not live in fear of death. This teaching is similar to that of the New Testament (Col. 3:1-4; Heb. 2:14-15) and gives added significance to Lucian's report of Christians who believed that they were immortal and thus unafraid of death.

Once again, these previous four sources are theologically oriented, freely incorporating many Gnostic tendencies, in addition to being generally later than most of our other sources. While these two qualifications do not necessitate unreliable reporting of historical facts about Jesus, we are to be cautious in our use of this data.

Other Lost Works

Acts of Pontius Pilate

The contents of this purportedly lost document are reported by both Justin Martyr (ca. AD 150) and Tertullian (ca. AD 200). Both agree that it was an official document of Rome. Two types of archives were kept in ancient Rome. The *Acta senatus* were composed of minutes of the senatorial meetings. These contained no discussions of Christ or Christianity as far as is known. The *Commentarii principis* were composed of the correspondence sent to the emperors from various parts of the empire. Any report from Pilate to

---

[77]For instance, see *The Second Treatise of the Great Seth* 55:9–56:19.

[78]*The Treatise on Resurrection* 49:15-27.

Tiberius would belong to this second group.[79]

Justin Martyr reported around AD 150 in his *First Apology* that the details of Jesus' crucifixion could be validated from Pilate's report:

> And the expression, "They pierced my hands and my feet," was used in reference to the nails of the cross which were fixed in His hands and feet. And after He was crucified, they cast lots upon His vesture, and they that crucified Him parted it among them. And that these things did happen you can ascertain in the "Acts" of Pontius Pilate.[80]

Later in the same work Justin lists several healing miracles and asserts, "And that He did those things, you can learn from the Acts of Pontius Pilate."[81]

Justin Martyr relates several facts, believing them to be contained in Pilate's report. The chief concern is apparently Jesus' crucifixion, with details such as **(1)** his hands and feet being nailed to the cross and **(2)** the soldiers gambling for his garments. But it is also asserted **(3)** that several of Jesus' miracles were also included in Pilate's report.

Tertullian even reports that Tiberius acted on the report:

> Tiberius accordingly, in whose days the Christian name made its entry into the world, having himself received intelligence from Palestine of events which had clearly shown the truth of Christ's divinity, brought the matter before the senate, with his own decision in favour of Christ. The senate, because it had not given the approval itself, rejected his proposal. Caesar held to his opinion, threatening wrath against all accusers of the Christians.[82]

Tertullian's account claims **(4)** that Tiberius actually brought

---

[79]Daniel-Rops, "Silence of Jesus' Contemporaries," p. 14.

[80]Justin Martyr, *First Apology*, XXXV. Quotations from Justin Martyr and Tertullian are from the *Ante-Nicene Fathers*, ed. by Alexander Roberts and James Donaldson (Grand Rapids: Eerdmans, 1973), vol. III.

[81]Justin Martyr, *First Apology*, XLVIII.

[82]Tertullian, *Apology*, V.

details of Christ's life before the Roman Senate, apparently for a vote of approval. The Senate then reportedly spurned Tiberius' own vote of approval, which engendered a warning from the emperor not to attempt actions against Christians. As noted by Bruce, this incident, which Tertullian apparently accepts as accurate, is quite an improbable occurrence. It is difficult to accept such an account when the work reporting it is about 170 years later than the event, with seemingly no good intervening sources for such acceptance.[83]

It should be noted that the *Acts of Pilate* referred to here should not be confused with later fabrications by the same name, which may certainly have been written to take the place of these records which were believed to exist.

There may well have been an original report sent from Pilate to Tiberius, containing some details of Jesus' crucifixion. In spite of this, it is questionable if Justin Martyr and Tertullian knew what any possible report contained. Although the early Christian writers had reason to believe such a document existed, evidence such as that found in the reference to Thallus is missing here. In particular, there are no known fragments of the *Acts of Pilate* or any evidence that it was specifically quoted by another writer. Additionally, it is entirely possible that what Justin thought original was actually a concurrent apocryphal gospel.[84] At any rate, we cannot be positive as to this purported imperial document. Like the Gnostic sources, we therefore are cautious in our use of this source.

Phlegon

The last reference to be discussed in this chapter is that of Phlegon, whom Anderson describes as "a freedman of the Emperor Hadrian who was born about AD 80."[85] Phlegon's work is no longer in existence and we depend on others for our information.

---

[83]See Bruce, *New Testament Documents*, p. 116, for an analysis of Tertullian's statement.

[84]Daniel-Rops, "Silence of Jesus' Contemporaries," p. 14.

[85]See Anderson, *Witness of History*, p. 19.

Origen records the following:

> Now Phlegon, in the thirteenth or fourteenth book, I think, of
> his Chronicles, not only ascribed to Jesus a knowledge of
> future events (although falling into confusion about some
> things which refer to Peter, as if they referred to Jesus), but
> also testified that the result corresponded to His predictions.[86]

So Phlegon mentioned that Jesus made predictions about
future events that had been fulfilled.

Origen adds another comment about Phlegon:

> And with regard to the eclipse in the time of Tiberius Caesar,
> in whose reign Jesus appears to have been crucified, and the
> great earthquakes which then took place, Phlegon too, I
> think, has written in the thirteenth or fourteenth book of his
> Chronicles.[87]

Julius Africanus agrees on the last reference to Phlegon,
adding a bit more information: "Phlegon records that, in the
time of Tiberius Caesar, at full moon, there was a full eclipse
of the sun from the sixth to the ninth hour."[88]

Origen provides one other reference, this time actually
quoting Phlegon on the subject of the resurrection: "Jesus,
while alive, was of no assistance to himself, but that he arose
after death, and exhibited the marks of his punishment, and
showed how his hands had been pierced by nails."[89]

From Phlegon we therefore learn the following items:
(1) Jesus accurately predicted the future. **(2)** There was an
eclipse at the crucifixion from the sixth to the ninth hours,
(3) followed by earthquakes, **(4)** all during the reign of Tiberius
Caesar. **(5)** After his resurrection, Jesus appeared and showed
his wounds, especially the nail marks from his crucifixion.

---

[86]Origen, *Contra Celsum* XIV in the *Ante–Nicene Fathers*.
[87]Ibid., XXXIII.
[88]Julius Africanus, XVIII.
[89]Origen, LIX.

Synopsis: Jesus and Ancient Christianity

When the combined evidence from ancient sources is summarized, quite an impressive amount of information is gathered concerning Jesus and ancient Christianity. It is our purpose in this section to make a brief composite picture of the historical data. We have investigated a total of seventeen sources that present valuable material with regard to the historical Jesus and early Christianity. As noted above, not all of these records are equally good documents, but even minus the questionable sources, this early evidence is still very impressive.[90] Few ancient historical figures can boast the same amount of material.

The Life and Person of Jesus

According to the sources that we have investigated above, the ministry of Jesus, the brother of James (Josephus), was geographically centered in Palestine (Tacitus, Lucian, *Acts of Pilate*). Jesus was known as a wise, virtuous and ethical man (Josephus, Mara Ben-Serapion), who was reported to have both performed miracles (*Acts of Pilate*) and made prophecies that were later fulfilled (Phlegon, cf Josephus). A result of his ministry was that he had many disciples, from both the Jews and the Gentiles (Josephus, Talmud).

Of the sources which we studied, the Gnostic works, in particular, comment on the person of Jesus. They relate that on one occasion he asked his disciples who they thought he was (*Gospel of Thomas*). Although there were varied answers to this question, these works agree that Jesus was both God and man. While he was a flesh and blood person (*Gospel of Truth*, *Treatise on Resurrection*), as indicated by the title "Son of Man" (*Gospel of Thomas*), he is also said to be the Son of God (*Treatise on Resurrection*, *Gospel of Truth*, *Gospel of*

---

[90]Sources that have raised various kinds of doubt are the *Toledoth Jesu*, the four Gnostic works and the *Acts of Pilate*, which make up approximately one-third of the total number of documents studied in this chapter.

Thomas), the Word (*Gospel of Truth*) and the "All" (*Gospel of Thomas*).

As pointed out earlier these Gnostic works are somewhat questionable sources for the historical Jesus because of their late and theological character. However, some secular sources for the historical Jesus report similar beliefs. They assert that Jesus was worshiped as deity (Pliny, Lucian), and that some believed he was the Messiah (Josephus) and even call him "King" (Mara Bar-Serapion). At the very least, that these beliefs were held by certain persons is a matter of historical record.

The Teachings of Jesus

An interesting tendency among some ancient authors was to view Jesus as a philosopher with some distinctive teachings (Lucian, Mara Bar-Serapion, cf. *Gospel of Thomas*). Lucian lists some of Jesus' teachings as the need for conversion, the importance of faith and obedience, the brotherhood of all believers, the requirements of abandoning the gods of other systems of belief and the worship of himself, which was either taught or at least the result of his teaching. It might also be inferred that the Christian belief in immortality and lack of fear of death reported by Lucian is also due to Jesus' teaching.

Pliny's report that believers took oaths not to commit unrighteousness is probably due to Jesus' warnings against sin. The *Gospel of Truth* adds that Jesus taught his listeners about his Father and that Jesus realized that his death was the means of life for many.

The Death of Jesus

The Jewish leaders judged that Jesus was guilty of teaching spiritual apostasy, thereby leading Israel astray (Talmud, cf. *Apocryphon of John*). So the Jews sent a herald proclaiming that Jesus would be stoned for his false teaching and invited anyone who wished to defend him to do so. But none came forward to support him (Talmud).

After suffering persecution (*Gospel of Truth*) and as a result of his teachings (Lucian), Jesus was put to death (*Gospel of Thomas, Treatise on Resurrection*). He died at the hands of Roman procurator Pontius Pilate (Tacitus), who crucified him (Josephus, Talmud, Lucian, *Gospel of Truth, Acts of Pilate*) during the reign of Emperor Tiberius (Tacitus, Phlegon).

Even some details of the crucifixion are provided. The event occurred on Passover Eve (Talmud) and included being nailed to a cross (Phlegon, *Gospel of Truth, Acts of Pilate*, cf. Tacitus), after which the executioners gambled for his garments (*Acts of Pilate*). There were signs in nature, too, as darkness covered the land for three hours due to an eclipse of the sun (Thallus, Phlegon), and great earthquakes occurred (Phlegon). One writer (Mara Bar-Serapion) asserted that Jesus was executed unjustly and that the Jews were judged accordingly by God.

The Resurrection of Jesus

After Jesus' death it is recorded that his teachings broke out again in Judea (Tacitus, cf. Suetonius, Pliny). What was the cause for this new activity and spread of Jesus' teachings after his death? Could Jesus have been raised from the dead? Various answers are mentioned. Mara Bar-Serapion, for example, points out that Jesus' teachings lived on in his disciples.

According to the *Toledoth Jesu*, the disciples were going to steal the body, so Juda the gardener reburied it and later sold the body of Jesus to the Jewish leaders, who dragged it down the streets of Jerusalem. Justin Martyr and Tertullian object, asserting that the Jews sent trained men around the Mediterranean region in order to say that the disciples stole the body. The earliest of the sources, Matthew 28:11-15, claims that after Jesus was raised from the dead, the Jewish leaders bribed the tomb guards in order to have them say that the disciples stole the body, even though they did not.

But we are also told that Jesus was raised from the dead and appeared to his followers afterwards. Josephus seems to record the disciples' belief in the resurrection of Jesus, noting that these witnesses claimed to have seen Jesus alive three days after his crucifixion. Phlegon said that Jesus appeared and showed the marks of the nail prints in his hands, and perhaps other wounds, as well.

The resurrection of Jesus is defended especially by *The Treatise on Resurrection*, but also proclaimed by *The Gospel of Truth* and *The Gospel of Thomas*. Afterward, Jesus was exalted (*Apocryphon of John, Gospel of Thomas*).

Christian Teachings and Worship

Christians were named after their founder, Christ (Tacitus), whose teachings they followed (Lucian). Believers were of all classes, ages, localities and of both sexes, forming a cross section of society (Pliny). For Christians, Jesus' death procured salvation (*Gospel of Truth*) for those who exercised faith in his teachings (Lucian). As a result, Christians believed in their own immortality and scorned death (Lucian), realizing that eternal life was a present possession (*Treatise on Resurrection*).

Additionally, Lucian relates several other Christian teachings. Believers had sacred writings that were frequently read. They practiced their faith by denying material goods and by holding common property. They went to any extent to help with matters pertaining to their community. However, Lucian does complain that Christians were gullible enough to be taken advantage of by unscrupulous persons.

Pliny relates that believers met in a pre-dawn service on a certain day (probably Sunday). There they sang verses of a hymn, worshiped Christ as deity, and made oaths against committing sin. Then they would disband, only to reassemble in order to share food together, which is very probably a reference to the love feast and Lord's Supper. Pliny also refers to the existence of positions in the early church when he mentions two female deaconesses.

The Spread of Christianity and Persecution

After the death of Jesus and the reported resurrection

appearances, the disciples did not abandon the teachings which they had learned from him (Josephus). By the middle of the first century, Christian doctrine, and the crucifixion of Jesus in particular, had spread around the Mediterranean. In fact, skeptics were already offering rationalistic explanations for supernatural claims only some twenty years after Jesus' death (Thallus).

More specifically, Christian teachings had reached Rome by AD 49, less than twenty years after the death of Jesus, when Claudius expelled Jews from the city because of what was thought to be the influence of Jesus' teachings (Suetonius). By the time of Nero's reign (AD 54–68), Christians were still living in Rome (Tacitus, Suetonius). We are also told that Christians were present during the fall of Jerusalem in AD 70 (Tacitus).

The spread of Christianity unfortunately involved persecution fairly early in its history. Sometimes it was tempered by a certain amount of fairness, but it was real and serious for many early believers, nonetheless. The Talmud relates an occasion when five of Jesus' disciples were judged to be worthy of death. Tacitus provides much greater detail. After the great fire at Rome, Nero blamed the occurrence on Christians, who are described as a group of people who were hated by the Roman populace. As a result, many believers were arrested, convicted, mocked, and finally tortured to death. Being nailed to crosses and being burnt to death are two methods that are specifically mentioned. Such treatment evoked compassion from the people, and Tacitus blamed these events on the eccentricities of Nero.

Christians were sometimes reported as lawbreakers (Pliny, cf. Trajan, Hadrian) for almost three centuries after the death of Jesus, after which Christianity became the official religion of the Roman Empire. Believers were blamed with meeting secretly, burning their children, and drinking blood.

For instance, Pliny's letter relates his methodology with Bithynian Christians. They were identified, interrogated, sometimes tortured, and then executed. If they denied that they were believers, as demonstrated by their worshiping

Caesar and the gods, they were freed. Pliny noted that true believers would never be guilty of such a denial of Christ.

Trajan's response encouraged moderation. Repentance and worship of the gods were sufficient for freeing these people. But they should not be sought out. Hadrian offered similar advice prohibiting the harassment of Christians and even ordered that their enemies be dealt with if they acted improperly against believers. However, if Christians were guilty, they would have to be punished.

Summary and Conclusion

This chapter has shown that ancient extrabiblical sources do present a surprisingly large amount of detail concerning both the life of Jesus and the nature of early Christianity. While many of these facts are quite well known, we must remember that they have been documented here apart from the usage of the New Testament. When viewed in that light, we should realize that it is quite extraordinary that we could provide a broad outline of most of the major facts of Jesus' life from "secular" history alone. Such is surely significant.

Using only the information gleaned from these ancient extrabiblical sources, what can we conclude concerning the death and resurrection of Jesus? Can these events be historically established on these sources alone? Of the seventeen documents examined in this chapter, eleven different works speak of the death of Jesus in varying amounts of detail, with five of these specifying crucifixion as the mode. When these sources are examined by normal historical procedures used with other ancient documents, the result is conclusive.[91] It is this author's view that, from this data alone, the death of Jesus by crucifixion can be asserted as a historical fact. This conclusion is strengthened by the variety of details that are related by good sources. As mentioned often, a few of the documents may be contested, but the entire bulk of evidence

---

[91]Cf. Grant, *Jesus: An Historian's Review*, pp. 199-200.

points quite probably to the historicity of Jesus' death due to the rigors of crucifixion.

The ancient references to the resurrection are fewer and somewhat more questionable. Of the seventeen sources, seven either imply or report this occurrence, with four of these works being questioned in our study. Before answering the issue concerning Jesus' resurrection, we will initially address the cognate point of whether the empty tomb can be established as historical by this extrabiblical evidence alone. There are some strong considerations in its favor.

First, the Jewish sources that we have examined admit the empty tomb, thereby providing evidence from hostile documents. Josephus notes the disciples' belief in Jesus' resurrection, while the *Toledoth Jesu* specifically acknowledges the empty tomb. Justin Martyr and Tertullian confirm Matthew 28:11-15 by asserting that Jewish leaders were still admitting the empty tomb over a century later. While these Jewish sources (with the exception of Josephus) teach that the body was stolen or moved, they still admit the empty tomb.

Second, there are apparently no ancient sources that assert that the tomb still contained Jesus' body. While such an argument from silence does not prove anything, it is made stronger by the first consideration from the hostile sources and further complements it.

Third, our study has shown that Jesus taught in Palestine and was crucified and buried in Jerusalem under Pontius Pilate. These sources assert that Christianity had its beginnings in the same location. But could Christianity have survived in this location, based on its central claim that Jesus was raised from the dead, if his tomb had not been empty?

It must be remembered that the resurrection of the body was the predominant view of first century Jews. To declare a bodily resurrection if the body was still in a nearby tomb points out the dilemma here. Of all places, evidence was readily available in Jerusalem to disprove this central tenet of Christian belief. The Jewish leaders had both a motive and the means to get such evidence if it were available. As expressed by historian Paul Maier, speaking of the birth of Christianity:

But this is the very *last* place it could have started if Jesus' tomb had remained occupied, since anyone producing a dead Jesus would have driven a wooden stake through the heart of an incipient Christianity inflamed by his supposed resurrection.[92]

Based on the evidence admitted by hostile documents, the absence of contrary data, and the important information concerning the location of the message in Jerusalem, we conclude that there is some probability for the empty tomb based on ancient extrabiblical sources alone. Maier confirms this:

Accordingly, if all the evidence is weighed carefully and fairly, it is indeed justifiable, according to the canons of historical research, to conclude that the sepulcher of Joseph of Arimathea, in which Jesus was buried, was actually empty on the morning of the first Easter.[93]

Dealing with different factual data, Michael Grant agrees from a historical viewpoint:

But if we apply the same sort of criteria that we would apply to any other ancient literary sources, then the evidence is firm and plausible enough to necessitate the conclusion that the tomb was indeed found empty.[94]

But what about the teaching that the disciples or someone else stole the dead body of Jesus? Does this account for the empty tomb and end the question of Jesus' resurrection? Here we need to move beyond the non-Christian sources for an answer.

Contemporary critical scholars, whether skeptical or not, are virtually unanimous in rejecting such hypotheses.[95] If the

---

[92]Paul L. Maier, "The Empty Tomb as History" in *Christianity Today*, 29/13, March 28, 1975, p. 5.

[93]Ibid., p. 6.

[94]Grant, *Jesus: An Historian's Review*, p. 176.

[95]See chapter 7 for a further treatment of these two theories and the critically attested historical facts that refute them.

disciples stole the body, they would not have been willing to die, in all probability, for a known lie or fraud.[96] Liars do not make good martyrs. Additionally, the changed lives of the earliest disciples and their belief that Jesus was raised, both of which are admitted by critics, are unexplained if they stole the body. This charge fails to address the two unbelieving skeptics who saw the risen Jesus, Paul and James the brother of Jesus, who would hardly have been convinced by such fraud. These and several other considerations such as the quality of the disciples' ethical teachings account for the dismissal of this view even by critical scholars. As far as the author knows, it has not been held by a reputable scholar for over 200 years.[97]

Equally faulty is the hypothesis that the body of Jesus was taken or moved by someone other than the disciples. The major problem, among others, is that it does not account for the strongest, critically ascertained fact in favor of the resurrection — the disciples' belief that the risen Jesus had literally appeared to them. Since one must search elsewhere to account for this major fact, this view cannot disprove the resurrection. Not only is this the case for the disciples, but even more so with Paul and James, who pose additional refutations.

Additionally, such views fail to provide a plausible person(s) to perform such an act, viable motives, a place for Jesus' final burial, or for the fact that the act was never admitted, discovered, or otherwise reported. But again, the appearances of Jesus are not even dealt with by these theses, and this constitutes the primary refutation.

Also, it should be remembered that the *Toledoth Jesu*, which purports the view that Jesus' body was dragged down Jerusalem's streets, is a much later source, and it is disdained as nonhistorical even by Jewish scholars. Its thesis fails

---

[96] See Eusebius, I:IX; II:XXIII; II:XXV for accounts of the martyrdoms of several of the disciples.

[97] For example, see Schweitzer's *The Quest of the Historical Jesus*, who lists no proponent of this theory since 1778.

because such an act would have killed Christianity centuries ago, but such an act obviously did not occur. Neither does it explain Jesus' appearances. It is no wonder that these fraud hypotheses have also had no reputable supporters in the last two centuries.[98]

However, we still cannot conclude that ancient extrabiblical sources, by themselves, historically demonstrate the resurrection, as is true with Jesus' death by crucifixion. The evidence indicates that alternative theories involving a stolen or moved body are invalid, and that the tomb was empty, but the cause of this event cannot be proven at this point alone. Still, the testimony of Josephus and Phlegon, in particular, are very helpful, and supplement the excellent case in Chapter 7 from the New Testament creeds and known facts.

We conclude that ancient extrabiblical sources both provide a broad outline of the life of Jesus and indicate that he died due to the effects of crucifixion. Afterwards he was buried and his tomb was later found empty, but the body had not been stolen or moved. While we have this mystery and some factual evidence in favor of Jesus' resurrection, additional data from other sources are needed in order to reach a final position.

---

[98]On the contemporary rejection of these fraud theories, see Karl Barth, *Church Dogmatics*, vol. IV, p. 340; Raymond Brown, "The Resurrection and Biblical Criticism," p. 233.

10 Ancient Christian Sources (Non-New Testament)

In addition to the New Testament, early Christian writers produced volumes of important works that give valuable insight into early Christian beliefs, doctrines, and customs, as well as various types of exhortation. Many of these writings also contain brief statements concerning the historicity of Jesus.

Our purpose in this chapter is not to investigate all these statements, but to study only those passages that exhibit an explicitly historical interest. Because of this emphasis on the historically-oriented claims, our treatment of these ancient Christian sources will be comparatively brief despite the large number of works that fit into this category.[1] We begin with the earlier writers, usually referred to as the "apostolic fathers" (about AD 90-125),[2] and then present some historical statements in a few writings that immediately followed this earlier period.

---

[1]Therefore, some well-known works such as the *Shepherd of Hermas* will not be included in this discussion at all, since it contains little that might be counted as historical information concerning Jesus.

[2]Quotations from the apostolic fathers are taken from J.B. Lightfoot, *The Apostolic Fathers*.

AD 90–125

Clement of Rome

One of the most important apostolic documents, Clement of Rome's letter to the Corinthian church is generally considered to be the earliest extra-New Testament Christian writing. Clement was the leading elder in the church at Rome and wrote *Corinthians* about AD 95 to help end a dispute between the church members and elders at Corinth.

Although *Corinthians* is largely doctrinal and moral in nature, it contains at least one important historical reference to Jesus and earliest Christianity:

> The Apostles received the Gospel for us from the Lord Jesus Christ; Jesus Christ was sent forth from God. So then Christ is from God, and the Apostles are from Christ. Both therefore came of the will of God in the appointed order. Having therefore received a charge, and having been fully assured through the resurrection of our Lord Jesus Christ and confirmed in the word of God with full assurance of the Holy Ghost, they went forth with the glad tidings that the kingdom of God should come. So preaching everywhere in country and town, they appointed their first-fruits, when they had proved them by the Spirit, to be bishops and deacons unto them that should believe.[3]

In this passage, Clement of Rome claims several facts. **(1)** The gospel or good news of the Kingdom of God was the major Christian message. **(2)** This gospel had been given to the apostles by Jesus himself even as it came from God. **(3)** Jesus' resurrection provided the assurance of the truthfulness of these teachings. **(4)** With the additional certainty of Scripture, the apostles spread the gospel. **(5)** Wherever the gospel was preached and local congregations were started, leaders were chosen to minister to the believers.

This certification of a chain of authority from God to Jesus to the apostles to the early Christian elders is interest-

---

[3]Clement of Rome, *Corinthians*, 42.

ing not only in that it was the basis for early doctrinal proclamation and church organization. Additionally, Clement of Rome anchors this authority in the belief that Jesus was raised from the dead and in the Scripture. A miraculous event in history was thus taken as the basic sign of authority behind the preaching of the earliest Christian message.

Ignatius

As bishop of Antioch and a leader in the early church, Ignatius was condemned to death in Rome. On the way to his execution he addressed seven letters to six churches and one individual (Polycarp). These letters are early witnesses to Christian doctrine and to early church hierarchy, being written about AD 110–115. They also contain several historical references to Jesus. In his epistle to the *Trallians*, Ignatius states:

> Jesus Christ who was of the race of David, who was the Son of Mary, who was truly born and ate and drank, was truly persecuted under Pontius Pilate, was truly crucified and died in the sight of those in heaven and on earth and those under the earth; who moreover was truly raised from the dead, His Father having raised Him, who in the like fashion will so raise us also who believe on Him.[4]

In this portion, Ignatius affirms several facts concerning Jesus. *(1)* He was of the lineage of David and *(2)* born of Mary. *(3)* As such, he really lived, ate and drank on the earth. *(4)* Jesus was crucified and died at the hands of Pontius Pilate. *(5)* Afterward God raised him from the dead, *(6)* as an example of the believer's resurrection. Again we perceive how the resurrection was the chief sign for believers, in this case that they would be raised from the dead like Jesus.

In his epistle to the *Smyrneans*, Ignatius refers twice to the historical Jesus. In the first instance, he asserts concerning Jesus:

---

[4]Ignatius, *Trallians*, 9.

He is truly of the race of David according to the flesh, but Son
of God by the Divine will and power, truly born of a virgin
and baptised by John that all *righteousness might be fulfilled* by
Him, truly nailed up in the flesh for our sakes under Pontius
Pilate and Herod the tetrarch (of which fruit are we—that is,
of His most blessed passion); that He might set up an ensign
unto all ages through His resurrection.[5] (Emphasis added by
the editor.)

Ignatius again affirms *(7)* that Jesus was physically of the
lineage of David, adding *(8)* that he was also the Son of God
as shown by the virgin birth. *(9)* Jesus was baptized by John,
(10) later being nailed (crucified) under Pontius Pilate and
Herod the tetrarch. *(11)* Afterward, Jesus was raised from the
dead.

In a second reference in *Smyrneans*, Ignatius concentrates
on Jesus' resurrection:

For I know and believe that He was in the flesh even after the
resurrection; and when He came to Peter and his company,
He said to them, *Lay hold and handle me, and see that I am not a
demon without a body.* And straitway they touched him and they
believed, being joined unto His flesh and His blood.
Wherefore also they despised death, nay they were found
superior to death. And after His resurrection He [both] ate
with them and drank with them.[6] (Emphasis added by the
editor.)

Speaking of the resurrection, Ignatius affirms that Jesus
(12) was raised in the flesh. *(13)* Afterward he appeared to
Peter and the disciples and told them to touch his physical
body, which they did. *(14)* Jesus then ate and drank with them
after his resurrection. *(15)* In a statement reminiscent of
Lucian, Ignatius also relates that upon believing, the disciples
despised death.

A last reference which Ignatius makes concerning the
historical Jesus is found in his epistle to the *Magnesians*:

---

[5]Ignatius, *Smyrneans*, 1.
[6]Ibid., 3.

Be ye fully persuaded concerning the birth and the passion and the resurrection, which took place in the time of the governorship of Pontius Pilate; for these things were truly and certainly done by Jesus Christ our hope.[7]

Here Ignatius assures his readers that they can be certainly persuaded of the facticity of Jesus' [16] birth, [17] death and [18] resurrection, the last two having occurred while Pontius Pilate was governor.

As in other references, Ignatius attempts to place such events firmly in the realm of history. His purpose, at least partially, is to provide an answer to the threat of Gnosticism, which often denied physical interpretations of some of these events.

Quadratus

One of the early apologists to begin answering claims raised against Christianity, Quadratus wrote his apology to Emperor Hadrian about AD 125. Unfortunately, this work is presently known only from one statement preserved by Eusebius in the fourth century.

Eusebius relates that Quadratus wrote his apology in order to answer malicious claims meant to harass Christians. It is stated that this defense was both sound in doctrine and revealed Quadratus' knowledge of the situation. Then Eusebius quotes a sentence from Quadratus' apology:

The deeds of our Saviour were always before you, for they were true miracles; those that were healed, those that were raised from the dead, who were seen, not only when healed and when raised, but were always present. They remained living a long time, not only whilst our Lord was on earth, but likewise when he had left the earth. So that some of them have also lived to our own times.[8]

This brief quotation from Quadratus' apology reports several

---

[7]Ignatius, *Magnesians*, 11.

[8]Eusebius, *Ecclesiastical History* IV:III.

important items concerning Jesus' miracles. *(1)* The facticity of Jesus' miracles could be checked by interested persons, since they were done publicly. With regard to the actual types of miracles, *(2)* some were healed and *(3)* some were raised from the dead. *(4)* There were eyewitnesses of these miracles at the time they occurred. *(5)* Many of those healed or raised were still alive when Jesus "left the earth" and some were reportedly still alive in Quadratus' own time.

AD 126–155

Barnabas

The epistle of *Barnabas* (sometimes referred to as *Pseudo-Barnabas*) has explicit antilegalistic overtones and expresses opposition to Judaism. Its purpose is to show that Jesus Christ is the fulfillment of the Old Testament law, but in doing so it often resorts to allegorical interpretations. Dates for this writing have varied widely, often from the late first century to the mid-second century. A commonly accepted date is AD 130–138.

In one major passage, *Barnabas* relates several facts concerning the life of Jesus:

> He must needs be manifested in the flesh. . . . He preached teaching Israel and performing so many wonders and miracles, and He loved them exceedingly. . . . He chose His own apostles who were to proclaim His Gospel. . . . But He Himself desired so to suffer; for it was necessary for Him to suffer on a tree.[9]

From this portion we note *(1)* that Jesus became a man. He *(2)* preached and taught Israel, *(3)* performed miracles and *(4)* expressed love for the people. *(5)* Jesus chose his apostles *(6)* to proclaim the message of the gospel. *(7)* It was necessary for Jesus to suffer on a tree (crucifixion).

---

[9]*Barnabas*, 5.

Justin Martyr

With the work of Justin Martyr, early Christian scholarship entered a new dimension. There is a marked difference between the characteristically devotional, doctrinal and practical exhortations of the apostolic writings and the apologetic works of Justin. These writings reflect his personal philosophical pilgrimage and his own polemic interests, which led to his reputation as the major Christian apologist of the second century. Included in his works are a number of historical references to Jesus.

In his *First Apology*, written soon after AD 150 and addressed chiefly to Emperor Antoninus Pius, Justin Martyr refers to various aspects of the life of Jesus. Referring to Jesus' birth, it is noted that he was born of a virgin, while his physical line of descent came through the tribe of Judah and the family of Jesse.[10] Later, after mentioning the location of Jesus' birth in the town of Bethlehem, Justin explains:

> Now there is a village in the land of the Jews, thirty five stadia from Jerusalem, in which Jesus Christ was born, as you can ascertain also from the registers of the taxing made under Cyrenius, your first procurator in Judea.[11]

These two references state several items surrounding Jesus' birth. **(1)** He was born of a virgin, **(2)** while he was a physical descendant of Jesse, of the tribe of Judah. **(3)** The village of Bethlehem was his birthplace, **(4)** which was located thirty-five stadia (approximately five miles) from Jerusalem. **(5)** The location and fact of Jesus' birth could be verified by consulting the records of Cyrenius, the first procurator of Judea.

Justin Martyr also refers to Jesus' public ministry and to the official documentation of his message. Earlier Justin's reference to the *Acts of Pontius Pilate* was discussed,[12] where it

---

[10]Justin Martyr, *First Apology*, XLVII.

[11]Ibid., XXXIV. Quotations from the works of Justin Martyr are taken from the *Ante-Nicene Fathers*, vol. 3.

[12]See chapter 9.

is asserted that Jesus' miracles such as his healing of diseases and raising the dead could be evidenced from Pilate's report.[13] Furthermore, in answer to the question as to whether Jesus did his miracles by magic, Justin answered in the negative, pointing to Jesus' fulfillment of prophecy as a vindication of his claims.[14] From these texts we note *(6)* that Jesus did miracles which were believed to be referenced in Pilate's report. *(7)* Fulfilled messianic prophecy was also taken as a further validation of his claims.

Justin also referred frequently to Jesus' death by crucifixion. On one occasion he spoke of Jesus as "Him who was crucified in Judea."[15] In a second reference to the so-called *Acts of Pontius Pilate*, he declares that Jesus was nailed to the cross through his hands and feet, and that some of those present cast lots for his clothing.[16] In a more extended reference to Jesus' death and resurrection, Justin Martyr declares:

> Accordingly, after He was crucified, even all His acquaintances forsook Him, having denied Him; and afterwards, when He had risen from the dead and appeared to them, and had taught them to read the prophecies in which all these things were foretold as coming to pass, and when they had seen Him ascending into heaven, and had believed, and had received power sent thence by Him upon them, and went to every race of men, they taught these things, and were called apostles.[17]

In these three references Justin reports *(8)* that Jesus was nailed to the cross through his hands and feet and *(9)* was crucified *(10)* while his garments were taken from him. *(11)* His friends denied and forsook him. *(12)* Later, Jesus rose from the dead and appeared to his followers, *(13)* teaching them concerning the prophecies which he fulfilled. *(14)* After Jesus

---

[13]Justin Martyr, *First Apology*, XLVIII.

[14]Ibid., XXX. For some specific Messianic prophecies, see XXXII-XXXV.

[15]Ibid., XXXII.

[16]Ibid., XXXV.

[17]Ibid., L.

ascended to heaven, **(15)** those who believed in him went out preaching to all men and **(16)** were called apostles.

In another work, *Dialogue with Trypho*, Justin Martyr writes specifically for Jews, in order to convince them that Jesus is the Messiah. Here we also find several historical references to Jesus. For instance, Justin asserts:

> For at the time of His birth, Magi who came from Arabia worshipped Him, coming first to Herod, who then was sovereign in your land.[18]

Here it is pointed out **(17)** that Arabian Magi visited Jesus at his birth and worshipped him, after **(18)** first stopping to see Herod, the ruler of the Jews.

Later, speaking of Jesus' crucifixion, Justin writes:

> For when they crucified Him, driving in the nails, they pierced His hands and feet; and those who crucified Him parted His garments among themselves, each casting lots for what he chose to have, and receiving according to the decision of the lot.[19]

Here Justin explicitly records several more events. He asserts **(19)** that Jesus was crucified, being nailed through both his hands and feet. **(20)** Again we find a reference to gambling for Jesus' clothes by those who crucified him, with each person keeping the items which he had won.

Following Jesus' death by crucifixion, the Gospel of Matthew reports that the Jews spread the story that the disciples came and stole his dead body (Matt. 28:11-15). Justin explains that this story was still being proclaimed elsewhere by the Jews:

> Christ said amongst you that He would give the sign of Jonah, exhorting you to repent of your wicked deeds at least after He rose again from the dead . . . yet you not only have not

---

[18]Justin Martyr, *Dialogue with Trypho*, LXXVII.
[19]Ibid., XCVII.

repented, after you learned that he rose from the dead, but, as I said before, you have sent chosen and ordained men throughout all the world to proclaim that a godless and lawless heresy had sprung from one Jesus, a Galilean deceiver, whom we crucified, but his disciples stole him by night from the tomb, where he was laid when unfastened from the cross, and now deceive men by asserting that he had risen from the dead and ascended to heaven.[20]

This interesting portion reports **(21)** that Jesus predicted that he would rise ahead of time,[21] and **(22)** exhorted the Jews to repent. **(23)** Even after Jesus rose from the dead the Jews did not repent but **(24)** spread the story that the disciples stole Jesus' body after he was crucified, and that the disciples then lied about the resurrection. **(25)** The disciples also taught that Jesus afterward ascended to heaven, which at least witnesses to the early Christian belief in this occurrence.

Lastly, Justin Martyr also witnesses to the facticity of the resurrection in another portion of *Dialogue with Trypho*:

> For indeed the Lord remained on the tree almost until evening, and they buried Him at eventide; then on the third day He rose again.[22]

Here Justin records **(26)** that Jesus hung on the "tree" until evening,[23] **(27)** that he was buried at that time and **(28)** that he rose from the dead the third day afterward.

Justin Martyr records many other events from the life of Jesus, but often he reports that his data was gleaned from the Scripture.[24] These references here will suffice to provide numerous examples of Justin's interest in Jesus' actual life on earth.

---

[20]Ibid., CVIII; cf. XVII.

[21]This is "the sign of the prophet Jonah" (see Matt. 12:38-40).

[22]*Dialogue with Trypho*, XCVII.

[23]Justin refers to it as a "cross" in CVIII, for instance.

[24]Cf. ibid., CV and CVI, for examples.

Synopsis of Christian Sources

In this chapter we have investigated five early Christian sources for the historicity of Jesus, all of which were extra-New Testament. Our intent was not to examine all the passages that spoke of Jesus, but only those which claimed to report historical data. Additionally, we limited our discussion to the life of Jesus, thereby overlooking material concerning early Christian origins. A synopsis of this material provides the listing of numerous details.

The Life of Jesus

These ancient Christian sources taught that Jesus really did live on earth in human history (Ignatius) after being born as a man (*Barnabas*). He was from the tribe of Judah (Justin), from the family of Jesse (Justin) and of the lineage of David (Ignatius). Jesus was born of Mary (Ignatius), a virgin (Ignatius, Justin), in the city of Bethlehem (Justin). It is even reported that Bethlehem was located about five miles from Jerusalem and that his birth could be verified by the records of Cyrenius, the first procurator of Judea (Justin). Later, he was visited by Arabian Magi, who had first visited Herod (Justin).

Concerning his public ministry, these sources record Jesus' baptism by John (Ignatius) and his choosing of apostles (*Barnabas*, Justin). There are also reports of miracles performed by Jesus (Quadratus, *Barnabas*, Justin). Here it is carefully pointed out that these miracles consisted of people being both healed and raised from the dead, concerning which it is asserted that some of the eyewitnesses to these events were still alive (Quadratus). It is also claimed that Pilate filed a report with the officials at Rome which corroborated these details (Justin). Additionally, we are told that Jesus fulfilled Old Testament prophecy, thereby validating his claims (Justin).

The Teachings of Jesus

These sources also record some of Jesus' important teachings. It is related that he preached and taught Israel, a people whom he loved (*Barnabas*). He exhorted the Jews to repent, yet they did not do so even after he rose from the dead, an event which Jesus had predicted ahead of time (Justin).

Jesus' major teaching was the nature of the gospel, which he received from God and later imparted to his apostles (Clement, *Barnabas*). It is asserted that the apostles were fully assured of the truthfulness of the message and that they, in turn, preached the Kingdom of God in various towns and countries. Where this message went, it was accompanied by the organizing of churches, complete with the choosing of leaders such as bishops and deacons (Clement).

The Death of Jesus

These early Christian writers were careful to point to the facticity of Jesus' death by crucifixion (Ignatius, *Barnabas*, Justin). They sought to link it firmly to history, such as with the assertion that this event occurred during the governorship of Pontius Pilate and the reign of Herod (Ignatius). Details of the crucifixion are also provided, such as Jesus being nailed to the cross (Ignatius, Justin) while his clothing was divided among his assassins (Justin). Jesus hung on the cross until evening, after which he was taken down and buried (Justin). During this period of time, his friends forsook and denied him (Justin).

The Resurrection of Jesus

These Christians were equally adamant in their belief that Jesus' resurrection is also a fact of history (Clement, Ignatius, Justin). This event occurred on the third day after Jesus' crucifixion in spite of the Jewish claim that the disciples stole the body (Justin).

Evidencing the fact that he had been raised from the dead, Jesus appeared to Peter and the other disciples

(Ignatius, Justin). During these encounters, Jesus allowed and even encouraged the disciples to touch his risen flesh, which they did (Ignatius). Jesus also ate and drank with his followers (Ignatius) and taught them concerning how he had fulfilled Old Testament prophecy (Justin). Later, Jesus ascended to heaven (Justin, cf. Quadratus).

These early Christian authors asserted that Jesus' resurrection provided the assurance that the gospel which he preached was ordained by God (Clement). This event was an example of the believer's resurrection and was the reason why the disciples despised death (Ignatius).

Summary and Conclusion

What value do these early extra-New Testament sources have in reconstructing a historical life of Jesus? Do such Christian authors provide any exceptional evidence for the death and resurrection? Actually, there are both positive and negative considerations in such questions.

Positively, the Christian sources presented in this chapter are early. Clement wrote at the end of the first century, or at approximately the same time as some of the later New Testament writings. Ignatius' seven books date from about fifteen to twenty years later. These men were also close to apostolic sources, as is evident from their own works,[25] and from other early testimony.[26]

Another factor is that some of these early authors were scholars or leaders in their own right. Clement and Ignatius were well-known bishops in the early church,[27] while Justin was a rather distinguished philosopher.[28] Additionally, these writers were frequently careful to cite evidence for their assertions. Clement and Ignatius referred to the resurrection

---

[25]See Ignatius, *Romans*, 4; cf. Clement, *Corinthians*, 47.

[26]For example, see Eusebius, *Ecclesiastical History* III: XV-XVI.

[27]Ibid., III:XV-XXII.

[28]Ibid., IV:XVI.

as the basis for Christian truth. Quadratus backed his testimony with eyewitness testimony concerning Jesus' miracles. Justin referred to miracles and fulfilled prophecy as evidence.

However, in spite of these early sources, scholarly testimonies and citings of evidence, there are also weaknesses in our usage of these sources. Initially, it is obvious that these writings rely on the New Testament for much of their data, as is specifically reported by Justin.[29] That they do so is certainly not a weakness in itself, for we have argued repeatedly that the New Testament is a good historical source. However, the point is that if they rely on the New Testament, then they are not totally *extra*-New Testament, and the object of this work is to ascertain what evidence of this latter kind is available.

It should also be remembered that the purpose of these writers was not a critical investigation of history *per se*, but the reporting of Christian origins. While such is certainly a fair and worthwhile approach, and can yield historical facts, additional evidence could also strengthen the case.

Such additional, corroborative data is partially available from the secular sources in Chapter 9, where many of the reports confirm the citings singled out here, especially with regard to the teachings and crucifixion of Jesus. There are also parallels concerning his life and the reports of his resurrection. Thus we continue to witness the ancient corroboration of Jesus' story. As we have said, he is actually one of the most-mentioned figures in the ancient world.

---

[29]Cf. *Dialogue with Trypho*, CV and CVI.

11 Summary and Assessment

Having finished our treatment of the ancient pre- and non-New Testament sources for Jesus' life, we turn now to a final assessment of this material.[1] Our first interest is to present an integrated summary of all the reports concerning Jesus' life, teachings, death, and resurrection from Part Two of this volume. Then we will give a final evaluation of the strength of these sources in establishing the facts.

Synopsis of Sources

Many aspects of Jesus' life have been reported by the four categories of evidence that we have examined. The ancient material from creedal (plus critically-ascertained facts), archaeological, non-Christian, and non-New Testament Christian sources presents quite a detailed look at the career of Jesus. We will begin this chapter by summarizing all of the reports from these four areas, which will help to give us a complete view of this data.

---

[1]Other relevant material on the life of Jesus is found in Part One.

The Life of Jesus

It is reported [1] that Jesus became a man (creeds: Phil. 2:6ff.; 1 John 4:2; *Barnabas*) and [2] lived on the earth in human history (Ignatius). [3] He came from the tribe of Judah (Justin) and [4] was of the lineage of Jesse and David (creeds: Acts 13:23; 2 Tim. 2:8; Justin; Ignatius).

Archaeological discoveries have shown that, before Jesus' birth, [5] a taxation was proclaimed by the Roman authorities, [6] who required that people travel back to their home cities. [7] Required nearly every fourteen years, just such a taxation apparently occurred at approximately the same time as Jesus' birth.

[8] Jesus was born of Mary (Ignatius), [9] who was a virgin (Ignatius; Justin), and [10] he had a brother named James (Josephus). [11] Jesus was born in the city of Bethlehem, located about five miles from Jerusalem, and it is recorded [12] that his birth could be verified by the records of Cyrenius, who was the first procurator of Judea (Justin). [13] Later, Jesus was visited by Arabian Magi, who had first seen Herod (Justin). [14] He was also from the town of Nazareth (creeds: Acts 2:22; 4:10; 5:38).

With regard to his public ministry, Jesus [15] was preceded by John (creeds: Acts 10:37; 13:24-25), [16] was baptized by him (Ignatius; cf. creed: Rom. 10:9-10), and [17] chose his apostles (*Barnabas*; Justin). Geographically, [18] Jesus' ministry began in Galilee and [19] extended to Judea in Palestine (Tacitus; Lucian; *Acts of Pilate*; creed: Acts 10:37).

[20] Jesus was known as a wise, virtuous, and ethical man (Josephus; Mara Bar-Serapion). [21] As the result of his ministry and teaching (creed: 1 Tim. 3:16), [22] he made many disciples from both the Jews and the Gentiles (Josephus; Talmud; creed: 1 Tim. 3:16).

We are told [23] that Jesus performed miracles (creeds: Acts 2:22; 10:38; *Acts of Pilate*; Quadratus; *Barnabas*; Justin). It is reported [24] that some people were healed and others raised from the dead and [25] that some of the eyewitnesses of these occurrences were still alive (Quadratus). It is also claimed [26] that Pilate filed a report with the Roman officials that corroborated these details (Justin). Additionally, Jesus both [27] fulfilled Old Testament prophecy, thereby validating his claims (creeds: Acts 2:25-31; 3:21-25; 4:11; 10:43; 13:27-37; Justin; cf. Josephus) and [28] made prophecies himself that were later fulfilled (Phlegon), [29] such as predicting his own resurrection (Justin).

The Person of Jesus

Many of the sources that we investigated comment on the person of Jesus.[2] In contemporary theology, the titles of Jesus are taken to be exceptionally important indications of who he thought he was, as well as how the early church identified him. The pre-New Testament creeds are crucial in this regard because of their early and authoritative nature. These confessional statements agree that Jesus was deity. We are told [30] that he was of the same nature or essence as God (creed: Phil. 2:6). He is specifically given the titles of [31] Lord (creeds: 1 Cor. 11:23; Acts 2:36; 10:36; Rom. 1:4; 10:9; Luke 24:34), [32] Son of God (creeds: Acts 13:33; Rom. 1:3-4) and [33] Christ (creeds: 1 Cor. 15:3; Acts 2:36, 38; 3:18, 20; 4:10; 10:36; Rom. 1:4; 1 Tim. 6:13; 2 Tim. 2:8; 1 Pet. 3:18; 1 John 4:2). Other titles from the Acts traditions include [34] Savior (Acts 5:31; 13:23), [35] the Holy and Righteous One (Acts 3:14; cf. 2:27; 13:35), and [36] Prince (Acts 5:31).

Secular sources report some similar data. [37] Jesus was worshiped as deity (Pliny; Lucian), [38] some believed that he was the Messiah (Josephus) and [39] called him "King" (Mara Bar-Serapion).

The Gnostic sources are even in agreement here. [40] We are told that on one occasion Jesus asked his disciples who they believed he was (*Gospel of Thomas*). Various answers are

---

[2]Our explicit intention in Chapter 10 was only to mention the post-New Testament Christian sources that reported historical facts during the life of Jesus. We did not mention the sources that also make claims concerning Jesus' deity. For examples, see Clement, *Corinthians*, 36; Ignatius, *Ephesians*, 7, 18; *Romans*, Introduction; *Smyrnaeans*, 1; *To Polycarp*, 8; Polycarp, *Philippians*, 12. In these examples from Ignatius and Polycarp, Jesus is specifically called God.

given in the Gnostic works, all of which agree [41] that he was both God and man. While he was a real flesh and blood person (*Gospel of Truth*; *Treatise on Resurrection*), as indicated (in the context) by the title Son of Man (*Gospel of Thomas*), he is also called [42] the Son of God (*Treatise on Resurrection*; *Gospel of Truth*) and [43] the "All" (*Gospel of Thomas*).

The Teachings of Jesus

It is recorded [44] that Jesus preached to and taught Israel, a people whom he loved (*Barnabas*). [45] He exhorted the Jews to repent, yet they refused to do so even after he rose from the dead (Justin).

[46] Jesus' major teaching was the gospel (creed: 1 Cor. 15:1-4), [47] which he received from God and later imparted to his apostles (Clement; *Barnabas*). [48] The apostles were fully convinced of the truthfulness of the gospel and they, in turn, preached the Kingdom of God everywhere (Clement).

The tendency among some of the secular sources was [49] to view Jesus as a philosopher with some distinct teachings (Lucian; Mara Bar Serapion; cf. *Gospel of Thomas*). For instance, Lucian refers to Jesus as a "sage." Lucian and Pliny, in particular, corroborate some of the major teachings of Jesus as mentioned earlier in the Christian sources.

Lucian asserts [50] that Jesus introduced new teachings in Palestine. These included [51] the need for conversion, [52] the denial of the gods, and [53] the brotherhood of all believers. Jesus' teachings additionally included and encouraged [54] worship of himself, [55] living according to his teachings, [56] the importance of faith, and [57] immortality, which led to a contempt for death among believers. Lucian also notes [58] that Christians had sacred Scripture which was frequently read.

In addition to the point mentioned earlier, that Jesus was worshiped by early believers as deity, Pliny also reports [59] an oath taken by believers not to commit sin, that typifies Jesus' ethical teachings. Additionally, Pliny tells us [60] that true believers could not be enticed or forced to worship the gods, and [61] that they worshiped on a certain day of the week before dawn, both of which also reflect Jesus' teachings.

Lastly, the *Gospel of Truth* adds two other items. [62] Jesus taught his listeners about his Father and [63] Jesus realized that his death was the basis for the life of many people.

The Death of Jesus

From the early creed in 1 Corinthians 11:23ff. we learn [64] that Jesus attended a dinner [65] on the evening on which he was betrayed. At this meal he [66] gave thanks for the food, and [67] shared both bread and drink, [68] which he referred to as the sacrifice of his body and blood for sin.

[69] The Jewish leaders determined that Jesus was guilty of teaching spiritual heresy and of leading Israel to apostasy (Talmud; cf. *Apocryphon of John*). [70] As a result, the Jews sent out a herald who proclaimed that Jesus would be stoned for his teachings, though anyone who wished was invited to defend him. However, no one came forward to speak for him (Talmud).

Jesus [71] appeared before Pilate (creeds: Acts 3:13; 13:28) and [72] made a good confession (creed: 1 Tim. 6:13), which may have been an affirmation of his messiahship. [73] After being persecuted (*Gospel of Truth*) and [74] as a result of his teachings (Lucian), [75] Jesus was put to death (creeds: 1 Cor. 15:3; Acts 3:13-15; 13:27-29; 1 Pet. 3:18; Rom. 4:25; 1 Tim. 2:6; *Gospel of Thomas*; *Treatise on Resurrection*). He died [76] at the hands of the Roman procurator Pontius Pilate (Talmud; Ignatius), [77] during the local rule of Herod (Ignatius). [78] More specifically, Jesus was crucified (Josephus; Talmud; Lucian; *Gospel of Truth*; *Acts of Pilate*; creeds: Acts 2:23, 36; 4:10; 5:30; 10:39; Phil. 2:6f.; Ignatius; *Barnabas*; Justin), [79] by wicked men (creed: Acts 2:23), [80] in the city of Jerusalem (creed: Acts 13:27-28; cf. 10:39), [81] during the reign of Roman Emperor Tiberius (Tacitus; Phlegon).

Even some details of Jesus' crucifixion are provided by these sources. [82] The event reportedly occurred on Passover Eve (Talmud). [83] Victims of crucifixion were apparently made to carry at least a portion of their crosses to the site, which sometimes resulted in stumbling to the ground (shroud). [84] Jesus had his wrists and feet nailed to the cross (cf. Tacitus; *Gospel of Truth*; *Acts of Pilate*; Ignatius; Justin; cf. Shroud; Yohanan). [85] Crucifixion could also involve the administering of a *coup de grace*, such as breaking the victim's legs (cf. Yohanan with ancient historical reports) in order to hasten death by asphyxiation, [86] which is the normal cause of death in crucifixion, as revealed by the need for the person to push up and down in order to breathe (cf. shroud; Yohanon with modern medical studies).

As long as the shroud is not a fake, and especially if it is Jesus' burial garment, it confirms several details of crucifixion involving more-or-less uncommon procedures. These include [87] the "crown of thorns," [88] the severity of the beating and whipping, [89] the absence of broken ankles, [90] the post-mortem chest wound, and [91] the blood and watery fluid that flowed from the wound.

While the crucifixion was in progress, [92] Jesus' executioners gambled for his garments (*Acts of Pilate*; Justin). [93] Mara Bar-Serapion asserted that Jesus was executed unjustly and that, as a result, the Jews were judged by God. [94] The creed in 1 Peter 3:18 also notes the contrast of a righteous person dying for sinners. [95] It is reported that darkness covered the land during the crucifixion (Thallus, Phlegon), [96] followed by earthquakes (Phlegon). [97] Jesus was on the cross until evening, [98] after which his body was removed and he was buried (Justin; creeds: 1 Cor. 15:4; Acts 13:29).

The man buried in the Shroud of Turin was also buried [99] hastily, [100] individually, and [101] in fine linen, all of which are uncommon procedures for a victim of crucifixion. Furthermore, [102] Jewish burial procedure sometimes involved sealing the tomb (Nazareth Decree). Even though it may not directly concern Jesus, grave robbing was punishable by death in Palestine (Nazareth Decree).

The Resurrection of Jesus

[103] During this time Jesus' friends left and denied him (Justin), experiencing despair at his death. [104] Then, three days after Jesus' death, the tomb in which he was buried was found empty (Justin; creeds: Acts 10:40; 1 Cor. 15:4, implied;

cf. *Toledoth Jesu*). [105] The Jews claimed that the disciples stole the body and proclaimed him risen (*Toledoth Jesu*; Justin), but such a view fails to explain the known facts.[3]

Numerous sources assert [106] that Jesus was raised from the dead (creeds: Luke 24:34; Acts 2:24, 31-32; 3:15, 26; 4:10; 5:30; 10:40; 13:30-37; 2 Tim. 2:8; Clement; Ignatius; Justin; *Gospel of Truth*; *Gospel of Thomas*; *Treatise on Resurrection*). Strong evidence for the resurrection appearances comes from the [107] early reports of this event, probably dating from the AD 30s, and from the eyewitnesses themselves, who reported having seen the risen Jesus personally (creeds: 1 Cor. 15:3ff.; Luke 24:34; Acts 2:32; 3:15; 5:30-32; 10:39-42; 13:28-31).

More specifically, reports indicated [108] that Jesus appeared to Peter (creeds: 1 Cor. 15:5; Luke 24:34) and [109-110] to the other disciples on more than one occasion (creeds: 1 Cor. 15:5, 7; Acts 10:39-42; 13:28-31; cf. Josephus; Ignatius; Justin), [111] as well as to over 500 people at once (creed: 1 Cor. 15:6). [112] Jesus invited them to touch his resurrected body (Phlegon), which they did (Ignatius), [113] and he even ate and drank in their presence (creed: Acts 10:41; Ignatius). During this time, Jesus also taught his disciples [114] concerning the Old Testament prophecy that he had fulfilled (Justin) and [115] told them to preach the gospel (creed: Acts 10:42). But Jesus did not appear only to believers. For instance, he was seen by two of the best known skeptics in the early church — [116] James, the brother of Jesus (creed: 1 Cor. 15:7) and [117] Paul (creed: 1 Cor. 15:8).

If Jesus is the man buried in the Shroud of Turin and the cloth is not a fake, there are additional evidences here for his resurrection from the dead. [118] There is no decomposition on the shroud, indicating a hasty departure of the body. But further, [119] the body buried in the cloth was apparently not unwrapped, while [120] the most probable cause for the image on the shroud is a scorch from a dead body.

It is asserted that after Jesus' resurrection and his subse-

---

[3]See chapters 7 and 9.

quent brief ministry on earth, [121] he ascended to heaven (creeds: 1 Tim. 3:16; Phil. 2:6f.; Justin; cf. Quadratus) and [122] was exalted (creeds: Acts 2:33; 5:31; 13:21; *Apocryphon of John*; *Gospel of Thomas*).

The Earliest Church

As a result of these events, [123] Jesus' disciples were transformed from persons who were afraid to be associated with him just a short time before to strong witnesses whose lives were changed (Tacitus; Suetonius; Mara Bar-Serapion; Josephus; Clement; cf. Pliny; cf. creed: 1 Tim. 3:16). [124] The gospel became the center of early Christian preaching (creed: 1 Cor. 15:1-4; Clement) and [125] salvation was taught through Jesus Christ (creeds: Acts 2:38-39; 3:19-23; 4:11-12; 5:32; 10:42-43; 13:26; 38-41).

[126] The resurrection of Jesus was the validation of his claims and showed that Jesus was approved by God as an accredited spokesman (creeds: Acts 2:22-24, 36; 3:13-15; 10:42; 13:32-33; Rom. 1:3-4; 10:9-10; Clement; Ignatius). [127] Early Christian preaching took place in Jerusalem, where Jesus had been crucified shortly before. [128] The church began and grew, [129] with Sunday as the primary day of worship (cf. Pliny; *Barnabas*).

Evaluation of Sources

The Life of Jesus

We have examined a total of 45 ancient sources for the life of Jesus, which include 19 early creedal, four archaeological, 17 non-Christian, and five non-New Testament Christian sources. From this data we have enumerated 129 reported facts concerning the life, person, teachings, death, and resurrection of Jesus, plus the disciples' earliest message. This is not to say that all of these sources are of the same quality (for a variety of reasons). But these facts (and those mentioned below) are spread out across all of the categories and types of writers and are rather evenly balanced.

There can be little doubt that this is a substantial amount of pre- and non-New Testament material for Jesus' existence and for numerous facts about his life. In light of these reports we can better understand how groundless the speculations are that deny his existence or that postulate only a minimal amount of facts concerning him. Much of ancient history is based on many fewer sources that are much later than the events that they record, as we have seen. While some believe that we know almost nothing about Jesus from ancient, non-New Testament sources, this is plainly not the case. Not only are there many such sources, but Jesus is one of the persons of ancient history concerning whom we have a significant amount of quality data. His is one of the most mentioned and most substantiated lives in ancient times.

The Person of Jesus

The deity of Jesus was widely reported in the ancient writings that we investigated. Of our 45 sources, 30 record this teaching, which surprisingly includes seven of the 17 secular sources.

It was pointed out in Chapter 4 that Jesus claimed to be deity, as indicated, for example, by such titles as "Son of God" and "Son of Man."[4] The pre-New Testament creeds (the six Acts texts, along with Rom. 1:3-4, 1 Cor. 11:23ff., 15:3ff., and Phil. 2:6ff., in particular), provide especially strong evidence for the deity of Jesus. This conclusion rests on the authoritative, apostolic sources for the creeds and the incredibly early time period to which they date, right after the conclusion of Jesus' ministry.

These creeds show that the church did not simply teach Jesus' deity a generation later, as is so often repeated in contemporary theology, because this doctrine is definitely present in the earliest preaching. The best explanation for these creeds is that they properly represent Jesus' own teachings, especially since he made similar claims.

---

[4]For a detailed case arguing for Jesus' unique claims concerning his deity and their corroboration, see Miethe and Habermas, chapter 27.

The Teachings of Jesus

There is remarkably little dispute about the teachings of Jesus as found in the list above.[5] That Jesus' central message was the Kingdom of God and the entrance requirements is rarely questioned, even by critics. That this is his chief theme is significant in light of his resurrection, for if Jesus was raised from the dead, confirmation is provided regarding the truthfulness of his most important teaching.[6]

The Death of Jesus

Of all the events in Jesus' life, more ancient sources specifically mention his death than any other single occurrence. Of the 45 ancient sources, 28 relate to this fact, often with details. Twelve of these sources are non-Christian,[7] which exhibits an incredible amount of interest in this event.

Not only is Jesus' death by crucifixion of major concern to these authors, but 14 of the 28 sources give various details about the crucifixion, from medical observations to political information concerning the current rulers, to historical specifications of the times in which Jesus died, to religious details about the reason for his death. These data witness to the facticity of Jesus' death by crucifixion, regarding both the reality of the event itself, as well as numerous details surrounding it. It is fair to assert that this is one of the best-attested facts in ancient history.

After Jesus' death, he was buried. This fact is not only strongly confirmed by five different sources,[8] but is generally a normal consequence of dying.

---

[5]See Norman Anderson, *The Teachings of Jesus* (Downers Grove: Inter-Varsity, 1983).

[6]For details on this message and its centrality, see Habermas, *The Resurrection of Jesus: An Apologetic*, chapters 4-5, Appendix 3, and Habermas and Moreland, chapter 9, for more on the confirmation of this theme.

[7]Of the remaining sources on the death of Jesus, twelve are from creedal texts, including the important traditions in the book of Acts.

[8]These sources include the early creeds in 1 Cor. 15:3ff. and Acts 13:29, as well as hostile sources such as *Toledoth Jesu* and the information implied

The Resurrection of Jesus

At this point in our evaluation we arrive at the crucial issue that brings us face to face with a miracle-claim. Again, it is not our purpose in this volume to make a judgment as to whether the resurrection is an actual miracle, as an act of God, but to evaluate whether it was an actual historical event. An examination of the details provides us with an affirmative answer — the facts demonstrate Jesus' resurrection from the dead according to the canons of history.

Of our 45 sources, 18 specifically record the resurrection, while an additional eleven more provide relevant facts surrounding this occurrence. Even if we were only to use the known facts that are accepted as historical by critical scholars, we still arrive at three major categories of evidence for the resurrection of Jesus.

First, alternative theories that have been hypothesized by critics to explain the resurrection on naturalistic grounds have failed to explain the data and are refuted by the facts. Combinations of these theories also fail on these grounds. This is further illustrated by the refutation of David Hume's thesis concerning miracles (as well as other related approaches), by the nineteenth century liberal critiques of each of these naturalistic theories, and by the twentieth century rejection of them as a whole.[9] Such refutations of critical theories are a major blow to those who would deny this event.

Second, even the accepted historical facts alone provide at least nine historical evidences for the resurrection, as enumerated above.[10] In particular, that this event was reported *early* (probably in the AD 30s) by the very *eyewitnesses* who attested to seeing the risen Christ (especially 1 Cor. 15:3ff. and the Acts creeds) is extremely strong evidence in favor of the literal

---

in the Nazareth decree. The Shroud of Turin is perhaps helpful, even if it did not belong to Jesus, since it evidences post-crucifixion burial.

[9]See chapter 7, pp. 159-165 for more details.

[10]See p. 160 for a list of these evidences that are based on the accepted historical facts.

resurrection.[11] The historical evidence for the empty tomb is also very strong (even from secular sources alone), as are the changed lives of the disciples and the conversions of Paul and James. Therefore, a historical case for this event can be built on both a failure of critical hypotheses on the one hand plus the presence of valid, positive evidences on the other.

Third, even if we were to utilize only the four minimal historical facts that are accepted by virtually all scholars who deal with this issue, we still have a significant basis on which to both refute the naturalistic theories and provide the major evidences for the resurrection. The primary strength of these four facts is that they have been established by critical methodology and thus cannot be rejected by those who have doubts concerning other issues such as Scripture. In other words, the minimum amount of historical facts is sufficient to establish the historicity of Jesus' resurrection. Doubts on other issues do not disturb this basic fact.[12]

If the Shroud of Turin is the burial garment of Jesus, we have another potential category of evidence for the resurrection, in that it would provide some strong scientific, repeatable evidence for this event. There is certainly no proof at this point, and the shroud could still turn out to be a fake, although the data appear to dictate otherwise. It would seem that, even if it did not belong to Jesus, the shroud is at least an actual archaeological artifact, thereby still providing some important information concerning death by crucifixion. The absence of bodily decomposition shows that the body was not in the cloth very long. Further, if the body was not unwrapped and if the image was created by a scorch from a dead body, we have some potential data that could be highly evidential considerations in favor of Jesus' resurrection from the dead.

These three major categories of arguments for the resurrection do not exhaust the ancient evidence for this event,[13]

---

[11]See pp. 152-157 for details.

[12]See chapter 7, pp. 161-167 for details.

[13]For instance, the evidence of the Nazareth Decree (see pp. 176-177) and the assertions of Tacitus and Suetonius that Jesus' teachings broke out

but they do demonstrate this fact as a literal event of history, according to normal historical methodology. This event is the final capstone and fitting conclusion for the unique life, person, teachings, and death of Jesus. In the earliest church, the resurrection served the purpose of confirming Jesus Christ's message and providing the basis for the truth of the Christian message.

The place that the resurrection might play in validating Christian theism today is a fit sequel for just such a study,[14] for the only time that such a resurrection is ever known to have occurred, it happened to the very person who made the most unique claims in the history of religions.

---

again in Palestine *after* his death are other avenues that might be explored. The direct testimonies of Josephus and Phlegon are the most helpful in arguing for this event from non-New Testament sources.

[14]See Habermas, *The Resurrection of Jesus: An Apologetic.*

Part Three
Appendixes

Appendix 1:
Historiography

History is much more than simply memorizing names and dates. Some of its inclusive aspects involve various sorts of theories about the nature of past events, analyzing trends, and the actual process of gathering evidence in order to ascertain what happened. A cognate discipline, philosophy of history, investigates the theoretical underpinnings of the discipline of history itself. In this chapter we will begin with a preliminary notion of history. Then we will provide a critique of those who question the amount of objective knowledge that can be gained from this discipline. Lastly, we will give an overview of the method of historical investigation.[1]

A Concept of History

The term "history" is used variously by different scholars. No uniform definition is agreed upon by everyone, while numerous approaches and interpretations are commonly utilized.[2] It is not our purpose to treat these contemporary

---

[1]For a slightly edited version of the first and third sections of this chapter, see Habermas' chapter "History and Evidence," in Miethe and Habermas, *Why Believe? God Exists!* (Joplin: College Press, 1993), pp. 237-245.

[2]For some of these interpretations, see Patrick Gardiner, "The Philosophy of History" in the *International Encyclopedia of the Social Sciences,*

notions. Still, there is at least some general agreement concerning the concept of history.

Historians generally recognize that their subject includes at least two major factors — the actual events in particular and the recording of these events. So this discipline is chiefly concerned with what has happened and how these events have been annotated and interpreted. This conception comprises the core understanding of history as it will be used in this book. Other elements are certainly involved, but these two major ideas are essential and recur most often, composing the foundation of historiography.

A couple of other factors are relevant to this discussion and should also be mentioned briefly. First, there is always a subjective factor involved whenever history is recorded. To give just one example, the historian must select the material that she will (and will not) present. The historical event itself is objective — generally we speak in terms of it occurring or not occurring. But the recording and interpreting of the event introduces various subjective factors.

For W.H. Walsh, the subjectivity of the writer is certainly present, but it does not keep us from obtaining historical truth. This subjectivity must be allowed for, but its effects can be offset.[3] Our approach towards history ought to be one of caution, since we need to recognize this subjective bias and then make the proper allowances for it.[4]

Perhaps an example of this subjective factor would be helpful. In ancient history, the writings of Tacitus provide a case in point. It is known that this Roman historian was prejudiced in his writing, presenting an "aristocratic bias" and being convicted that moralizing was the "highest function" of history. Other times inaccuracies tarnish his text, as when he credits speeches to people who never gave them or incorrectly

---

ed. by David L. Sills (New York: The Macmillan Company and The Free Press, 1968), vol. 6, pp. 428-433.

[3]W.H. Walsh, *Philosophy of History* (New York: Harper and Brothers, 1960), pp. 101, 103.

[4]William Wand, *Christianity*, pp. 432-433.

reports details in battle accounts. Moses Hadas maintains that the interpretations of Tacitus "must often be challenged" since he "could see only through his own lenses which were strongly colored."[5]

Does this mean that Tacitus must be rejected as a trustworthy source for ancient Roman history? Do these subjective elements found in his writings invalidate the information that he seeks to impart to his readers? As strange as it may seem, Hadas paradoxically states that Tacitus was Rome's greatest historian.[6]

Then he explains:

> One may well ask how trustworthy the resultant history is. A modern historian guilty of such faults would surely lose all credit. . . . With allowance made for rhetorical embellishment customary in his day, and within the limits of distortion which his own views of morality and politics make inevitable, Tacitus never consciously sacrifices historical truth.[7]

Michael Grant illustrates how Tacitus is not an isolated case in ancient times. The Greek Herodotus blended legends and anecdotal material into his histories, while another Roman, Livy, allowed for the operation of omens. Even worse, both Livy and Tacitus are examples of ancient historians who wrote about events that took place long before their time, sometimes as much as five centuries earlier. The results indicate frequent inconsistencies and contradictions in these ancient writings.[8]

But modern historians do not despair about reconstructing ancient times. As Hadas explained, scholars can make allowance not only for the subjective facets involved in the recording and interpretation of events, but even for incorrect data. The reconstructing of ancient history relies on the

---

[5]See Moses Hadas' "Introduction" to *The Complete Works of Tacitus*, pp. IX-XIX.

[6]Ibid., p. IX.

[7]Ibid., XVII-XVIII.

[8]Grant, *Jesus: An Historian's Review*, pp. 183-189.

ability of the scholar to determine the facts of the past in spite of these deterrents.[9]

We employed some of these same principles when we investigated the resurrection of Jesus in the above chapters. Although the events occurred many centuries ago, historical investigation is still capable of ascertaining objective data.

Second, history cannot reach a point where it is positive of its findings in all instances. As with physics, medicine, and other inductive disciplines, there is also a certain amount of dependence on probability in history, as well.[10] Ernest Nagel, for example, concedes that his deterministic view of history opposes the almost unanimous convictions of contemporary physicists. Such scientific conclusions have had an effect on historians, for the accepted scientific view against a deterministic universe has helped to turn historians in the same direction.[11]

Nagel tabulates five primary reasons for the general rejection of historical determinism by so many historians today. First, there are no developmental laws or patterns in history. No principles or precepts exist that would determine certain outcomes in advance of their occurrence. Second, history cannot be predicted, in spite of frequently-repeated ideas to the contrary. Past events or other such data do not determine the future. The third argument concerns the appearance of novel events and configurations of new ideas that recur throughout history.

Fourth, unexpected or chance events outside the ordinary are also a part of history. The fifth argument is the conflicting results that occur when one attempts to apply the concept of a deterministic world to the freedom and moral duty of human beings. Such freedom requires a creative aspect in history arising from human choice.

---

[9]Hadas, "Introduction," pp. XVII-XVIII; cf. Grant, *Jesus: An Historian's Review.*

[10]Wand, *Christianity*, pp. 51-52.

[11]Ernest Nagel, "Determinism in History" in William H. Dray, ed., *Philosophical Analysis and History* (New York: Harper and Row, 1966), p. 355.

Some examples of Nagel's five points might be helpful. Who could have predicted the wide dissemination of views brought about by a novel culture from a war-like community in third century BC Macedonia? Or who could have anticipated the creative civilization that would grow from a barbaric people situated on the banks of the Tiber River that would finally emerge in the first century BC? These and other similar findings have convinced many historians to reject the deterministic view of history. Again, Nagel asserts that the opposition to determinism in modern physics has also been a key factor, exercising a direct influence on most historians.[12]

So historians generally recognize the necessity of couching conclusions in probabilistic terms. Wand points out that we cannot be as sure of historical investigation as some have thought in the past. Our judgments must be made according to which facts are most likely in terms of the historical evidence.[13]

However, we must carefully note a critical detail of special importance. The concept of probability does not preclude our achieving certainty in matters of well-established historical findings. Events that are validated by careful historical research (and especially those established for long periods of time) in the absence of viable contrary findings are proven facts. The best-established historical events are those that are confirmed by careful research into the relevant data, especially when it has repeatedly withstood the eye of critical scrutiny. The possibility of future reevaluation does not preclude present certainty. After all, we cannot hold in abeyance all of history, science, or other inductive areas of study, in the constant fear that something may be challenged!

If additional data do cast doubt on an event, it might be necessary to reopen the investigation. But precluding such contrary material, the fact may be viewed as certain, or as provisional proof. For instance, we need not doubt the death

---

[12]Ibid.

[13]Wand, *Christianity*, pp. 25-27, 51-52, 156.

of Julius Caesar by assassination, Napoleon's defeat at Waterloo, or the election of Abraham Lincoln as the sixteenth president of the United States of America. These facts are well-established at this time and thus proven to be certain.[14]

In this sense, the historian may achieve objective data when he has accurately performed his investigation, applied the appropriate standards of criticism, and determined the outcome according to the canons of reliability. The scholar also needs to be open to additional challenges, entailing further defense and/or adjustment.

It has not been our purpose to deal exhaustively with the concept of history.[15] Yet, a contemporary treatment of the subject ought to include at least these components. We will refer to history as both the occurrence of past events, as well as the recording and interpreting of them. Recognizing the inevitable influence of a subjective element when history is written, allowance must be made for it in order for objective data to be obtained. Realizing also that history deals with probabilities, we need to ascertain as nearly as possible those facts that best fit the data.

As is the case with probabilities and uncertainties, any event is possible. Such is the nature of inductive studies. Therefore, events ought not be ruled out (either scientifically or historically) before they are researched. A thorough investigation of the evidence is required. Events that are firmly established by historical investigation may be regarded as certain, proven by the available data.

---

[14]We are not using "proof" in the sense of apodictic certainty such as that achieved in certain types of mathematics or deductive logic, but in the sense of other sorts of inductive studies. For details, see Gary R. Habermas, "Probability Calculus, Proof and Christian Apologetics," *The Simon Greenleaf Review of Law and Religion*, vol. VIII (1988-1989), pp. 57-88.

[15]For a more complete treatment, see Earle E. Cairns, *God and Man in Time* (Grand Rapids: Baker, 1979), pp. 11-29.

Historical Analysis and Objectivity[16]

But some scholars have downplayed the objective element, preferring to emphasize the more subjective role of the historian. This was especially the case with certain trends from the late nineteenth through the mid-twentieth centuries. W.H. Walsh enumerates some of these subjective factors, dividing them into four categories: the personal preferences of the researcher, group prejudices, differing concepts of historical interpretation, and worldview conflicts.[17] More in agreement with this emphasis, Charles Beard produces similar reasons.[18]

But since the middle of this century, most historians have preferred a synthesis of the objective and subjective outlooks. These scholars both pursue past facts by utilizing the more objective tools of historical research, while still attempting to take seriously the limitations imposed by various sorts of subjective factors. In brief, though various outside influences are admitted, we still have at our disposal significant historical means of researching the past and deciding what occurred.[19]

There are numerous reasons why so many contemporary scholars opt for this synthesis between discovering objective facts in spite of subjective limitations. Personal biases can distort the interpretation of data and thereby affect one's conclusions. However, to hold that these factors cannot be

---

[16]For a more detailed version of the following discussion, see Gary R. Habermas, "Defending the Faith Historically," forthcoming.

[17]W.H. Walsh, "Can History be Objective?" in Hans Meyerhoff, *The Philosophy of History in Our Time* (Garden City: Doubleday, 1959), pp. 216-224.

[18]Charles Beard, "That Noble Dream," in Fritz Stein, ed., *The Varieties of History* (Cleveland: World, 1956), pp. 323-325.

[19]For this historical dialogue, see especially the essays by Carl Becker, Charles Beard, Morton White, Ernest Nagel, and W.H. Walsh in Meyerhoff, *Philosophy of History*, Section II. Compare the selections by Walsh, White, Isaiah Berlin, Christopher Blake, and William Dray in Patrick Gardiner, *Theories of History* (New York: Macmillan, 1959), Part II and the contributions by Walsh and J.A. Passmore in William H. Dray, ed., *Philosophical Analysis and History*.

overcome and are so serious that they must necessarily nullify all historical conclusions is to stumble into a host of errors. Recent historians and philosophers who study this subject have noted numerous problems with relativistic hypotheses, which have accounted for the fact that this outlook has "suffered a decline in status."[20]

1. Self-contradiction

First, and quite devastating to relativistic claims, the statement that all historical knowledge is relative is self-contradictory. Nagel argues that when such a claim is made, at least one objective conclusion is known, so there could well be others.[21] Christopher Blake explains the criticism in slightly different terms: "either Relativism is wrong or, if it is correct, then it is itself only a relative verdict . . . ."[22]

Amazingly, even Charles Beard (frequently recognized as the "foremost spokesman" for historical relativism[23]) fully admits this problem. In fact, it could scarcely be stated in any stronger or more forceful terms than his:

> Contemporary criticism shows that the apostle of relativity is destined to be destroyed by the child of his own brain. If all historical conceptions are merely relative to passing events . . . then the conception of relativity is itself relative. When absolutes in history are rejected the absolutism of relativity is also rejected. . . . the conception of relativity will also pass, as previous conceptions and interpretations of events have passed. . . . the skeptic of relativity will disappear in due course. . . . the apostle of relativity will surely be executed by his own logic.[24]

---

[20]Meyerhoff makes this remark (*Philosophy of History*, p. 119) while discussing the views of Carl Becker and Charles Beard.

[21]Nagel in ibid., p. 214.

[22]Blake in Gardiner, *Theories*, p. 332; cf. pp. 335, 343; David Hackett Fischer, *Historian's Fallacies: Toward a Logic of Historical Thought* (New York: Harper and Row, 1970), pp. 42-43.

[23]This is Meyerhoff's comment (in *Philosophy of History*, p. 138).

[24]Beard in ibid., p. 147.

2. *Logical fallacy*

Second, to assert that subjective biases must nullify or overcome objective procedures is to argue in a non-sequitur manner. Morton White insists that, "The mere fact that historians are biased is no argument against the existence of impersonal standards . . . ." To hold that bias nullifies all historical knowledge is fallacious, just as it would be to declare that a physician's feelings about her patient's sickness prevents her from making a proper diagnosis.[25] Ernest Nagel concurs: "the bare fact that inquiry is selective [is] no valid ground for doubting the objectively warranted character of its conclusions . . . ."[26]

3. *Inconsistency*

Third, another indication of the inadequacy of relativistic approaches to historiography is that these historians fail to carry out the skepticism of their own position, perhaps because there would be no history to write. So, in spite of their relativism, they pursue the writing of the actual occurrences of history. White criticizes Beard's skeptical approach, in that it did not affect Beard's "own scientific work" on "the essence of history."[27] For instance, Beard considered his own work on an economic understanding of the Constitution[28] to be "objective and factual."[29] Meyerhoff also recognizes this problem, stating that "Beard never reached a satisfactory middle ground" between the objective and subjective elements in his own historiography.[30]

---

[25]White in ibid., pp. 194-195. White (p. 199) borrows the analogy of the physician from Sidney Hook.

[26]Nagel in Meyerhoff, *Philosophy of History*, p. 210.

[27]White in Ibid., pp. 200-201.

[28]Charles Beard, *An Economic Interpretation of the Constitution* (New York: Macmillan, 1935).

[29]White in Meyerhoff, *Philosophy of History*, pp. 190-196, 200-201. White goes further in charging Beard with contradicting himself on whether or not history can be done in a neutral manner (pp. 196-197).

[30]Meyerhoff, *Philosophy of History*, p. 138.

4. Correcting subjectivity

Fourth, bias can be allowed for, recognized, and dealt with. Nagel declares: "The very fact that biased thinking may be detected and its sources investigated shows that the case for objective explanations in history is not necessarily hopeless."[31] Historians can avoid the damaging effects of partiality. Even though various prejudices can never be completely uprooted, Walsh reminds us that "every reputable historian acknowledges the need for some sort of objectivity and impartiality in his work" in order to separate facts from propaganda, feelings, and personal preconceptions.[32]

5. Historical Facts

Fifth, the inductive measures that are normally applied in historiography yield knowable conclusions. Even though he reaches a moderate conclusion on the issue, Walsh explains: "Historical conclusions must be backed by evidence just as scientific conclusions must."[33] Beard even agrees here: "The historian . . . . sees the doctrine of relativity crumble in the cold light of historical knowledge."[34]

Perhaps surprisingly, historians who are often categorized as relativists actually agree on the ability to obtain past knowledge.[35] Karl Mannheim, identified by Gardiner as "[p]erhaps

---

[31]Nagel in ibid., p. 213.

[32]Walsh, *Philosophy*, p. 19; cf. other comments by Walsh in Meyerhoff, *Philosophy of History*, pp. 217, 222, 224; in Dray, *Philosophical Analysis*, pp. 60-61, 74; in Gardiner, *Theories*, pp. 60-61, 74.

[33]Walsh in Gardiner, *Theories*, p. 301. Most historians agree with this point. See D. Fischer, *Fallacies*, pp. 42-43; Passmore in Dray, *Philosophical Analysis*, pp. 79-80, 88; Berlin in Gardiner, *Theories*, pp. 324-329; Blake in Gardiner, *Theories*, pp. 331-332, 339; White in Gardiner, *Theories*, p. 365.

[34]Beard in Meyerhoff, *Philosophy of History*, p. 148.

[35]For some impressive passages in those who are often identified as the best known relativists, see Wilhelm Dilthey (in Gardiner, *Theories*, p. 224), Benedetto Croce (in Gardiner, *Theories*, p. 228 and in Meyerhoff, *Philosophy of History*, p. 47), Robin Collingwood (in *Essays in the Philosophy of History*, ed. by William Debbins [New York: McGraw-Hill Book Company, 1965], pp. 102-103 and in Meyerhoff, *Philosophy of History*, pp. 79-84), Beard (in *An Economic Interpretation of the Constitution*, and in Meyerhoff, *Philosophy of*

the most forthright proponent of historical relativism in recent times,"[36] agrees that the presence of subjective concerns "does not imply renunciation of the postulate of objectivity and the possibility of arriving at decisions in factual disputes."[37] Supporting a case for objective facts, Blake comments that there is a large amount of historical research that is accepted by the entire historical community.[38]

For reasons such as these, we may conclude that attempts to treat historiography in a relativistic manner are confronted by numerous problems, including more than we have presented here,[39] and have failed. Granted, there are undoubtedly subjective factors that often influence the historian's work. This is not doubted by those who defend the objectivity of historical inquiry.[40] But objectivity is also possible in the

---

History, pp. 141, 149), and Carl Becker (in Meyerhoff, *Philosophy of History*, pp. 122-128, 134, 136; cf. Carl L. Becker, *The Heavenly City of the Eighteenth-Century Philosophers* [New Haven: Yale Univ. Press, 1932; reprint 1969], chapters I-II). It is important to note that it is precisely for this reason that the label "relativists" is a misnomer for these idealistic historians.

[36]Gardiner, *Theories*, p. 269.

[37]See Karl Mannheim in Gardiner, *Theories*, pp. 244, 247.

[38]Blake in Gardiner, *Theories*, p. 331.

[39]Examples of these critiques are not hard to locate in the relevant literature. In an insightful comment, Fischer thinks that relativists confuse knowledge itself with the *means* by which knowledge is acquired. (See Fischer, *Fallacies*, pp. 44-45.) White adds that this is "a confusion which is typical in the philosophy of history, the confusion between the psychology of historical interpretation and its logic." (See White in Meyerhoff, *Philosophy of History*, p. 199.) Another problem is that while relativists recognize both the existence and necessity of objectively-known facts, these are still under-emphasized due to the role of interpretation. (For a helpful comparison on this subject, contrast Collingwood's distinction [in Gardiner, *Theories*, pp. 251-258] between the "outside" and the "inside" of an event.) Isaiah Berlin levels still another charge: terms like "subjective" and "relative" either "need correlatives, or else they turn out to be without meaning themselves." In brief, what is the standard to be used in comparison (Berlin in Gardiner, *Theories*, pp. 324, 328)? Blake agrees with Berlin, complaining that there is otherwise "no alternative recognisable [sic] sense" of meaning for the subjective vocabulary (Blake in Gardiner, *Theories*, p. 335).

[40]As Nagel clearly admits (in Meyerhoff, *Philosophy of History*, p. 215).

sense defined above, the result of an accurate investigation of data, followed by an application of the appropriate standards of criticism, including entertaining alternative theses, all within the standards of probability. Any additional challenges need to be answered, entailing further defense and/or adjustment.

Historical Research and Investigation

How does one actually **do** the work of the historian? How is such research to be conducted?

The occurrence of past events can usually be discovered (within a certain probability) by a careful investigation of the facts. These former events are only accessible by a study of the available historical evidence. Although the historian usually did not personally participate in what he is studying (assuming he wasn't originally there), he can inspect the relevant data such as the eyewitnesses, written documents, and various other records, structures, and archaeological finds. Upon such confirmation the historian must build his case. Such tools comprise the working principles of historical research.[41]

Of course, what the existing data reveal is not automatically accepted as true, especially if there are conflicts in the testimony. The historian has the job of critically investigating the available sources in order to ascertain as closely as possible their accuracy. Results can be obtained by determining which conclusions best fit the evidence. The historian builds on such groundwork.[42] We therefore decide on the evidence at hand — choosing the most probable conclusion.

---

[41]Walsh, *Philosophy*, p. 18. Some illuminating examples of historical investigations of the past are supplied by Delbrück's methods of determining how ancient battles were fought in the times of the Greek and Roman empires. By examining the historical data, Delbrück successfully obtained information such as the size of the opposing armies, how they actually maneuvered, and other facets of specific battles in ancient times. For instance, see Edward M. Earle, ed., *Makers of Modern Strategy* (Princeton: Princeton Univ. Press, 1943), especially pp. 264-268 for Delbrück's historical techniques.

[42]Walsh, *Philosophy*, pp. 18-19.

Historical data must be available if the historian is to investigate the past in such a manner. These sources are often divided into two types: primary and secondary. Primary sources "are underived, firsthand, or contemporary with the event," and are much more crucial.[43] They may consist of eyewitness testimony given in various forms.

Secondary material witnesses to primary sources, directed to past persons and events. These may take the form of works like textbooks, monographs, edited volumes, and syllabi. As such, they help elucidate and expand the previously existing materials.

Primary sources consist of both literary and non-literary remains. The former include written documents, either official or unofficial. Pliny the Younger's famous correspondence, penned while he was a Roman governor in Asia Minor during the early second century AD, is an example of writings composed by a state official or representative. An unofficial primary document would include informal works of a firsthand nature, such as books, newspapers, journals, or periodicals. Julius Caesar's accounts of his battles in Gaul, written before his rule in first century BC Rome, is an example.

Documents written by eyewitnesses or that reflect their influence are, of course, extremely important in historical study, whenever they are available. Examples of such eyewitness sources are provided by American interest in the 1950s and 60s in published interviews with still-living Civil War veterans.[44] Literary remains in the form of inscriptions on stone, metal, or other materials (termed epigraphy) are also available in some cases.

Primary non-literary remains include material such as recordings obtained directly from eyewitness interviews, oral tradition, photographs, and archaeological artifacts.

---

[43]Cairns, *God and Man*, p. 34. For further details regarding our following discussion, compare also pp. 33-42, although we will diverge at certain points.

[44]See Otto Eisenschiml and Ralph Newman, *Eyewitness: The Civil War as We Lived It* (New York: Grosset and Dunlap, 1956).

Eyewitness testimony using recorded interviews obviously cannot extend much over 100 years, at the most. Tradition, whether oral or written, sometimes reaches back into antiquity, with sources such as reports, legends, heroic stories, and ballads. Reliable traditions grounded in eyewitness testimony would be an important source. On the other hand, Americans are acquainted with George Washington and the cherry tree or the exploits of Davy Crockett. The weakness with this sort of tradition is that it must be trustworthy and not simply hearsay or storytelling.

Archaeological artifacts can be quite valuable as witnesses to our past. Remains like architecture, monuments, grave sites, burial chambers, furniture, artwork, clothes, coins, tools, or other implements can often help determine both historical backgrounds and events. For example, Jewish burial chambers have actually revealed very specific data concerning burial customs, human physical characteristics, and varieties of death inflicted by enemies. Excavations of Qumran near the Dead Sea have uncovered not only the scrolls themselves, but also numerous facts from about the time of Jesus regarding the ascetic and communal lifestyle of the sectarian Essenes. Uncovering Greek cities such as Athens, Corinth, and Ephesus have provided invaluable evidence concerning the art, religious beliefs, and lifestyle of these ancient cultures.

The gathering of the primary and secondary sources does not complete the study; neither does the historian automatically conclude that such a collection of data is synonymous with the facts themselves. Rather, these sources must be organized and subjected to criticism before conclusions can be drawn.[45] In the case of written documents, for example, both external and internal historical criticism is implemented.

External criticism is applied for the purpose of checking the writing itself and is divided into two parts. Higher criticism assesses the authenticity of the document regarding elements such as its background, authorship, date of writing,

---

[45]For details of Cairns' treatment, see *God and Man*, chapter 2.

place of composition, the audience, and reason for writing. Further, is the text reliable? Does it bear signs of corresponding to fact? Lower criticism concerns the question of whether we essentially have the text as it was originally composed. It involves questions of manuscript evidence: the dates of existing copies, their comparison to the original, and the presence of any documentary interpolations or omissions.

Internal factors are also helpful in assessing a document's reliability. They include the competence and character of the author, as well as his ability to separate facts from feeling, opinion, or other subjective distortion.

If the sources are unwritten, criticism could take such forms as the use of dating methods, other scientific testing procedures such as chemical analysis, and comparisons to relevant written accounts. The testing of eyewitness interviews and oral tradition would follow lines of criticism closer to those used for documentary sources, complete with external and internal phases, including authorship, the date of the testimony, its credibility, and whether it has been modified by time or circumstances.

After the historian gathers his materials, organizes them, and applies external and internal criticism, he is ready to prepare and formulate his conclusions. The results should conform to all the known data and provide the most comprehensive and probable judgment on the issues. The outcome is then open to careful scrutiny from other scholars, which should prompt the cautious historian to be able to defend the results, based on the factual data available.

Summary and Conclusion

We began by maintaining that a concept of history includes at least the events themselves and the records of these occurrences. Additionally, there is always a subjective element in reporting the past and conclusions from this discipline must be couched in probabilistic terms. But when proper procedures are followed, the objective data of history can be uncovered within these parameters. Those who have argued against the historian's ability to uncover objective facts are opposed by numerous difficulties.

We also outlined how the historian's methods and tools, especially the use of primary sources, are still able to achieve accurate knowledge of the past. Most historians agree with this conclusion. Cairns summarizes as follows:

> Through scientific study of his artifacts and documents, the historian can be reasonably certain concerning an event . . . . There is a surprising amount of consensus among historians on the basic facts and on many conclusions about the past.[46]

It is within these parameters that we have sought in this volume to address the historicity of Jesus. We have especially endeavored to ascertain the facts surrounding his death and resurrection.

---

[46]Ibid., p. 97.

Appendix 2:
An Apologetic Outline

Throughout this volume, our presentation has been topical and directed either to specific critical challenges or to historical issues in the life of Jesus, rather than to a systematic overview of apologetics. In this appendix, our major purpose is to organize our answers, both to those who, in Part I, have attempted to explain away the unique elements in the life of Jesus, as well as to include the historical material from Part II. This will hopefully assist the reader in gaining a more systematic sense of the issues discussed in this book.

The material in this chapter will be organized according to topical, outline form for easier reference and will be divided into three major categories: the New Testament, Jesus, and miracle-claims. We will not be concerned here with the original challenges themselves, but only with the positive responses that were made to each one. In this way, the chapter will be a tighter unit and will not be disjointed as were our earlier discussions. Accordingly, comparatively few endnotes will be utilized. Instead, reference will be made back to the portion where the discussion originally occurred so that those sources can be checked.

A. The Trustworthiness of the New Testament

The condition of the New Testament was a recurring theme in Part I, where it was necessary to answer certain charges, especially against the reliability of the Gospels. So even though our evidence for the life, death, and resurrection of Jesus has been almost entirely gleaned from pre- and non-New Testament sources, we still made several responses to those who questioned the canonical Christian documents.

1. The New Testament has better manuscript evidence than any other ancient book (pp. 54-56).
   a. There are over 5,000 New Testament manuscripts and portions of manuscripts. By comparison, the majority of classical works have less than 20 manuscripts.
   b. The dates of the New Testament manuscripts are close to the original writings. One Gospel fragment (Ryland's) dates from about 25 years after the Gospel of John and most of the New Testament (Chester Beatty and Bodmer Papyri) from 50–150 years after the originals. Most classical works date from 700–1400 years after the originals.
   c. None of the canonical New Testament is lost or missing.[1] By comparison, 107 of Livy's 142 books of history have been lost and about one half of Tacitus' 30 books of *Annals* and *Histories* is missing.
2. Good arguments can be given that each of the Gospels was either written by an eyewitness, or significantly influenced by firsthand testimony, as recognized by many contemporary scholars (p. 107).
   a. The apostle Matthew is often taken to be either the author or the major source behind the first Gospel.
   b. It is often recognized that Peter is the major apostolic influence for Mark's Gospel.

---

[1] It needs to be carefully noticed that we are distinguishing here between those documents that compose the canonical New Testament writings, rather than answering questions about whether there are other books (such as certain Pauline letters, for example) that we no longer have. In other words, in this volume we are speaking about having a complete set of those writings that have been judged to be canonical, not speculating concerning whether others should have (or would have) been included.

    c. That Luke is the author of the third Gospel and Acts is well supported by the data, including both his reliance on eyewitness sources (Luke 1:1-4), and his companionship with Paul.

    d. There is a wealth of evidence that the fourth Gospel was either written by or crucially influenced by the eyewitness testimony of John.

3. Even without proving eyewitness authorship, the Gospels measure up well by normal historical standards used in ancient historiography. They are very close to the events that they record, with three out of four being dated within one generation and all four within seventy years of Jesus' life, all during the lives of eyewitnesses (pp. 106-108).

4. The Gospels are trustworthy sources, as explained by A.M. Hunter (p. 108).

    a. These Christian authors, like their Jewish counterparts, were careful to preserve traditional material.

    b. The Gospels are close to eyewitness sources.

    c. The Gospel authors were honest reporters.

    d. The picture of Jesus presented in the four Gospels is virtually the same.[2]

5. The Gospels and Acts exhibit a specific interest in reporting historical facts, not mythology. This is especially the case when the life of Jesus is reported (pp. 52-54).[3]

6. Contemporary historians frequently oppose the application of radical criticism to New Testament studies. According to A.N. Sherwin-White and Michael Grant, such attacks fail at a number of crucial points (pp. 52-54).[4]

---

[2]See Archibald M. Hunter, *Bible and Gospel*, pp. 32-37.

[3]Although the case cannot rest on self-claims alone, it is helpful to note the numerous times the New Testament insists that it is reporting eyewitness data. For a few examples, see Luke 1:1-4; John 1:14; Acts 2:22-38; 17:30-31; 1 Cor. 15:1-20; Heb. 2:3-4; 2 Pet. 1:16-18; 1 John 1:1-3.

[4]See A.N. Sherwin-White, *Roman Society*, pp. 186-193; Grant, *Jesus: An Historian's Review*, pp. 179-184, 199-201.

    a. Numerous ancient works exhibit intentions and methodologies similar to that of the New Testament authors, and yet these ancient works are well accredited as historical works.

    b. There are no ancient writings in the category that radical critics place the Gospels.

    c. The Gospels are much closer to the events that they describe than numerous events recorded in ancient histories, which sometimes occurred hundreds of years before the earliest sources.

    d. Some ancient histories strongly disagree with each other, yet much history is ascertained from them.

    e. Radical critics often ignore the cause for the earliest apostles' experiences, while historians attempt to ascertain what lies behind these episodes.

    f. New Testament books such as Acts have been largely confirmed by external tests of historicity.

    g. Even if form criticism is applied to the Gospels, this does not preclude the ascertaining of much historical material that is contained in them.

7. Older studies that attempt to discern numerous Hellenistic influences on the New Testament authors are somewhat outdated, with much attention at present being focused on the Jewish background of these books (p. 56).

8. Older attempts to late-date the Gospels, often into the second century AD, are no longer well-accepted by critical scholars. Such efforts would be convenient for some of the critics, but are disproven by the facts (pp. 35-36; 42-43).

9. The Gospels and Acts were recognized as inspired books almost immediately after being written (pp. 110-113).[5]

    a. 1 Tim. 5:18 quotes Luke 10:7 and refers to it as "Scripture."

---

[5]For the references in 9:b-f, and item 10 below, see J.B. Lightfoot, *The Apostolic Fathers*.

b. Clement of Rome (about AD 95) speaks of the "Gospel" and quotes portions found in all three synoptic Gospels, referring to them as the words of Jesus (Corinthians 13, 46).

c. Ignatius (Smyrnaeans 3) and Polycarp (Philippians 2, 7), both writing about AD 115, refer to verses in the synoptic Gospels as the words of Christ.

d. The Didache (8, 15-16; ca. late first or early second century) refers to the "Gospels" twice and quotes portions found in all three synoptic Gospels each time.

e. Barnabas (ca. AD 135) refers to the text of Matthew 22:14 as "Scripture" (4) and quotes a portion found in all three synoptics as the apostles' "Gospel" (5).

f. Papias' fragments (Exposition of Oracles of the Lord; ca. AD 140 or even earlier) assert that Matthew wrote one of the Gospels, while Mark wrote another Gospel, based on the eyewitness testimony of the apostle Peter (III). Two other fragments (XIX, XX) testify that the apostle John dictated his Gospel to Papias himself. (Luke was not questioned by Papias, but any mention of the third Gospel is simply missing from his work).

10. Paul's epistles were also recognized as inspired Scripture almost immediately after being written (p. 113).

a. 2 Peter 3:15-16 calls Paul's epistles "Scripture."

b. Clement of Rome (Corinthians 47), Ignatius (Ephesians 10; To Polycarp 5), and Polycarp (Philippians 1, 3-4, 6) all refer to Paul's writings as inspired.

B. The Historicity of Jesus

1. The trustworthy Gospels (A above) exhibit much interest in the historical Jesus and give accurate accounts of his life, death, and resurrection (p. 37).

2. Numerous pre- and extrabiblical sources record much ancient testimony concerning Jesus within 125 years after his death (Part II).

a. Early Christian creeds that pre-date the New Testament, as well as the historical facts that virtually all critical scholars admit, provide an extremely strong case for the death and resurrection of Jesus (Chapter 7).

b. Archaeology contributes a few finds that illuminate and provide background for Jesus' career (Chapter 8).

c. Secular historians, government officials, religious works, and other sources report many details about Jesus from non-Christian viewpoints (Chapter 9).

d. Ancient Christian sources preserve a number of historical statements about Jesus (Chapter 10).

3. In spite of the excellent pre- and extrabiblical evidence for the historicity of Jesus, there are also good reasons why there are not even more such sources (p. 66).

4. To reject Jesus' miracles *a priori* is to ignore correct inductive procedure where all facts are investigated before a decision is made (pp. 50-51; 58-59).

5. To reject Jesus' doctrinal teachings *a priori* as valid for today is to pick and choose portions of the Gospels. Further, if Jesus was raised from the dead, there is, at a minimum, some implied significance for Jesus' teachings, as well (p. 64).

6. Without a significant historical basis in the life of Jesus, Christianity would have had no impetus for its origins (pp. 49-50).

7. The ancient mystery religions cannot account for early Christianity (pp. 33-35):

a. The *early* testimony of creeds such as 1 Corinthians 15:3ff., Luke 24:34, and those in the book of Acts reveal that the crucial facts of the Gospel were reported directly after the historical events themselves.

b. More importantly, the *eyewitness* testimony of 1 Corinthians 15:3ff. and other texts links the Gospel testimony to the original persons involved, rather than any legendary stories.

    c. There is no clear and early evidence for a resurrection occurring in a mystery religion before the late second century AD.

    d. There are numerous differences between Jesus and the mystery religions.

    e. The mystery religions had very little influence in Palestine.

    f. The trustworthy Gospels give an historically accurate portrayal of Jesus.

8. Jesus died on the cross, as indicated by several facts (pp. 72-75).

    a. David Strauss' famous critique showed that the swoon theory was self-contradictory. Even if this hypothesis were true, it still would not account for the disciples' conviction that they had actually seen the risen Jesus.[6]

    b. The nature of crucifixion, including the discovery of Yohanan's skeleton, reveals both the nature and assurance of death by this method.

    c. The explanation for Jesus' heart wound indicates that it would have killed him even if he had still been alive.

    d. The death of Jesus is the most recorded event in ancient, non-Christian history (Chapter 9).

    e. The trustworthy Gospels give accurate accounts of Jesus' death.

9. After his death, Jesus was raised bodily and appeared to his followers (pp. 159-161).

    a. Naturalistic hypotheses that have sought to explain in normal terms the supernatural element of Jesus' resurrection have failed to do so, chiefly because they are refuted by the known historical data. Several other reasons also indicate this failure.

    b. There are numerous positive evidences for the resurrection that indicate that Jesus rose from the

---

[6]Strauss, *A New Life of Jesus*, pp. 408-412.

dead and appeared to many of those who followed him.

   c. A case for the resurrection can be built by using only those mimimal facts that are clearly established by the historical method. On a smaller scale, these facts can refute the alternative hypotheses and provide the best evidences for the resurrection.

   d. The Shroud of Turin may supply some additional scientific evidence for Jesus' resurrection (p. 254).

10. There are numerous differences between both Jesus' teachings and those of the Qumran community, and between Jesus and the Essene Teacher of Righteousness, in particular (see pp. 78-80 for lists). More important, linking Jesus to the Qumran community would not necessarily be detrimental to Christianity at all (pp. 80-81).

11. Jesus' message was not changed by Paul or by other followers (pp. 81-88).

   a. In both the synoptics, as well as in John, Jesus claimed to be deity. Often this was done by his words, such as his claims to be Son of God and Son of Man.[7] At other times he showed his deity by his actions, such as forgiving sin, fulfilling Old Testament messianic prophecy and by claiming authority much greater than that of the Jewish leaders.[8]

   b. Numerous pre-Pauline creeds such as Philippians 2:6-11, Romans 1:3-4, 1 Corinthians 11:23ff., and many from the book of Acts designate Jesus by the loftiest titles, thereby indicating the early teaching of his deity. These show further that this doctrine definitely did not originate with Paul.

---

[7]Examples include Mark 2:10-11; 10:45; 13:32; 14:36; 14:61-63; Matt. 11:27.

[8]See Mark 2:1-12; Matt. 5:20-48; cf. Isa. 9:6-7; 53; Dan. 9:24-27.

   c. Paul also taught the deity of Jesus,[9] so there is no conflict with the Gospels.

   d. Neither Jesus nor Paul taught that Christianity was a new religion. Both held that Christianity was a fulfillment of Judaism.[10]

   e. Jesus' central teaching of the Kingdom of God and its entrance requirements of faith in his person and teachings is found in all four Gospels[11] and in Paul's epistles.[12]

   f. Paul was known as the apostle to the Gentiles.[13] Not only did Jesus command his disciples to take the gospel to the Gentiles,[14] but this was actually a fulfillment of Old Testament prophecy, not a new doctrine.[15]

   g. The fact that Paul's message was checked and approved by the original apostles (Gal. 2:1-10) reveals that he was not teaching a message contrary to Jesus'. Such official apostolic recognition was not only given to Paul's original message but also to his epistles, which were written later and immediately recognized as Scripture (2 Pet. 3:15-16; see Clement of Rome, Ignatius, and Polycarp in A,10 above).

   h. Such an approach to the New Testament usually involves picking and choosing certain texts while ignoring others.

   i. Since Jesus literally rose from the dead, any verification of the truthfulness of his teachings would

---

[9]For instance, see Rom. 1:3-4; 9:5; 10:9-10; Phil. 2:6-11; Col. 1:19; 2:9; Titus 2:13.

[10]Matt. 5:18; Luke 16:16-17; Rom. 10:4, 9-11; Col. 2:16-17, for examples.

[11]Cf. Mark 1:14-15; Matt. 18:3-6; 25:31-46; Luke 18:28-30; 24:45-48; John 1:10-13; 6:47; 20:30-31.

[12]Cf. Rom. 6:23; 10:9-10; 1 Cor. 15:1-4.

[13]Acts 9:15-16; 22:21; Rom. 11:13-14; Gal. 2:9.

[14]Matt. 28:19-20; Luke 24:47; John 10:16; Acts 1:8.

[15]See Gen. 12:3; Isa. 19:18-25 for two examples.

even extend to Paul's message and writings, since they are in agreement with the Gospels at these points.

12. Jesus was not an international traveler during his "silent years" or after his death (pp. 89-98).

    a. There is no viable historical evidence for such international ventures.

    b. The swoon theory fails and is rejected by critical scholars (see B,8 above).

    c. These endeavors almost always involve a long trail of illogic and incredibly mysterious connections.

    d. The trustworthiness of the Gospels refute these theses.

C. Miracle-claims

1. No event can be rejected *a priori* unless one assumes an omniscient viewpoint. Since this is impossible, the facts must be examined (pp. 58-59).

2. The laws of nature do not disallow any events, but are simply descriptions of how things usually occur. Hume was incorrect in endeavoring to utilize man's experience of these laws against the existence of miracles (p. 58).

3. Twentieth century science has changed, and while it certainly does not prove miracles, neither does it disallow them (p. 59).

4. There are several reasons why those who deny or question the objectivity of historical knowledge are mistaken (Appendix One).

5. Correct inductive research methodology demands a systematic investigation of all relevant data before a decision is made. Such a process is observed in fields as diverse as science, medicine, law, and journalism, as well as history. In a similar way, miracle claims must also be checked out before a philosophical or historical judgment is made (pp. 60-61).

6. Although many would place miracle-claims completely in the realm of faith, such is to ignore their possibly objective theistic and historical nature (p. 61).

a. If it is taught that miraculous events have occurred in history, as is the case with New Testament miracle-claims, then at least the objective, historical side of such a claim can be investigated. In other words, if it actually happened, at least the portion of the event that touched the space-time world can potentially be examined.

b. In the New Testament, the resurrection of Jesus is not only the central tenet of Christianity, but it is asserted that if Jesus did not rise from the dead, then faith is actually in vain (1 Cor. 15:1-20, especially vv. 14, 17). Paul even supports his point that Jesus was raised by citing eyewitnesses, historical testimony to this fact (vv. 5-8). Under these circumstances, one could hardly claim that objective, factual interests in the resurrection are foreign to the New Testament.[16]

c. This objection also commits errors that are associated with the "leap of faith." If carried to its logical conclusion, it provides no objective basis for faith, including any reasons why faith should be exercised in any certain beliefs, or even that faith should be exercised at all. As such, it is difficult to distinguish between belief and credulity.

7. Alternative theories that have been proposed to account for Jesus' resurrection on naturalistic grounds have failed to account for the known historical facts (pp. 62-63).

8. There are many strong historical reasons to believe that Jesus was raised from the dead (p. 160).

---

[16]As we saw, even Bultmann asserts that Paul was attempting to produce objective evidence for the resurrection in this passage, even though Bultmann disapproved of such a procedure (Bultmann, *Theology of the New Testament*, vol. I, pp. 82, 295).

Conclusion

We will not belabor the chief conclusion in this appendix, namely, that attempts to debunk the historicity of Jesus in whole or in part have failed for numerous reasons, such as those outlined above. Usually such attempts ignore a myriad of evidence that serve to disprove these alternate hypotheses. Perhaps this is why most critical scholars also shun such theses.

Evidence such as that pointed out in this chapter does reveal the negative conclusion concerning the failure of these misconceptions about Christianity. It also establishes some of the positive evidence in favor of the trustworthiness of Scripture, the historicity of Jesus, and the nature of miracle-claims. Such evidence is quite formidable.

Appendix 3:
A Selected Scholarly Bibliography for Non-Christian Sources

(Each source, including primary documents, is listed in alphabetical order.)

A. Tacitus

Barnes, Timothy D. "Legislation Against the Christians." *Journal of Roman Studies* 58 (1968), 32-50.

Boissier, Gaston, *Tacite*. Paris: Hachette, etc., 1903.

Hadas, Moses. Editor. *The Complete Works of Tacitus*. Transl. by Alfred J. Church and William J. Brodribb. New York: Random House, 1942.

Mendell, Clarence W. *Tacitus, the Man and His Work*. New Haven: Yale Univ. Press, 1957.

Sherwin-White, A.N. "The Early Persecutions and Roman Law Again." *Journal of Theological Studies* 3 (1952), 199-213.

de Ste. Croix, G.E.M. "The Persecutions: Christianity's Encounter with the Roman Imperial Government." *The Crucible of Christianity*. Ed. by Arnold Toynbee. New York: World, 1969.

Syme, Sir Ronald. *Tacitus*. 2 vols. Oxford: Clarendon, 1958.

B. Suetonius

Janne, H. "Impulsore Chresto." *Mélanges Bidez: Annuaire de l'Institute de Philologie et d'Histoire Orientales*. II (1934), 531-553.

Ramsay, Sir William. *The Church in the Roman Empire.* New York: Putnam's 1893.

Safrai, S. and M. Stern. Editors. T*he Jewish People of the First Century.* Vol. 1. Philadelphia: Fortress, 1974.

Scramuzza, Vincent. *The Emperor Claudius.* Harvard Historical Studies, 44. Cambridge: Harvard Univ. Press, 1974.

Suetonius, Gaius. *The Twelve Caesars.* Transl. by Robert Graves. Baltimore: Penguin, 1957.

Wiefel, W. "The Jewish Community in Ancient Rome and the Origins of Roman Christianity." *The Romans Debate.* Ed. by K.P. Dornfried. Minneapolis: Augsburg, 1977.

C. Josephus

Bentwich, Norman. *Josephus.* Philadelphia: Jewish Publication Society, 1914.

Bienert, Walther. *Der alteste nichtchristliche Jesusbericht: Josephus über Jesus.* Halle: Akademischer Verlag, 1936.

Bruce, F.F. *Jesus and Christian Origins Outside the New Testament.* Grand Rapids: Eerdmans, 1974.

Goldstein, Morris. *Jesus in the Jewish Tradition.* New York: Macmillan Press, 1950.

Josephus, Flavius. *The Works of Flavius Josephus.* Transl. by William Whiston. Grand Rapids: Kregel, 1974.

Klausner, Joseph. *Jesus of Nazareth.* London: Collier-Macmillan, 1929.

Lacqueur, Richard. *Der jüdische Historiker Flavius Josephus.* Damstadt: Wissenschaftliche Buchgessellschaft, 1970.

Montefiore, H.W. *Josephus and the New Testament.* London: Mowbrays, 1962.

von Schlatter, Adolf. *Die Theologie des Judentums nach dem Bericht des Josephus.* Gutersloh: C. Bertelsmann, 1932.

Shutt, R.J.H. *Studies in Josephus.* London: SPCK, 1961.

Williamson, Geoffrey A. *The World of Josephus.* Boston: Little, Brown and Company, 1964.

D. Thallus

Bruce, F.F. *The New Testament Documents: Are They Reliable?* Grand Rapids: Eerdmans, 1960.

Quasten, Johannes. *Patrology*. 3 vols. Utrecht-Antwerp: Spectrum, 1953, II: 137-138.

E. Pliny the Younger and Emperor Trajan
Pliny the Younger. *Pliny: Letters*. Transl. by William Melmoth. 2 vols. Cambridge: Harvard Univ. Press, 1935.
Sherwin-White, A.N. *The Letters of Pliny: A Historical and Social Commentary*. Oxford: Clarendon, 1966.
————. "Why Were the Early Christians Persecuted? An Amendment." *Past and Present* 27 (1964), 23-27.
Vindman, L. *Étude sur la correspondance de Pline le Jeune avec Trajan*. Praha: Rozpravy Cheskoslovenské Akademie Ved, 70 (1960), 87-106.

F. Emperor Hadrian
Eusebius Pamphilus. *Ecclesiastical History*. Transl. by Christian F. Cruse. Grand Rapids: Baker, 1955.

G. Talmud
Epstein, I. Translator. *The Babylonian Talmud*. London: Soncino, 1935.
Goldstein, Morris. *Jesus in the Jewish Tradition*. New York: Macmillan, 1950.
Hereford, R.T. *Christianity in Talmud and Midrash*. London: Williams and Norgate, 1903.
Jocz, Jacob. *The Jewish People and Jesus Christ*. London: SPCK, 1954.
Pranaitus, Iustin B. *The Talmud Unmasked: The Secret Rabbinical Teachings Concerning Christians*. New York: E.N. Sanctuary, 1939.
Schechter, Soloman. *Studies in Judaism*. Philadelphia: Jewish Publication Society, 1908, 1924.
Strack, Hermann L. *Einleitung in Talmud und Midrasch*. München: Beck, 1921.
Wright, Dudley. *The Talmud*. London: Williams and Norgate, 1932.

H. Toledoth Jesu
Klausner, Joseph. *Jesus of Nazareth*. London: Collier-Macmillan, 1929.

Maier, Paul L. *First Easter*. New York: Harper and Row, 1973.

I. Lucian of Samosata

Aerts, F. *Pereginus Proteus, een Kynieker uit de Ze eeuw na Kristus*. Dissertation: Löwen, 1931-1932.

Bagnani, G. "Pereginus Proteus and the Christians." *Historia* 4 (1955), 107-112.

Betz, E. "Lukian von Samosata und das Christentum." *Novum Testamentum* 3 (1959), 226-237.

——————. *Lukian von Samosata und das Neue Testament, religionsgeschichtliche und paränetische Parallelen*. Berlin: Akademie-Verlag, 1961, 124-130.

Bompaire, Jacques. *Lucien écrivain; imitation et création*. Paris: E. de Boccard, 1958.

Caster, Marcel. *Lucien et la pensée religieuse de son temps*. Paris: Societé d'edition "Les Belles lettres," 1937.

Labriolle, P. De. "Lucien et les Chrétiens." *Les Humanitées* 4 (1929), 148-153.

Lane, William L. "Unexpected Light on Hebrews 13:1-6 from a Second Century Source." *Perspectives in Religious Studies* 9 (1982), 267-274.

Lucian of Samosata. *The Works of Lucian of Samosata*. Transl. by H.W. Fowler and F.G. Fowler. 4 vols. Oxford: Clarendon, 1905.

Schwartz, Jacques. *Biographie de Lucien de Samosate*. Bruxelles: Latomus, 1965.

Zeller, E. "Alexander und Peregrinus, ein Betrüger und ein Schwärmer." *Vortrage und Abhandlungen* 2 (1877), 154-188.

J. Mara Bar-Serapion

Bruce, F.F. *Jesus and Christian Origins Outside the New Testament*. Grand Rapids: Eerdmans, 1974.

K. Gnostic Sources (in general)

Baur, Walter. *Orthodoxy and Heresy in Earliest Christianity*. Ed. by Robert Kraft and Gerhard Krodel. Philadelphia: Fortress, 1971.

Evans, Craig. "Jesus and Gnostic Literature." *Biblica* 62 (1981), 406-412.

Grant, Robert M. *Gnosticism and Early Christianity*. Revised edition. New York: Harper and Row, 1966.

Jonas, Hans. *The Gnostic Religion*. Boston: Beacon, 1963.

Robinson, James M. Editor. *The Nag Hammadi Library*. New York: Harper and Row, 1981.

L. Gospel of Truth

Arai, S. *Die Christologie des Evangelium Veritatis*. Leiden: E.J. Brill, 1964.

Grobel, Kendrick. *The Gospel of Truth*. London: Black, 1960.

Malinine, Michel, H.C. Peuch, and G. Quispel, *Evangelium Veritatis*. Zürich: Rascher, 1956.

Ringgren, Helmer. "The Gospel of Truth and Valentinian Gnosticism." *Studia Theologica* 18 (1964), 51-65.

Schenke, H.M. *Die Herkunft des sogenannten Evangelium Veritatis*. Göttingen: Vandenhoeck and Ruprecht, 1959.

M. Gospel of Thomas

Gärtner, Bertil. *The Theology of the Gospel According to Thomas*. Transl. by Eric J. Sharpe. New York: Harper and Brothers, 1961.

Schrage, Wolfgang. *Das Verhältnis des Thomas-Evangeliums zur Synoptischen Tradition und zu den Koptischen Evangelien-übersetzungen*. Berlin: A. Topelmann, 1964.

Turner, H.E.W. and Montefiore, H. *Thomas and the Evangelists*. London: SCM, 1962.

Wilson, Robert M. *Studies in the Gospel of Thomas*. London: Mowbray, 1960.

N. Acts of Pontius Pilate

Justin Martyr. *First Apology: Ante-Nicene Fathers*. Ed. by Alexander Roberts and James Donaldson. Grand Rapids: Eerdmans, 1973.

Tertullian. *Apology: Ante-Nicene Fathers*. Ed. by Alexander Roberts and James Donaldson. Grand Rapids: Eerdmans, 1973.

Index

Scripture Index

Romans

1 Corinthians

About the Author

Gary R. Habermas received his B.R.E. from William Tyndale College, M.A. from the University of Detroit, D.D. from Emmanuel College, Oxford, England, and Ph.D. from Michigan State University. He has ministered in three churches, the last being the Chicago Avenue United Brethren Church in Kalamazoo, Michigan. He taught Apologetics and Philosophy at Big Sky Bible College and served as Associate Professor of Apologetics and Philosophy of Religion at William Tyndale College. From 1981 to the present he is Professor in the Department of Philosophy and Theology (Chairman since 1988) at Liberty University in Lynchburg, Virginia. Gary is also the Director of the M.A. program in Apologetics.

Gary, his wife, Eileen, and their children live in Lynchburg, Virginia. Gary has been a member of the Virginia Philosophical Association, the Conference on Faith and History, the Evangelical Theological Society, and the Evangelical Philosophical Society as national President, Vice-President, and Secretary-Treasurer. His hobbies include reading, writing, sports in general (and ice hockey in particular), and chess.

The 18 books by the author include:

Beyond Death: Exploring the Evidence for Immortality (Crossway, 1998).

In Defense of Miracles: A Comprehensive Case for God's Action in History co-edited with Doug Geivett (InterVarsity, 1997).

Prolegomena to Theology (Harcourt Brace, 1996).

Why Believe? God Exists! : Rethinking the Case for God and Christianity with Terry Miethe (College Press, 1993).

Dealing With Doubt (Moody Press, 1990).

The Shroud and the Controversy: Skepticism, Science, and the Search for Authenticity with Kenneth Stevenson (Thomas Nelson, 1990).

Did Jesus Rise from the Dead? The Resurrection Debate with Antony Flew, edited by Terry Miethe (Harper and Row, 1987).

Ancient Evidence for the Life of Jesus: Historical Records of His Death and Resurrection (Thomas Nelson, 1984); retitled, *The Verdict of History: Conclusive Evidence for the Life of Jesus*, 1988.

Verdict on the Shroud: Evidence for the Death and Resurrection of Jesus Christ with Kenneth Stevenson (Servant Books, 1981; Dell Publishing, 1982); one foreign edition.

The Resurrection of Jesus: An Apologetic (Baker, 1980; University Press of America, 1984).

Gary has published over 100 articles in journals, magazines, and reference works such as: *Religious Studies, Baker Dictionary of Theology, Journal of the Evangelical Theological Society, Bulletin of the Evangelical Philosophical Society, Christian Counseling Today, Christian Scholar's Review, Bibliotheca Sacra, The Simon Greenleaf Review of Law and Religion, Journal of Church and State, Criswell Theological Review, International Christian Leadership Journal* (formerly *His*), *Grace Theological Journal, Christianity Today, Catholic Digest, Saturday Evening Post, Conservative Digest,* and *New Covenant.*

Dr. Habermas has contributed chapters in the following books:

"Did Jesus Perform Miracles?" in *Jesus Under Fire: Modern Scholarship Reinvents the Historical Jesus*, edited by Michael Wilkins and J.P. Moreland (Zondervan, 1995).

"A Plea for the Practical Application of Christian Philosophy" in *A Christian's Guide to Faith and Reason* by Terry Miethe (Bethany House, 1987); retitled *Living Your Faith: Closing the Gap Between Mind and Heart* (College Press, 1993).

"A Public Debate" in *Arguing Persuasively* by Ronald and Karen Lee (Longmans, 1989).

"Averroes, Rationalism and the Leap of Faith" in *Shalom: Essays in Honor of Dr. Charles H. Shaw*, edited by Eugene Mayhew (William Tyndale, 1983).

"Skepticism: David Hume" in *Biblical Errancy: An Analysis of Its Philosophical Roots*, edited by Norman Geisler (Zondervan, 1981).